The Entrapments of Form

The Entrapments of Form

CRUELTY AND MODERN LITERATURE

Catherine Toal

FORDHAM UNIVERSITY PRESS *New York* 2016

THIS BOOK IS MADE POSSIBLE BY A COLLABORATIVE GRANT
FROM THE ANDREW W. MELLON FOUNDATION.

Library of Congress Cataloging-in-Publication Data

Toal, Catherine.
   The entrapments of form : cruelty and modern literature / Catherine Toal. — First
edition.
      pages   cm
   Includes bibliographical references and index.
   ISBN 978-0-8232-6934-1 (hardback)
   ISBN 978-0-8232-6935-8 (paper)
   1. French literature—19th century—History and criticism. 2. American literature—
19th century—History and criticism. 3. Cruelty in literature. 4. Modernism
(Literature)—France. 5. Modernism (Literature)—United States. I. Title.
PQ295.C7T63 2016
840.9'353—dc23

                                                                        2015026934

Printed and bound in Great Britain by
Marston Book Services Ltd, Oxfordshire

18 17 16   5 4 3 2 1

First edition

CONTENTS

The Entrapments of Form

Introduction: The "Strange and Familiar Word"

In remarks on his manifestos for the theater, Antonin Artaud complained that "when I said the word 'cruelty,' everyone immediately took it to mean 'blood.'"[1] His protest contains a brief history of his chosen term. Firstly, the supposed misunderstandings of his intention carry etymological echoes. Clément Rosset reminds us that "*cruor,* from which *crudelis* (cruel) is derived, as well as *crudus* (raw, undigested, indigestible) designates flayed and bleeding flesh."[2] As Artaud's synonym suggests, cruelty can also denote a state or condition, one predicated at the very least on an analogy with physical suffering. The speech act Artaud performs at the same time alludes to the extreme violence—and the dyad of victim and perpetrator—often inextricable from cruelty. His criticism of the wantonness of the audience conjures up the relish assumed to attend its infliction. Claiming the position of injured party, Artaud effects a polemical reversal characteristic of the word's deployment: initially "everyone" believed he meant "blood"—now, he retaliates. Finally, his very attempt to maneuver the noun toward a new meaning sketches the possibility of an abstract usage, but alongside this, the stubborn, perhaps ineradicable persistence of a corporeal overtone.

If we ask where "cruelty" originated, the answer, reverberating with a well-known proverb, is Rome. This response refers not only to the linguistic provenance of our English word, but emerges from the relative infrequency of cognates in Ancient Greek poetry and prose.[3] Neither does an evocation of Rome refer merely to the inherited image of an imperium famed for spectacles combining fatal chastisements with public entertainment and for legendary examples of despotic willfulness. As the historian Daniel Baraz has pointed out, the first explicit philosophical treatment of cruelty appears in Seneca's *De Ira* (On Anger), and in his *De Clementia* (On Mercy), the latter text addressed to the young Nero.[4] Baraz argues that only the second book of *De Clementia* offers a distinctive definition of cruelty. In the first, and in *De Ira*, it is invoked interchangeably with the already near-synonymous *saevitia* and *feritas*, each of which can be translated either as "savagery" or "ferocity." The unique phrase used in *De Clementia* is *atrocitas animi in exigendis poenis* or "brutality of the mind in the infliction of punishment."[5] Andrew R. Dyck comments on the use of the word *atrocitas* by Cicero that it "expresses instinctive abhorrence," deriving from "*ater* (black) with the *ox/ ωψ* suffix 'looking like,'" and "though not a technical term, is often used of criminal cases."[6] Variously rendered also as "harshness," "barbarousness," "monstrousness," *atrocitas* here is invoked by Seneca to convey the crossing over of the magistrate into the sphere of criminality, an implication that resonates throughout the historical deployment of cruelty in legal discourse.

However, in parallel with this restricted if highly consequential usage, we can discern affinities in the etiology of cruelty given in the two treatises that are decisive and illuminating for its later meanings. *De Ira* describes *crudelitas* as the consequence of an "oft-repeated indulgence" of anger that transforms an otherwise aversive emotion into an experience of pleasure, thereby "making a pastime of ferocity."[7] The phrase Seneca uses here is *per otium saevi*, which specifically suggests the (shocking) transfer of a quality exhibited when animals prey on one another to the nonpurposive activity of leisure. In the more overtly political context of *De Clementia*, such a transformation of anger into pleasure is linked with the disposition of the tyrant and his inventively excessive treatment of enemies and offenders. Both texts therefore consider cruelty a kind of trespass into an illicit realm, *De Ira* providing the affective diagnosis of the political disposition proscribed by *De Clementia*. Together, they explain how a form of conduct with its roots in the disturbance of anger could congeal into pleasure (and into indifference toward others' fate), and thus become a deviant operational mode for justice running contrary to its utility.

The themes Seneca sets in play (and the positions he takes) are obviously already familiar from Ancient Greek ethics: the importance of habit, and the dangers of tyranny in the soul and in the polity. However, their appearance in Greek writings does not constellate around a similar set of concerns. Seneca drastically oversimplifies when he condemns Aristotle as "the defender of anger."[8] Nonetheless, Aristotle's reference to an historical example also drawn upon by Seneca in both of his treatises, the deeds of the tyrant Phalaris, reveals a marked and telling divergence. For Seneca, Phalaris—reputed to have treated offenders in a manner that was "inhuman and incredible"—represents a dangerous pinnacle of human viciousness (called cruelty) that should serve as a cautionary warning against all tendencies to aggression and hostility.[9] Aristotle, by contrast, neutrally mentions the tyrant's "desire to eat the flesh of a child" and his "appetite for unnatural sexual pleasure" and ranges his conduct alongside the cannibalistic practices of barbarian coastal tribes and "morbid pleasures," such as "plucking out the hair" or "gnawing the nails," as well as the problem of "fits of anger."[10] In Aristotle's discussion, Phalaris falls into the sphere of the "perverse," that is, proclivities either imprinted by nature or by habits so ingrained that they lack general interest for the aims and concerns of moral deliberation. Although it could hardly be called a disagreement over an identical object, the disparity between Seneca's and Aristotle's use of the example of Phalaris calls to mind a pair of alternatives occurring in the moral-philosophical treatment of cruelty: its relegation to the margins as an instance of deviance, versus its disturbing centrality as a primary possibility within the range of human potential.

As is well known, Plato's depiction of the dangers of tyranny is far less equanimous than Aristotle's. In the infamous passage in *Republic* on the formation of the tyrant, cannibalism—later proverbial for cruelty—is a vivid, condemnatory metaphor rather than an enumerated aberration.[11] Andrew Lintott reminds us that, if *Republic* does contain a nascent concept of cruelty, it is not one that includes consideration of the effects of the tyrant's depredations on the wider community; indeed, the *demos* are held responsible for his rapine.[12] Nevertheless, as Lintott notes, juxtaposing Greek with Roman sources: the latter show a consistent tendency to condemn only the mistreatment of persons of high status as "cruelty."[13] Greek historiography, by contrast, entertains scruples about exercising eliminatory force against weak and rival populations. The new departure in Seneca's two texts lies in the direct foregrounding of a vice that for the Greeks was "a comparatively unimportant ethical category."[14] Evidently written from the

position of an intimate who might himself become the victim of imperial impetuosity, *De Clementia* implicitly includes in its focus on the
disposition of the agent an attention to the fate of the object. It is this
element that effects a disruption of the Aristotelian system of virtues.

Aristotle's proposals are intended to guide the conduct of the head
of the household, the fundamental unit for the protection of which
the state is organized. They contain many caveats, but essentially they
rest on the proposition that each virtue, proper to a sphere of action,
represents a mean or middle way between either a deficiency or an
excess. Seneca describes cruelty as the "opposite" of mercy, but it has
no relationship of excess or deficiency to its antithesis. Mercy, the
virtue being extolled, is also avowedly a deficiency, the willingness
to refrain from inflicting a punishment that might be due. Furthermore, mercy does *not* represent the opposite of *severitas* (strictness),
on the grounds that the latter can only be a virtue. However, *severitas* is not recommended. *Misericordia,* or pity, which, contrary to
the view of the "ill-informed" is decidedly not a virtue, figures the
temptation into which "mercy" can fall and raises the new problem
of vices that masquerade as virtues. *Severitas*, more obtrusively, may
degenerate into cruelty.[15] We will later see cruelty overturn the Aristotelian hierarchy of virtues. In *De Clementia*, its prominence signals
a threatened unmooring of political prerogative from functional purpose. Although inflected by aristocratic interest, Seneca's plea raises
a query that haunts the social imaginary: the degree to which the
censure "cruelty" even comes to apply in recognition of the suffering
of those outside the protections of status.[16] More generally, the dis-
quisitions *De Ira* and *De Clementia* instantiate a divide in the concept's reach—yet one with unstable overlap—between the private life
of conduct and the remit—or corruption—of the state.

Though proving the durability of the Senecan antithesis with clemency, reflections on cruelty in the founding works of Christian theol-
ogy give a new shape to the term. This shape can appear alien, but it
lurks within our contemporary perspective. A summation of its components can be discovered in a less overtly doctrinal text, the *Confes-
siones* of Augustine, where a brief vignette describes the surrender,
despite initial resistance, of the youthful Alypius of Thagaste to an
obsession with gladiatorial spectacles. According to the anecdote,
Alypius closes his eyes to the games, only to be plunged by hearing the
frenzy of the crowd into a state of intoxication at the "bloodthirsty
pleasures" (*cruenta voluptate*).[17] As the scenario indicates, Augustine's

references to cruelty are not directly concerned with action. Just as this anecdote bears on spectatorship, instances of dramatic violence in *De Civitate Dei contra Paganos* are never cited principally for the purposes of discerning right from wrong agency. Like Alypius's story, they serve the larger aim of descrying effects of worldliness on the mind and fortifying it against such influence. A quest of this kind not only radicalizes the Ancient discourse on the soul, divorcing it from practical reason, it introduces a distinctive peculiarity.

The historian of Late Antiquity Peter Brown observes that for Augustine, it was not the fact of sexuality itself that resulted from the Fall, but rather the "uncontrollable" quality of sexual arousal.[18] The rapturous contagion of the crowd's response to the "cruel and murderous" gladiatorial games makes a clear link between that excitation and the erosion of the will attendant on physical desire. In another text, the disquisition *De nuptiis et concupiscentia* (*On Marriage and Concupiscence*), Augustine uses the phrase *libido crudelis* (cruel lust) to condemn those who induce abortions to avoid the procreative consequences of sexual relations within wedlock. As Daniel Dombrowski notes, the expression is not simply a reformulation of an earlier characterization, *libidinosa crudelitas* (lustful cruelty): "Since Augustine also accuses those who have merely used contraceptive devices of being cruel, we can be sure that it is not cruelty to a human being inside the womb that he is worried about."[19] Rather, the idiom and its context suggest that postlapserian sexual propulsion as such has attracted the epithet "cruel." Semantic patterns in *De Civitate Dei* display an intricate connection between the critique of Roman worldly dominance and a sense of the "cruel" sway of covetous and indulgent appetite.[20] We might say that Augustine inaugurates the first hint of a theme that will become a prominent motif in aspiring scientific treatments of cruelty, namely its kinship to the sources of the sexual instinct.[21] Preeminently, however, his wielding of its adjectival and other variants erases any primacy of doer and deed, becoming an overarching articulation of the fallen condition, and therefore one of its symptoms.

The central theological discussion of cruelty in the Middle Ages confirms Hans Blumenberg's outline of Christianity's strategy of intellectual legitimation as the pretension to provide answers to the enigmas of Ancient philosophy.[22] Thomas Aquinas reconceptualizes *De Ira* and *De Clementia*—in the section "de crudelitate" from the *Summa Theologiæ*—in the form of two questions: "Is cruelty the contrary of clemency?" and "Does cruelty differ from savagery or ferocity?"[23] Pursuing an extraordinary means of demonstration, each of the two answers relies on a culinary metaphor with a philological inspiration. The first, noting the link between cruelty and "rawness," argues that "Things well-prepared and cooked we are wont to find pleasant and agreeable to the taste, but when they are raw they are harsh and horrible. We have seen that clemency implies a certain mildness or sweetness of disposition concerned with the diminution of punishments. Accordingly cruelty and clemency are direct opposites." The second answer, more violent in its mention of eating, observes that savagery and ferocity are terms "used by comparison with wild beasts" and asserts their distinction from cruelty on the basis that animals of this kind "attack man and feed on his body, and not as moved by justice, for this consideration is proper to reason alone."[24]

Despite the ostensible agreement with Seneca, the conclusions of Aquinas's discussion bring about a transformation of emphasis. The first culinary metaphor clearly shifts attention away from conduct toward states of mind. Legal theorist Paulo D. Barrozo argues that Aquinas foregrounds subjective intention in contradistinction to Seneca's at least incipient regard for the "suffering victim."[25] In the second, more complex answer, a strange formulation succeeds the image of predatory, devouring animals: brutality or savagery applies to "those who punish another, not because of some fault he has committed, but because of the pleasure they take in his being hurt." *De Clementia* clearly proposes a differentiation between the violence of "savagery" and the juridical context to which a narrower definition of cruelty applies. Aquinas, on the contrary, situates punishment in relation to both propensities and thereby narrows the definition of cruelty still further: cruelty "not only looks at the fault of its victim, but exceeds due measure in punishing." Cruelty as "human wickedness" is opposed to the "human virtue" of clemency. "Savagery and ferocity," by contrast, are opposed to a "superhuman virtue" one of the "gifts of the Holy Ghost" known as "piety."

This new opposition confines the Senecan pairing to the worldly realm, transcending it with an antithesis between fallen nature and divine grace. In each of its maneuvers, Aquinas's second answer seals off the lines of psychological and pragmatic inquiry that Seneca pursued. The introduction of reference to "inflicting punishment" into the account of the operation of "brutality or savagery" precludes the tracking of an affective momentum for such tendencies. Similarly, the definition of cruelty as an estimation of culpability that merely "exceeds" in punishing omits altogether the mind of the agent, or any contemplation of the criteria that might justify leniency or quittance. Both the nutritive relishing of "clemency" as a flavor of temperament and the wholly technical definition of cruelty suggest a lack of concern with the quotidian business of the juridical realm, either its logics or consequences. Effectively, the inclusion of "punishment" within the depiction of savagery sets up an equivalence between chastisement and the preying of wild beasts. The subliminal connection created by Aquinas's metaphor may signal a disregard for worldly judgment, an uncanny return of the sense of violence the analysis represses, or an intimation of divine wrath. Above all, "De crudelitate" tells us that the naming of this "human wickedness" need not amount to an examination of its workings.

As Daniel Baraz points out, Aquinas's deliberations figure a rare philosophical intervention on the topic of cruelty in the Middle Ages, where it most often featured as the stereotypical attribute of ideological or territorial adversaries, or in stories of the persecution of martyrs.[26] Paradoxically, the era itself is renowned for casual and invasive violence: in everyday life, in theatrical performance and ritual practice, and in the tormenting of criminal and doctrinal offenders.[27] However we reckon the cause of the amelioration of these outrages, or whether we consider that they have simply been rezoned and reorganized,[28] it remains striking that "cruelty" as a term resurfaces in the political theory of early modernity, specifically as the antipode to the new role of impartial stewardship envisaged for the state. Its destiny confirms Jacques Derrida's parenthetical characterization of it as a "strange and familiar word,"[29] a comment prompted by the uncanny recollection of archaic barbarism, and by an unstable power of slander or indictment. Able to expose practices tolerated—or not thus classified—to date, it belongs both inside and outside the realm of our possible cultural judgments.

This volatility is fully exploited by a text that represents the founding work of modern statecraft and one of the few apparent defenses of cruelty, Machiavelli's *The Prince* (1532). The chapter on criminal rises to power advocates "cruelty well committed"—which means that it should not be "persisted in" but "committed all at once."[30] It will immediately be seen that Machiavelli's caveat contradicts the very nature of cruelty conveyed by Seneca: endless, incurable, destructive spiral. A later chapter treats the opposition with clemency entirely in terms of reputation, arguing that a new prince cannot avoid acquiring a reputation for cruelty and mentioning punishment only in connection with threats to the regime itself. This abuse of Senecan terminology is a statement of the true costs of the acquisition of hegemony. The earlier chapter highlights the equal dependency of the dynastic prince and the nonaristocratic usurper on the elimination of opposition. The later one indicates that "cruelty" is not only required at the commencement of a regime, but also for subduing menaces to unity and security, and as a demonstrated prospect of last resort, hindering their emergence.

Both discussions combine the emphasis on monopoly of violence with the importance of perception. The successful criminal usurper, whose killing spree extends to the term of his natural mortality, achieves power "but not glory."[31] Here, Machiavelli exerts constraint on the latitude of the prince by means of an Ancient Roman value.[32] The chapter focused on reputation stresses the support to loyalty found in invariant behavior toward subjects, slowness to retaliation, and execution on justified grounds. It is obvious that these provisions contain the seeds of the impartial stewardship of the modern state— along with the stipulation that the ruler should refrain from rapine, which takes on cruelty's former quality of interminable escalation. Machiavelli's use of the word "cruelty" literally expresses the crude beginnings of the articulation of sovereignty, with its predication on violence. His rewriting of Seneca, part of a larger strategy of misquotation of Ancient and biblical sources,[33] bolsters legitimacy by divulging its ultimate foundation.

Judith Shklar reads Machiavelli as a defender of oppression, and instead credits Montaigne with founding the ideals of liberalism, most importantly the necessity of "putting cruelty first" among the vices, which includes requiring that the state safeguard its citizens from injury.[34] Montaigne's essays on cruelty pursue this theme with three essential gestures: the recommendation that the corpses of criminals be submitted to mutilation; that immediate death is to be preferred to torture; that it is more valorous to leave enemies alive than to kill them.[35] These not exactly consistent stipulations sum up his solicitous care for the body subject to the ravages of sectarian war, the invasions of corporeal punishment, and the havoc wreaked by the private quest for honor. Together, they promote a sovereign authority limited to coercions decreed by necessity, and protect the body itself from any designs inimical to its integrity as a fact of animate life. However, their fantastical scale, compassing harassed decease and acquitted vitality, hints at complications in the advocacy of a governmentality and personal ethic averse to the infliction of physical suffering.

These complications enter chiefly through Montaigne's own presence in the text and through the intrusion of examples concerning the bodies of others. Both kinds of interpolation appear as a counterweight to the astonishing violence of the contemporary context, at the point when Montaigne presents himself as "cruelly hating cruelty," and when he cites instances of self-dispatch on the part of victims of monarchical atrocity: in "De la cruauté," the condemned prisoner who tries every available means of suicide in mistaken anticipation of horrible tortures prior to an execution; in "Couardise, mère de la cruauté," the valiant Theoxena, uncomfortably close to the "mother" of the title, who stabs and then drowns her son, her stepchildren, herself, and her husband to escape the murderous precautions of tyranny. These stories are too burlesque to be taken as emphatic of the pathos of victimhood and the exigencies to which it is forced. In their escalation of slapstick, they hint at a quality of enjoyment that is manifest in a different way, but one that demands the same conclusions, in Montaigne's biographical interventions on cruelty, where he adduces himself as an example.

Shklar interprets confessionally Montaigne's asseveration that he "cruelly hates cruelty," believing that the adverbial aggravation refers to the dangers of a misanthropic rejection of a world filled with abuses.[36] The suddenness of this confession, however, is all the more striking in contrast to the discourse that precedes it, on the relationship between virtue and goodness, where virtue, that Ancient standard, appears like a masochistic astringency that, when fully internalized, can become perverse pleasure. Goodness, an inherent quality of character, represents no exceptional achievement and thus deserves no praise. We are asked by Montaigne to understand his repugnance toward cruelty as being of the latter type, an inheritance of nature and good upbringing rather than personal effort. Yet the proffering of disposition as stubborn fact also requires no proof of its postulations. The "I" of the essay moves directly from contemplation of the horrors of religious wars to the experience of the hunt, evidently the sole ground on which the aversion to cruelty will be tested. Not only is it obvious that the speaker participates in hunting despite its eviscerations, the distress and destruction of sentient life produce a heady admixture of pleasure and unpleasure, whose intensity is not even equaled by the sexual act with which it is digressively compared.

Montaigne's reflections on cruelty trace its threading through life. His famous adverbial phrase, rather than conveying the danger of self-righteousness, roots the horror of aversion in the palpability of incursions into sentience. The discussion of virtue, overthrowing an Aristotelian teleology, divorces excellence from ends, placing it in a dangerously autonomous dialectic of pleasure and pain. The anecdotes of self-dispatch, though critiques of the excesses of power, also suggest an autonomized masochism, or at the very least a common surrender to the dictates of violence. Not that there are no moral symmetries upheld by the essays—for instance, the association between a habit of cruelty and a timorous obsession with control—but, as Shklar also implies, Montaigne confronts us with an organic malady that no reform of the state can fully abolish, one so banally endemic that it can seem pointless to speak about it at all.

Ruling cruelty out of the bounds of discourse is the solution favored by Thomas Hobbes's *Leviathan* (1651). He professes to find it simply unintelligible: "That any man should take pleasure in other mens great harmes, without other end of his own, I do not conceive it possible."[37] *De Cive* (1651) compares cruelty to drunkenness.[38] Of course for Hobbes, the irrelevance of cruelty derives not from banal ubiquity but from an inimical relation to the universal aim of humanity: the pursuit of self-preservation, whether pertaining to sustenance or to consequence. The state takes over and finds legitimacy in this purpose, hence the exclusion of a propensity aligned with destructiveness as not only undesirable but unthinkable. References to cruelty on the part of the theorists of modern power denote the phases of the consolidation of sovereignty for which they assume responsibility. Machiavelli frankly adduces the basis of dominance by using a word that would occur to victims. Montaigne wishes to halt the state's infringements on corporeality, an investigation that must at the same time reveal how moral—being also bodily—impulses entwine with their opposites. Hobbes, more entirely focused on the subtending of the state, has no place for corrugations in the will to survive. Although his sovereign force may be the same principle as Machiavelli's "cruelty," his disqualification of the term belongs to a greater confidence in the prospective minimization of physical coercion.

In the stage of speculation on the basis of human community that followed the European wars of religion, an emphasis on sentiment and ties of affection overlays a primary focus on utility. David Hume's *An Enquiry Concerning the Principles of Morals* (1751) explicitly links justice with sociability rather than (as Hobbes did) with the imperative of security or (as Locke suggested) the rewards of labor. The concerns of "moral sense" philosophy can be attributed not only to the establishment of stable political compromise but also to the need for a justification and defense of its benefits at the fundamental level of feeling and natural impulse. The consolidation of social bonds on the basis of affect led to the elaboration of a further layer to the social contract: its predication on the phenomenon of appropriate responses to the sight of others' emotions and circumstances. Such a test is classically encapsulated by Adam Smith's proposed hypothesis of the "impartial spectator," the uninvolved bystander whose disinterested assessment of a situation must regulate both the behavior of the person directly concerned and the reaction of anyone apprehending it from the outside.

As James A. Steintrager has shown, it was the eighteenth century that added pleasure in the suffering of others to the standard definition of cruelty. He argues that the possibility of such pleasure caused immense difficulties for British and French moral philosophers: they wished to define it as a "monstrous" attitude outside normal human tendencies—yet it obviously has a share in "sensibility."[39] The moral sense theorists articulate various solutions to this problem. Shaftesbury, in *An Inquiry Concerning Virtue, or Merit* (1699), extends the Senecan critique of anger (and verges on a kind of Frommian moral psychoanalytics) by proposing that pleasure in others' suffering affords only temporary but not lasting relief from an essentially miserable condition of misanthropic social exclusion.[40] Adam Smith draws upon the visceral intensity of the reaction to the tearing of flesh (which excites our "dread of death") to uphold the idea that sympathy with the victim of cruelty is always overpowering.[41]

If the eighteenth century faced a dilemma with respect to cruelty, wishing to exclude it from the range of accountable possibilities while thinking of it largely in visual and affective terms, it also stages a peculiar semantic explosion around the word itself. "Enlightenment" lacks a specific theory of cruelty, but the use of the category to polemicize against the effects of superstition or tyranny constitutes a characteristic feature of its jargon. Paradigmatic of such gestures is Voltaire's *Traité sur la tolérance* (1763). In that text, "barbarism" signifies the infliction of extravagant and unjustified physical injury, while "cruelty" connotes the cyclical recurrence of violence perpetrated through ignorance and prejudice, or the nightmare temporality of irrationality.[42] Ubiquitous invocations of cruelty obviously raise the question of descriptive aptness, and of the beneficence of proposed alternatives to the abuses it names. John Langbein contends that the *philosophes'* attack on regimes of punishment in the eighteenth century was not decisive in the abolition of the Roman-canon law system of proof and its use of torture.[43] This legal method had already been effectively phased out through the introduction of the possibility of conviction on circumstantial evidence. More fraught even than the issue of whether philosophical rhetoric had a real object of reference or simply used the accusation of cruelty to forge a bid for cultural authority is the issue of whether eighteenth-century innovations ameliorated the perceived cruelty of medieval and early modern systems of discipline.

In *Du système pénitentiaire aux États-Unis et de son application en France* (1833), Gustave de Beaumont and Alexis de Tocqueville articulate a viewpoint deeply influenced by Enlightenment logic when they condemn "revolting cruelties" such as "branding and mutilation" because these permanent physical marks leave no possibility of forgetting the past and, therefore, of improvement in the future.[44] However, they endorse, specifically rejecting its characterization as "cruel," the Pennsylvania method of absolute solitary confinement, an invention that continued to attract exactly that epithet later in the nineteenth century, most famously in Charles Dickens's *American Notes* (1842).[45] Michel Foucault's *Surveiller et Punir* (1975), which takes the Pennsylvania panopticon as the archetype of modern methods of formation and control, exhibits a starkly counter-Enlightenment view of the apparently opposed phenomena of physical injury and confinement. Of the early modern use of torture he comments, noting its relationship to investigative and religious criteria of proof and justification: "It was certainly cruel, but it was not savage." Of the panopticon he remarks, "It was a cruel and cunning cage."[46] While the first observation makes an acknowledgment that diminishes the importance of the quality named, the second cites cruelty as a decisive and unavoidable feature of modern regimes of punishment. The uncertainty about whether Enlightenment reformism really produced improvement results in the most uniquely radical modern perspective on cruelty (one that guided Foucault's researches), Nietzsche's *Zur Genealogie der Moral* (1887). Above all, this text challenges the eighteenth-century anathematization of physical injury, arguing that all civilizational and educational projects are realized by means of cruelty, and indeed that its untrammelled presocial expression figures a lost natural healthiness and purity. The zenith of a modern skepticism regarding the Enlightenment wish to eliminate physical pain in the name of progress arrives with Ernst Jünger's treatise on that subject, *Über den Schmerz* (1934), which argues that the anaesthetized modern subject has become a helpless tool in the hands of technological power, which he calls a "cruel spirit."[47]

This book charts two alternative but intertwined directions of thought and aesthetic experiment that emerged from the Enlightenment discourse on cruelty, and that together shape its modern contours and their departure from the original philological connection with blood and flayed flesh. Nietzsche's valorization of cruelty finds its precedent in the work of the Marquis de Sade, which performs a scandalous extension of the eighteenth-century celebration of "nature" by proclaiming cruelty an ineradicable and morally neutral component of the arrangement of the cosmos. In two grammatically similar definitions, offered in *La Philosophie dans le boudoir* (1795) and *Juliette* (1797) respectively, Sade appropriates central keywords of the era to create formulations applicable to each sex. "Cruelty is nothing but the energy of man not yet corrupted by civilization,"[48] declares the *Philosophie*, while the tale of the female libertine deems the phenomenon "nothing but one of the branches of sensibility."[49] In the first definition, a monstrous propensity becomes part of the mechanistic dynamism of a materialist universe. In the second, it achieves precisely the status resisted by moral sense theorists: a simple variant of empathic capacity. Sade's definitions are obviously not the entirety of his engagement with the infamy they attempt discursively to eradicate. Their relationship to the rest of his work represents at once an opportunistic exploitation and critical dismantling of the revolutionary promise of civic equality.

The nascent "United States" offer the spectacle of an appropriation of the standard rhetoric of Enlightenment concerning cruelty to proclaim the legitimacy of a revolutionary project. The 1776 Declaration of Independence, unlike the Declaration of the Rights of Man and Citizen in 1789, adopts the emotive, accusatory tone and the historical perspective of philosophical polemic. Condemning "cruelty and perfidy scarcely paralleled in the most barbarous ages," its draft version equated lack of political representation for the entire colonial population with the introduction of chattel slavery on the continent, holding the metropolitan power responsible for both facts.[50] The position of victimization cultivated in the primary document of national foundation (both through its comparisons and its suppressions) has far-reaching relevance for the representation and understanding of cruelty in American literature and culture, which upholds an official rejection of the quality as alien to the very character of the nation while generating narrative mechanisms that betray the operation of systematic, if mysteriously unattributable, killing and violence. In the French context, Sade's definitions inaugurate a tradition of celebrating cruelty, one that figures a retreat into the aesthetic realm of the kind of critique of revolutionary promise that he articulates in largely discursive and demonstrational form. These two divergent pathways out of the legacy of Enlightenment—the extolling of a trait and mode of action inimical to its reformist aims, and a formal adoption of its values—intertwine at key points and develop in tandem. Together, they fashion the fundamental outline of cruelty in modern literature.

A look at the context of Sade's definitions of cruelty—and not only the content of his narratives—indicate that these formulations both render injury indifferent and obfuscate the actual aim of the archetypal libertine scenario. The definition given in the *Philosophie* occurs near the treatise "Français, encore un effort si vous voulez être républicains," which essentially seeks to convert the republican state into an apparatus for the servicing of libertine desire (foreign wars are prohibited; all murder except the judicial is permitted; and so forth). That offered by *Juliette* appears in the vicinity of a discourse addressed to the Society of the Friends of Crime, inveighing against the "cruel" nature of love, or the power acquired by women falsely elevated to the status of uniqueness by infatuated admirers. Both of these examples evidence an apprehension at the prospect of occupying a position of parity with others (whether shared citizenship in the state, or the condition of petitioning but unfavored lover). In the notations that end Sade's unfinished *Les 120 Journées de sodome*—the tableaux sketched there are paradigmatic for his entire oeuvre—the libertine agent seeks repeatedly to solicit the complicity of his victims in their own destruction (through promises of survival through the betrayal of a loved one). The strategy and the complicity make no difference to the actual outcome (murder), but they nullify along the way bonds of love or affection and the unique significance that individual persons can thereby be assumed to have for one another.

The libertine puppeteer of the process occupies the artificial position of inflicting reduction to a condition of equivalence, while remaining immune from it himself. This basic mechanism, rather than the litanies of torture, rape, and killing, constitutes the novelty and the essential driving force of Sadean narrative. In its frozen, predetermined character and the twist it enacts, predicated on the difference between a godlike orchestrating agent and a manipulated victim, the tableau figures the new shape of cruelty. No longer only a matter of malicious injury to the flesh, it turns on the question of equality. It becomes a travesty performed on the promise of the "rights of man," reiterating and reinforcing the subject's needless relegation to the status of indifferent and disposable matter.

In American literature, we find the archetypal Sadean tableau in Herman Melville's *Benito Cereno* (1855), which produces a dramatization of the contradiction noted by Tocqueville, between the mutual "sympathy" Americans generally show in social intercourse and the "cruelty" with which they treat their slaves.[51] Melville's text is part of a long genealogy of instances of unattributed or mysterious killing in American literature, stretching from Charles Brockden Brown's *Wieland* (1798) to Henry James's *The Turn of the Screw* (1898). The most obtrusive instance in this series, Poe's "perverse," a narrative arrangement that is essentially an automatized device for the perpetration of seemingly accidental or unmotivated killing, transforms the Sadean tableau in French literature over the course of the nineteenth century. Baudelaire's prose poems, under the influence of Poe's short narratives, present the dyad of victim and perpetrator and the dynamic of entrapment involving both in a way that renders ambiguous the locus of agency and innocence. Lautréamont, reader of Baudelaire and Poe, and committed in *Maldoror* (1869) to "painting the delights of cruelty,"[52] constructs a narrative in which poetic rhetoric itself obfuscates the act of murder, challenging the very boundary between an aesthetic work and a crime. The motif of unattributed murder is the key to a further entwinement between French and American literature, one that raises the question of the treatment (ethical and representational) of narrative protagonists. Henry James noted "an impression of something I can find no other name for than cruelty" in the approach of his aesthetic antagonist and inspiration, French naturalism.[53] The condensation of the prototypical Jamesian narrative configuration (of characters and desire) into the form of the "very mechanical"[54] *Turn of the Screw* reveals that the dissectional mercilessness of naturalism and the ostensibly more indulgent "point of view" are counterparts rather than opposites.

The first section of this book traces the three instances of interaction between American and French literature described above. Chapter 1, "The Forms of the Perverse," charts the Sadean legacy and its fusion with the influence of Poe. Chapter 2, "Some Things Which Could Never Have Happened," explains Melville's staging of Tocqueville's claim. Chapter 3, "Murder and 'Point of View,'" situates the fraught, decisive phase in the evolution of Henry James's aesthetic in the context of his interpretation of French contemporaries. The second section of this study, beginning with Chapter 5, "The Marquis de Sade in the Twentieth Century," shows the contribution of these exchanges to the forging of a distinctively twentieth-century definition of cruelty. In the French context, postwar readings of Sade strikingly revise the content, while adopting the grammatical form of his definition, proposing that "cruelty is nothing but the negation of the self."[55] This definition has roots in Artaud's reconceptualization of cruelty for the theater and, further back, in Proust's analysis of the connection between sadism and melodrama. Artaud's writings, and their resonance with allusions to the category of cruelty in the work of Ernst Jünger, suggest that this new idea of it has its source in an apprehension of the nature of modern warfare, or in a complete erasure of the interpersonal dyad of victim and perpetrator by the specter of technologically organized destruction. The reiteration of a definition of cruelty as "the negation of the self" comes to an end with Lacan's essay "Kant avec Sade," which seeks to return his contemporaries' attention to the problem of enforced complicity and the feature of theatricality in Sade. Lacan's provocative linkage of Sade's endorsement of calumny with the history of anti-Semitism (and implicitly, with its most catastrophic consequences)[56] brings his argument closer to a quite different structural and historical understanding of cruelty, articulated by the Frankfurt School through a rewriting of *Zur Genealogie der Moral*.[57]

Chapter 6, "American Cruelty," argues that American philosophy in the twentieth century offers definitions of cruelty similarly distant from the word's etymological meanings, consistently defining it as a failure of love, or a failure to "notice" the suffering of others.[58] This gesture contributes to a crisis of cultural and political response in the face of legal attempts to justify the use of torture by means of a diminution of the consequential meaning of the adjective "cruel" in the national and international regulation of punishment, detention, and the codes of war. American philosophy routinely draws upon "literature" to explore the meaning of cruelty, claiming that philosophy itself refuses to fulfill such a duty. The resulting interpretative findings endure in a tendency to treat the confrontation with terrorism, or cultural struggles for hegemony, in "aesthetic" terms, as problems of sensibility or visual representation. This book is also a study of literature. However, it neither searches out the complicity of aesthetic forms with disavowed affects, nor identifies moral lessons in the interaction of protagonists. Instead, it elucidates the hidden structures that decide the modern outline of cruelty as a concept and an eventuality.

CHAPTER ONE

The Forms of the Perverse

Nineteenth-century American literature presents a strange case at its origin: Edgar Allan Poe, fated to a terrific posthumous career in France, and only recovered for serious Anglophone study once aesthetic appraisal and canon-formation ceased to be paramount scholarly tasks.[1] Well known is the story of Poe's immediate legacy in his homeland: the grave left without a tombstone for twenty years; the series of damning or ambivalent judgments. Whitman confessed to a long period of "distaste" for Poe's work. T. S. Eliot condemned his "slipshod" and "puerile" creations. Henry James relegated enthusiasm for Poe to "a decidedly primitive state of reflection."[2] Yet it is never noted that the progress of Poe's impact in France reveals no less of an incongruity between evaluation and tenacious significance. Evidence suggests mainly the influence of Poe's poetry and philosophy of composition on the symbolists, but only his stories (except for "The Raven") were translated by the writer responsible for his infiltration into French culture, Baudelaire.[3] Further peculiarities appear here: Mallarmé translated Poe's poetry into prose; "Eureka," the most anomalous Poe text, an abstract narrative, was of greatest importance for Valéry.[4]

Critics tend to rely on the assumption of a powerful personal identification as the genesis of Poe's French influence.[5] What is often overlooked is the broader intertwining influence of American literature on French literature in the forging of literary modernity. Régis Messac's Le 'Detective Novel' et l'influence de la pensée scientifique charts the pathway from Brockden Brown's Wieland and Cooper's wildernesses through Poe's stories to the Paris of Balzac and Lautréamont.[6] The mark left by Messac's study on Walter Benjamin's *Passagen-Werk* suggests that the fundamental shape of literary modernity is inconceivable without the transatlantic shift Baudelaire's translations mediate.[7] This present chapter is not another study of those translations, but rather a proposal for how their misreadings and gaps illuminate the precise nature of Poe's narrative patterns, and their wider relationship to the mediation of the colonial project in US literature. I also examine here how continuing engagement with Poe's work in the later nineteenth century contributed decisively to the revision, within nineteenth-century French literature, of one of its primary reference points—the libertine aesthetic of the Marquis de Sade, with its expounding of "cruelty"—thereby shaping the character of French prose poetry.

The unevenness of Baudelaire's engagement with Poe makes it difficult to identify with accuracy the point of greatest compelling interest raised for him by the American writer's work. But one consistent element is indeed present. Even in his earliest essay on Poe, largely plagiarized from other sources,[8] Baudelaire declares his fascination with "l'esprit de PERVERSITÉ" (the spirit of perversity).[9] Quoting extensively from the disquisition in "The Black Cat" on this phenomenon (from Isabel Meunier's translation) in the only original section of the essay, Baudelaire also alludes to it in the revised version "Edgar Poe, sa Vie et ses Œuvres" (1856), where he admires the meticulousness of Poe's analysis of this tendency: "qui flotte autour de l'homme nerveux et le conduit à mal" (that hovers about the nervous man and leads him to evil).[10] "Notes nouvelles sur Edgar Poe" (1857) reaches the zenith of such admiration, extolling Poe's "imperturbable affirmation" (resolute affirmation) of "la méchanceté naturelle" (natural evil), or later, of "la perversité primordiale de l'homme" (the primordial perversity of man).[11]

Baudelaire's "perversité" is clearly not Poe's "perverseness." The former is shot through with the following influences: Sade, Maistre, suspicion of Rousseau. Poe's perverse is formulated with a degree of lightness (as the contrast between his "imp" and Baudelaire's "démon" already indicates). For Poe, it seems to be more important that the phenomenon achieve a certain kind of negation, rather than that it stipulate positive depravity: perversity is the actualization of what should *not* be, acting "for the reason that we should *not*"—going against the teleology of the productive, the healthful, the norm.[12]

Even more striking than the ways in which Baudelaire interprets and translates the meaning of Poe's "perverse" is the assimilation of form to content in the treatment of those stories of Poe's that theorize the category. Both "The Black Cat" and "The Imp of the Perverse" culminate in murder. Each story, however, distracts from and seems to figure this outcome as ancillary. "Imp" does so through its prefatory range of "silly" or less serious examples of perverseness (the narrative itself, a long circumlocution, constitutes one). "The Black Cat" does so by displacing lethal aggression toward the narrator's wife onto a relation with a household pet. Baudelaire fuses the plot-result of "Imp of the Perverse"—in which the narrator condemns himself by compulsive confession of his crime—with one of its opening speculative claims: "l'impossibilité de trouver un motif raisonable suffisant pour certaines actions mauvaises et périlleuses, pourrait nous conduire à les considérer comme le résultat des suggestions du Diable, si l'expérience et l'histoire ne nous enseignaient pas que Dieu en tire souvent l'établissement de l'ordre et le châtiment des coquins;—*après s'être servi des mêmes coquins comme de complices!*" (The impossibility of finding a reasonable motive for certain bad and perilous actions might lead us to consider them the result of the Devil's promptings, if experience and history had not taught us that God sometimes derives from them the establishment of order and the punishment of reprobates;—*having made use of these same reprobates as accomplices!*).[13] Poe's own statement is more noncommittal: "We might, indeed, deem this perverseness a direct instigation of the Arch-Fiend, were it not occasionally known to operate in furtherance of good."[14] Similarly, in Baudelaire's intended dramatization of "The Black Cat" ("L'Ivrogne"), the protagonist consciously wishes to do away with his wife and is straightforwardly propelled to the deed by drunkenness.[15]

Of course, there is an element in Poe's "perverse" that justifies—or inspires—the darker shading Baudelaire gives it. The very duplicity of the stories, their representation of murder as incidental to their own unfolding, creates a violence that is meaningless, laconic, and enjoyed as such. For instance, "The Black Cat" narrator's summary disposal of his spouse: "I . . . buried the axe in her brain"; "she fell dead upon the spot without a groan."[16] All Poe's narratives of the perverse present an elaborate prefatory or pretextual apparatus that makes possible the precipitation of mindless, trivialized, and banal corporeal destruction. The most obvious example is "The Murders in the Rue Morgue," where the complexity of ratiocination, the deductions of the detective, are antithetical to the brutality of the acts perpetrated by the unthinking, nonhuman culprit.

American literature contemporaneous with Poe shares this "perverse" form, generating murderous violence for which narratives disavow or alienate responsibility. Recognition of this subterranean scheme resolves continual debates concerning the ideologically pugnacious racism, or, on a contrary view, the multifaceted critical potential, of formative American literature.[17] The mechanism of the "perverse" constitutes an acknowledgment of the devastation—only now receiving adequate historical accounting—wreaked on the indigenous populations of the American colonies.[18] At the same time, it achieves a sense of exoneration, befitting the negligible role played by individual protagonists in vaster historical processes, but also actively seeking an escape from guilt. Lastly, it marks an enjoyment that both betrays the existence of such guilt and expresses an illegitimate accession to the benefits of colonial incursion and its extraordinary depredations. With this structure, the "perverse" also contradicts the traditional mythopoeic understanding of American literature as the concatenation of colonial experience, its progressive development from first encounters with the "wilderness" to full-fledged postlapserian allegory.[19] The "perverse" shows literary forms at odds with themselves—invested in their own dissolution, as much as taking tentative steps toward a putative national cultural consolidation.

While American literature betrays an integral affinity with Poe's "perverse," Baudelaire's translations of Poe reveal the pressure of a tension between his initial understanding of the "perverse" and its actual patterning in Poe's texts. In the *Petits poèmes en prose* Baudelaire finally creates forms that enact the ambiguities and duplicities of the American perverse. The full implications of this achievement are disclosed by a poet who receives the imprint of both Poe and Baudelaire's influence. Lautréamont's *Les Chants de Maldoror* adapts perversity's denial of its own teleology to create a poetic rhetoric that feigns lack of awareness of the murderous acts lurking within its own narrative unfolding. In his last essay on French literature, written to Max Horkheimer in 1940, Walter Benjamin argued that the species of violence figured by *Maldoror* amounted to a kind of dreamwork of "Hitlerism."[20] Benjamin's remark prompts investigation of the labyrinthine nineteenth-century journey of the "perverse," a form that has always distorted the boundary between aesthetics and politics, producing strange refractions of external catastrophe.

PERVERSITY TO CRUELTY

Baudelaire's translations show numerous points at which the tension between his interpretation of Poe's "perverse" and the latter's actual form, as well as the possibility of future reinterpretation, are evident. "The Murders in the Rue Morgue," which does not contain an explicit theorization of perversity, shows the fundamental nature of its importance as a pattern in Poe's work. The structure of the plot is organized around the fulfillment of what should "not" be the case. Dupin, the detective protagonist, sleeps by day and wakes by night; the witnesses of the murder testify that the perpetrator was a foreigner, but do not know which language he spoke, only that it was "not" their own.[21] Linguistic constraints compel Baudelaire to diminish negative emphasis, for instance with respect to the perverse aim of the detective's investigations: "all apparent impossibilities *must* be proved to be not such in reality"; "il fallait démontrer que l'impossibilité n'était qu'apparente."[22]

Most strikingly, Baudelaire cannot translate the negative formulation that expresses Dupin's judgment of the police inspector because, running counter to the language of the text itself (as the murderer's "speech" does to that of its auditors), it is in French in the original. A quotation from Rousseau's *La Nouvelle Héloïse*, the phrase was, in that novel, a statement about philosophers.[23] Dupin uses it to depict the police inspector as a witless bungler of perversity, who seeks to "explain" (rather than bring into existence) what is "not," and to "deny" rather than thwart, what is: "de nier ce qui est, et d'expliquer ce qui n'est pas" (to deny what is, and to explain what is not).[24] Baudelaire cites the phrase in "Notes nouvelles sur Edgar Poe" to condemn the proponents of socialism.[25] Although this usage seems again to convert Poe's perverse into a theological doctrine opposed to mid-nineteenth-century pieties, the reiteration of the untranslatable phrase attests to a preoccupation with something elusive in the motif. Also, Baudelaire effectively turns the phrase against Rousseau himself, since he considers "Jean-Jacques" the hapless progenitor of Fourierist utopianism. Such a deployment of the quotation would not be possible without Poe's citation (perhaps it even contains an anticipation of a link between utopianism and a police state), and it represents a formal operation of perversity, rather than the mere transposition of a meaning.

An obstacle of French/Anglo-American (cultural as well as linguistic) translation also causes Baudelaire to omit a parenthetical remark on the word "affaire": "[The word 'affaire' has not yet, in France, *that levity of import* which it conveys with us.]"[26] Apparently trivial, this phrase in fact sums up the negating triviality of the case itself, which contains a similar dramatic, objectifying violence to that represented in "The Black Cat." Rather than focusing on the horrifically dismembered female victims, the story transfers its attention to the sailor who is the owner of the orangutan who killed them. The narrator tells this character's story as if it were his own, provoking the ratiocinating Dupin's entire empathy: "I pitied him from the bottom of my heart."[27] In other words, "The Murders in the Rue Morgue" presents a similar dynamic to "The Black Cat" and "Imp of the Perverse," centered on a protagonist (or subject, in the broader sense) who is the vehicle of a violence for which he appears not fully responsible, a violence that generates casualties consigned to a disposability, a merely corporeal fate, that he manages to escape.

Poe's longer narratives, *Arthur Gordon Pym* and *The Unparalleled Adventure of One Hans Pfaall,* disclose the primacy, for the perverse, of these casually accumulated corpses. Both journeys appear to follow an ambitious arc (Baudelaire comments on the ludicrous seriousness with which Poe presents Pfaall's extraterrestrial quest),[28] yet are resolutely circular. The College of Astronomy of Rotterdam is "not a whit better, nor greater, nor wiser" for Pfaall's research, while the moon-dwellers he meets are no less unsympathetic than the earthlings he left behind.[29] Arthur Gordon Pym famously encounters the specter of "whiteness" at the world's south, as if meeting in the end a mere projection of the identity of himself and his fellows.[30] What does remain progressive throughout each narrative is the accumulation of collateral victims that succumb to the vicissitudes of the voyages: the creditors mangled and burnt by Pfaall's balloon takeoff; the innumerable shipmates and comrades dispatched by *Pym*'s misfortunes. *Pym* is noteworthy for dispensing also with the main protagonist, though not through death within the action—rather through the remark of an editor, who intervenes to tell us that the manuscript has broken off.[31] This maneuver demonstrates the infinitude of the series of collateral victims, but also the externality of the main protagonist to this series, because he can only be done away with through a textual gesture.

With its layers of intrepid relentlessness, *Arthur Gordon Pym* finds an echo in contemporaneous efforts toward the aggressive expansion and strengthening of federal sovereignty.[32] The narrative sketches the empty form of this political ambitiousness—the spatial and geographical signal of its extension—while repeatedly exhibiting its main symptom: the cumulative, ostensibly incidental loss of life. The main protagonist's special status, his evasion of any reduction to the condition of casualty of history, marks him as the beneficiary of this violence, the one around whom it is spectacularly performed, while also simultaneously acknowledging and eluding a burden of guilt. *Pym* is unusual in staging a crisis in the predicament of the perverse protagonist, in the scene where Parker, a newly acquired comrade, suggests that one of the surviving band be cannibalistically sacrificed to provide sustenance for the rest—and selected for the purpose by the drawing of lots.[33] Pym is—unlike the others—deeply opposed to the plan. The differences in Baudelaire's rendering from the original text illuminate the distance between his understanding of the perverse and the dynamic it possesses in Poe, as well as the direction of his future appropriations of Poe's narratives.

Where Poe's Pym confesses that the "stern recollection" of the incident "will imbitter every future moment of my existence," Baudelaire's speaks of "le cruel souvenir [qui] empoisonnera chaque instant de mon avenir."[34] The adjective "cruel" is also added to the experience itself: "le moment le plus cruel de ce terrible drame, le plus plein d'angoisse, fut pendant que je m'occupais de l'arrangement des lots" ("the bitterest anxiety which I endured at any period of this fearful drama was while I occupied myself in the arrangement of the lots").[35] It can easily be seen that Poe's Pym regards the threat of being sacrificed to others' survival as salutary deviation from the normal course of events, rather than as a tragic imposition of contingent circumstance. The cannibalism episode figures the crisis point of the perverse because it threatens to dispose of the protagonist according to a rigid structural logic in which he will have no determining power—exactly like the anonymous victims that strew the narrative as a whole. In the end, the logic neatly turns against its initiator, and Parker is the choice of the randomness of the lottery.

The divergence between Baudelaire's emphasis and Poe's original serve to recall distinctions between them that emerge—despite his assimilation of them to the same phenomenon—in Adorno's observations concerning their relationship to the "novel" or the "new."[36] Drawing on Poe's "Descent into the Maelstrom" and the last line of Baudelaire's poetic series "La Mort," "which chooses a fall into the abyss, whether hell or heaven," Adorno suggests that the "cult of the new" in modernity discloses the fact that in the abstract world of the industrial age "there is nothing new any more." The new is simply "the formula by which stimulus is wrung from dread and despair," one that "makes evil flower" and becomes "a compulsive return of the old." Hence Poe's allegory of the novel or new consists in the "breathlessly spinning yet at the same time frozen movement of the hapless boat in the vortex of the maelstrom" ("atemlos kreisenden, doch gleichsam stillstehenden Bewegung des ohnmächtigen Bootes im Wirbel des Maelstroms"). The example he cites from Baudelaire is of the poem "Une martyre," which allegorically celebrates "the sacredness of lust in the horrifyingly liberating still-life of crime." Adorno goes on to claim that the intoxication induced by encounter with the naked, beheaded corpse in the poem resembles the paralyzed fascination with which victims of National Socialism consulted the newspapers to read about their prospective fate. He proposes that, in the Third Reich, "sensationalism" mediated (and stunned the public into consuming and accepting) news of unspeakable atrocity and of gradual military collapse to the degree that its audience forgot "wem das Ungeheure angetan wird, einem selbst oder anderen" (whom the enormity was committed against, oneself or others).

Scrutinizing this provocative theoretical overview, we should note that in the comparison between the two authors, the appearance of *circular* movement is specific to the examples drawn from Poe—whereas Baudelaire evokes frozen corporeality suffused with lust, or an unrepresented fall into the unknown. Circular movement sums up the structure of "perverse" narrative form, which endlessly repeats a threat posed to the protagonist and his hairsbreadth evasion of annihilation, a prospect that provokes the addictive "stimulus" Adorno theorizes, while also releasing an enjoyment of others' dispatch by the mechanical maelstrom (their reduction to a mere corporeality that the hero escapes). Such a dynamic forms the condition of the crisis staged in *Pym* that Baudelaire reconceives as existential drama. In his translation, Baudelaire focuses on the precise moment of the drawing of lots ("le moment le plus cruel"—whereas Poe specifies a general time period) in conformity with his fascination with still-life or endgame instances of horror infused by will and desire. Secondly, we might say that Adorno's reference to the "similarity" of "Une martyre" to the media culture of the Third Reich overleaps the history of Baudelaire's gradual engagement with Poe's work through translation, which eventually generates an interpretation of its "perverse" form directly concerned with investigating "whom the enormity is committed against." In the *Petits poèmes en prose*, Baudelaire seeks to explore the occlusion of "cruelty" in the perverse, assimilating it to a self-conscious tradition of analysis (and valorization) of this more definite category. American literature contemporaneous with Poe performs a contrary maneuver, using the mechanism of the "perverse" to displace the problem of agency and the assignment of victimhood. Baudelaire's achievement at once exploits and exposes this element of dissimulation, while illuminating the chasm between the reflexivity of his undertakings and the disavowals of an emergent literature operating under the determinative pressures of political exigency.

THE AMERICAN PERVERSE

Before turning to Baudelaire's revision of Poe's "perverse," I want to demonstrate the latter's deep-rootedness in the varieties of formative literary experiment contemporaneous with Poe's formulation. A prefatory articulation of the "perverse" emerges with Charles Brockden Brown's invention of the figure of "Carwin the Biloquist," uncanny, embodied prefiguration of Poe's "Imp" in being a nonmetaphysical, inexplicable causal agent, operating through the medium of voice, who alienates individuals from healthful intentions. Appropriately to the retrograde trajectory of the perverse, Carwin appears in narrative action *before* the eponymous *Memoirs* recounting his biography[37]— in the earlier *Wieland or The Transformation*. Set immediately prior to the Revolutionary War, *Wieland* necessarily possesses a kind of foundational status, and efforts to lend it ideological coherence are legion. No reading, however, has yet been able to account for the numerous anomalies that beset Brown's construction of his plot.[38] A focus on the motif of "biloquism" ignores the death that lies outside Carwin's machinations—that of the elder Wieland, by extraordinary natural or unnatural causes—and the contradiction posed by the mystery surrounding it. The narrator, Clara Wieland, condemns her brother for his (oddly unprecedented) religious credulity—following the acts of murder he commits heeding Carwin's commands as the voice of God—but their father's demise is not without hints of divine retribution for failure to fulfill an assumed religious mission to the Indians. A further complication lies in the eventual reduplication of the figure of Carwin in the person of Maxwell, responsible for the flight of the mother of Louisa Conway (heroine of an obtrusive subplot) to America. Clara criticizes the mother's vulnerability to Maxwell's adulterous designs, creating a strangely conventional parallel for her earlier assessment of Wieland's gullibility, as well as a peculiarly insistent shift of responsibility to the object away from the initiator of a seduction. The common element linking this addendum to the central narrative is the figure of Louisa Conway herself, the most comprehensive victim of Wieland's killing spree, and the person with whom Clara herself most closely identifies. Above all, *Wieland*'s most unusual feature is the grisly first-person recounting of the murder acts, justified by the conceit that the perpetrator does not have a proper consciousness of what he has done and by the narrator's inclusion of his testimony as "evidence."

John Carlos Rowe argues that Brown surreptitiously justifies frontier warfare by raising the specter of nameless formidable threat.[39] However, this conclusion ignores the way in which *Wieland*'s violence—always attributed to motiveless (and distinct) external sources—seems relentlessly retributive toward the settlers, rebuking every instance of removal to American soil until return to Europe is finally effected. Clara blames her own attachment to the place where so much destruction has occurred on a "perverse constitution of mind," suggesting that the colonial project itself is judged misbegotten and accursed. Along with the ascription of punitive lethalness to incalculable outside forces, the other two main features of *Wieland*'s affective scheme—the existential enjoyment of appalling brutality without guilt, and the insistence on a position of absolute innocence and victimhood—signal, like Poe's perverse, an acknowledgment of the illegitimacy of colonial violence and of accession to its benefits, along with a wish for exculpation.

The hydraulics of Poe's perverse are shared by a writer more polished than Brown—also involved, in his own uniquely paradoxical way, in the regressions and advances attending the development of a self-consciously "American" literature. Washington Irving's central motifs certainly inform the classic accounts of US culture: the decisive encounter between two male protagonists in a wilderness space—a feature of his short stories—bears on the mythopoesis of Leslie Fiedler's *Love and Death in the American Novel;* and Ann Douglas's emphasis on the pose of bachelor writerly idleness that represented one consequence of a sentimentalized departure from the astringency of Calvinism.[40] What has not yet been noted in this motif of Irving's is the way in which the wilderness encounter results in the death yet continued virtual existence of one of the male figures: the "specter bridegroom" takes on the identity of his fallen comrade; Ichabod Crane may or may not pursue a career as a bureaucratic functionary beyond Sleepy Hollow.[41] The clue to the meaning of the encounter is provided by its manner of appearance in "Rip van Winkle," where it is discernible through the relationship between the Postscript—in which we are told about a hunter who is "dashed to pieces" once he disturbs the bower of the Indian Manitou—and the long somnabulistic interlude in Rip's biography.[42] The hunter's fate is an alternate for Rip's own: Rip's survival parallels the phantasmal continued existence of the "specter bridegroom," and the rumored afterlife of Ichabod Crane. By separating the two destinies, "Rip van Winkle" reveals the source of the motif: incursion into Indian territory. The wilderness encounter stages a kind of punishment for this incursion, but also makes possible a type of irresponsible survival. Comically paradigmatic for this is the flesh-and-blood imposture of the specter bridegroom, released from the shackles of fairytale and feudal convention, who wins his betrothed on no other grounds than physical appeal. Irving's motif therefore incorporates both retribution and enjoyment—the mischievous acknowledgment of an escape from consequences.

The interplay between killing off and unencumbered afterlife dominates Irving's work in other senses as well. Contemporary—and later—critics of his derivativeness ought rather perhaps to have taken comfort in the fact that his sketches show little interest in the content of English literary tradition, but instead treat books themselves as "alive" and concentrate on the scenes of their inspiration and production (Shakespeare's childhood haunts; the purported tavern locales of the *Henriad*).[43] Such a strategy implicitly negates and annihilates the substance of the books themselves, thereby making way for new— American—matter. In their focus on these material frameworks, however, the sketches are also their own self-negation and abolition: the evident fakeness of the Falstaffian mementos Irving's narrator discovers means that his dilation on them is idle; the sketch is nothing more than a contentless, yet self-sustaining, frivolous invention. Ann Douglas attributes the ephemerality of the sketch to its market status as a disposable commodity.[44] Yet the genre's artifactual transitoriness appears to have deeper affective roots, since it often dwells on instances of loss and mourning, giving the impression that it is driven by the internal purpose of bringing human extirpation about. More significantly, Irving's sketches, like his fiction, play with the double result of dying off and continued existence and appear to generate both outcomes simultaneously. "The Wife" has an anonymous narrator attend on the suspiciously one-dimensional situation of a "friend," a wealthy man eager to provide his perfect bride with every luxury, who falls bankrupt and worries about how she will react to the news. The narrator's final comment, on the apparently happy outcome of the communication—"yet never has he experienced a moment of more exquisite felicity"–carries an ominous intimation of deterioration within its saccharine reassurance.[45] Similarly, Irving's version of the life of Sarah Curran, "The Broken Heart," recounts her experience subsequent to the execution of her lover, the Irish patriot Robert Emmet, in a manner that makes rude indifference and speedy recovery from grief factually compatible with pining.[46]

A key to the treatment of loss in the sketches is found in Irving's narrations of Indian resistance and decline.[47] Here, life and death are not brought into claustrophobic and insinuating proximity, rather Irving returns to a past when the tribes of the eastern seaboard were, as Wai Chee Dimock puts it, "a force to be reckoned with,"[48] and expresses outrage at their sufferings. The effort at retrospective revival and the difference in tone, suggest that this history may be the political referent for the process explored symbolically—and with more ambivalence and complicity—in the fictions, where destruction is, as it is for Brown and Poe, a source of pleasure nevertheless marked for retributive expiation. The relation between these narratives and Irving's other texts—or between the theme of Indian removal and its repeated fictional "working through"—can be summed up in Irving's use of the word "perverseness." In the History of New York, this word is used to describe any phenomena that thwart the smooth realization of the colonial enterprise (the "perverseness" shown by those accused of witchcraft at Salem in dying under torture; the "perverseness" of the incontrovertible laws of nature herself).[49] Irving's "perverse" use of perverseness therefore connects the term to an ostensibly progressive expansionist enterprise that is simultaneously condemned as an actualization of what should "not" be. His repeated fictional triggering of a mortality that signals at once punishment and enjoyment, situates him with Brown and Poe as the inventor of a literary mechanism that attests to the role of originary devastation in shaping the existence of the colonial subject.

The structural features of the perverse are also apparent in the novels of an author who diverges both from Irving's overt humanitarian outrage and Poe's studied political neutrality,[50] and who possesses another kind of relation to the fitful and uncertain development of a confident national literary imaginary. Evaluative repugnance (which Poe shared)[51] for James Fenimore Cooper's dilatory prose has long since been replaced by cultural analysis of the significance of his themes and representational choices—little has been said about the possible ideological or affective uses of his ineluctable stylistic quirk. For instance, in Cooper's final Leatherstocking novel, *The Deerslayer*, persuasive readings focus on its telescoping of historical time to justify Indian extermination,[52] and on its negotiation of the transition from classical republicanism through a fixation on (female) sexual "virtue."[53] However, the narrative does more than address these conflicts through the balancing acts of its plot. The very dissociation between descriptive ponderousness and the events of the action succeeds in creating the impression that incidents happen without the knowledge and even outside the framework of the narrative itself. "Event" in Cooper is inextricable from violence, and the violent acts that punctuate *Deerslayer* often take place without being "seen" or depicted. The hunter Harry Marsh's shooting of a Huron Indian girl going to meet her lover on the watch is conveyed only through sound and aftermath. Similarly, the destruction of the Huron Indian camp by British forces at the end of the novel is transmitted in a discreet, veiling reference to its cacophony and fury.

It will be evident from these examples that the narrative's ignorance of violent acts amounts to a surreptitious justification of aggression against the indigenous population. The dislocation between narration and act generates the sense that violence always originates elsewhere, and—when represented—from the Indian adversaries, as in the case of Deerslayer's encounter with a Huron Indian who tries to steal his canoe. Attempting to explain property rights to the thief (in a vignette Philip Fisher rightly identifies as an encapsulation of the Lockean defense of America's conquest)[54] and to part amicably, Deerslayer only resorts to lethal violence when finally attacked himself. Both elements—the endowment of violence with a suddenness that makes it appear unanticipated by the narrative and its exclusive link in visual portrayal with Indian agency—are summed up in a paradigmatic lethal arc, when a tomahawk is thrown at Deerslayer in captivity, and he returns it in the same movement, killing his assailant and (as Fisher also observes) making the latter appear the author of his own destruction.[55] The killing is portrayed much like the murder of the wife in Poe's "The Black Cat": abrupt, infused with a certain emotionless, calculative relish: "The keen little axe struck the victim in a perpendicular line with the nose, directly between the eyes, literally braining him on the spot."[56] Cooper's dilatory prose seems, like Poe's prefatory theorizing, the economic payment for such moments of violent dispatch, which in this text fantasize the autogenic extirpation of the Indian.

In addition to precipitating violent acts that it does not "see"—and locating the origins of white aggression in Indian maleficence—the narrative assigns the most egregious atrocities to a suprafictional source. At the center of the novel—though unremarked by critics, as if they are participating in the author's wish not to witness it—is the scalping and killing of the hunter Hutter by Huron Indians. This horror is attributed to "providence," deemed to have punished Hutter for his foray into the Huron Indian camps in search of scalps that he can sell to the "colony."[57] Ostensibly, the allusion to divine judgment condemns alike freelance opportunists and corrupted settlers. In its positioning within the text, however, the unwitnessed event confirms an assessment made in the novel's numerous long-winded debates over cultural and racial difference turning on the practice of scalping: that the Huron Indians are "pervarse and wicked."[58] It thus becomes an indirect justification of the destruction of the tribe's camp in the denouement. Cooper pursues the unique strategy of opposing "pervarseness" through the adoption of a perverse structure, in which violence always emerges from an extraneous source, facilitating at once enjoyment of its chance collateral fatalities and liberation from guilt. His ending underlines the latter aim through a similar tactic deployed by Brown: the younger "simple-minded" innocent girl in Hutter's care, Hetty, is killed in the attack on the camp, epitomizing a white Christian victimhood that distracts from interested belligerence and extermination.

As the quotations selected in a sequence of the section "Der Flaneur" in Walter Benjamin's *Passagen-Werk* suggest, Cooper exercises an enduring and multilayered influence on nineteenth-century French literary culture, with Balzac, Dumas, and their commentators extolling the relevance of forest wilderness and "savage" menace to the complexity of urban life.[59] It is also evident from the same sequence that Poe is the intervening figure in such a process of spatial translation, since the role of the "detective" links the "hunter" with the scrutinizing yet aesthetically entranced flaneur. Baudelaire participates in this process of cultural transposition, leaving behind the emphasis on "natural evil" expounded by his early essays on Poe to examine, in the *Petit poèmes en prose*, the duplicity and obfuscations of perversity. In so doing, he not only (notoriously) creates forms that are at once high and low culturally and that challenge the separation of art from the sensationalism of violence, but also he goes beyond an exoticized appropriation of American sources by exploiting Poe's manipulative disavowals. The results and final significance of Baudelaire's investigations are revealed by an author who promotes the alignment of literature with urban savagery and effects a second transatlantic revolution in French poetics (Lautréamont).

THROWING POE OUT THE WINDOW

The first persuasive effort to encapsulate Poe's influence on the prose poems is Jonathan Culler's reading of "Le Mauvais Vitrier," a rewriting of "The Imp of the Perverse," which actually features Poe as the weapon ("pot") thrown at the glazier who cannot provide aesthetically pleasing wares and so is forced to do so by means of their dramatic shattering.[60] Culler argues that the missile represents a device—the turning of a word into an allegory—suggested to Baudelaire by Poe through the role of words in "Imp"'s "psychological" explanation of perversity, where the protagonist's urge to speak (and confess) furnishes the plot that rounds out the anecdote. However, "The Imp of the Perverse" is not an explanation or diagnosis. Its closing elucidatory statement, "I have said thus much, that in some measure I may answer your question, that I may explain to you why I am here," reveals the whole narrative to have been a circumlocution and an example of procrastination, namely, an enactment of the phenomenon it theorizes.[61] "Le Mauvais Vitrier" in fact parodies this refusal of explanation, as well as its deliberately disingenuous obfuscation of the tendency of perversity toward harm and injury. Obsessively citing and discounting a range of possible authoritative sources of insight (professional and subjective), the poem integrates references to violence into these cancellations of intelligibility. For instance, while Poe counts procrastination as one (relatively harmless) instance of everyday perverseness, Baudelaire emphasizes procrastinators' sudden commission of violent acts: "Tel qui, craignant de trouver chez son concierge une nouvelle chagrinante, rôde lâchement une heure devant sa porte sans oser rentrer, tel qui garde quinze jours une lettre sans la décacheter . . . se sentent quelquefois brusquement précipités vers l'action par une force irrésistible, comme *la flèche d'un arc*" (he who, fearing that he will receive some distressing news from his concierge, drives desultorily around for an hour in front of his own door without daring to enter; he who keeps a letter for fifteen days without opening it . . . feels sometimes suddenly prompted to action by an irresistible force, like an arrow from a bow).[62]

The act that the poem dramatizes is minutely calculated, despite the preparatory emphasis on inexplicability and suddenness. This contradiction alludes to the way in which Poe presents murder as incidental to perverseness, a side-event, yet which is clearly the central "aim" of the text, a tension that creates perversity's insidious status and formal outline. However, the actual structure of the act shows that Baudelaire's revision of Poe achieves another purpose: the rewriting of the Sadean tableau of torture. Sonya Stephens remarks that "the poet does not smash the glass directly, but forces the glazier down on to it to ruin himself with the weight of his own body."[63] Sade's accounts of sexual and physical violation are preoccupied with this motif of soliciting and securing complicity in the acts from the victims. His insistence on this element becomes transparent in the condensations of his scenarios delineated by the notations that end the (incomplete) text *Les 120 Journées*.[64] Here, victims are always depicted as being trapped into futile betrayals by the false promise of survival or by the manipulation of bonds of love and kinship. This intermediate stage in murder, where the victim contributes to the enormity of the act that will be perpetrated anyway, seems necessary to the assertion of the prerogative and artificial godlike power of the libertine.

A difference of perspective between Walter Benjamin and Jacques Derrida illuminates the manner in which Baudelaire is rewriting Sade. Benjamin argues that Baudelaire was "ein zu guter Leser von Sade" (too good a reader of Sade) to write detective stories or identify with the position of detective because "der Kalkül, das konstruktive Moment, stand bei ihm eindeutig auf der Seite des Asozialen. Es ist ganz und gar in die Grausamkeit eingebracht" (calculation, the moment of fabrication, was in his case related to an asocial tendency. It was completely immersed in cruelty).[65] Derrida queries, first of all, whether there is really an absence of Sadean cruelty in Poe, and whether it is possible to say that one never "identifies" with the figure of the detective.[66] More generally, he reflects, Baudelaire is deeply concerned with a process and experience presumably fundamental to the detective's work, that of "knowing." Sade is important to him in this respect on a primordial, almost theological level, figuring both daring openness to and also the point of origin for a lapserian state: "il faut toujours revenir à De Sade [sic], c'est-à-dire à l'Homme Naturel, pour expliquer le mal" (it is always necessary to return to Sade, that is to natural man, to explain evil).[67] Sade—and eighteenth-century libertinism more generally—also represents, for Baudelaire, a condition of conscious awareness of one's own evil. As Derrida notes, Baudelaire contrasts this position relentlessly with that of Georges Sand, egoistically convinced of her own goodness and thus closed to all sense of its possible vitiation. She is, according to Baudelaire, Satan as *ingénu*.[68]

But while Sade may, with full awareness, affirm what is normally considered "evil," his tableaux can hardly be considered exploratory in anything other than a corporeally outlandish sense; they are "calculated" and "constructed," to draw on Benjamin's terms, and always bolster the determining power of the libertine (who in theory must be prepared to fall victim to the schemes of others, but in practice rarely does). Sade's "cruelty" can be compared, in structural terms, to that articulated by the main protagonist of Baudelaire's cherished novel, *Les Liaisons dangereuses*, when the Marquise de Merteuil enjoins the Comte de Valmont to regard the Présidente de Tourvel—"voyez la cruauté!" (behold cruelty!)—as "une femme ordinaire, une femme telle qu'elle est seulement" (an ordinary woman, a woman just as she is, simply).[69] The reduction of others to a condition of equivalence, and the accrual of artificial power derived therefrom, is the guiding purpose and aesthetic gesture of Sade's novels as well. The *Petits poèmes en prose*, on the other hand, continually question this position of sadistic dominance, along with the status and nature of victimhood. The poems repeatedly reverse initial impressions of where responsibility, sympathy, and suffering lie, making the reader complicit with the actions, oversights, and interpretations the poems perpetrate. Poe's "perverse" is the decisive contributor to this strategy because it is predicated on a duplicitous presentation of the relation between agency and violence.

One prose poem demonstrates the combination of Poe's influence with Sade's reconfiguration. "Une mort héroïque" possesses the three elements that structure Poe's story "Hop-Frog": a king, his persecuted jester, and an ambiguous narrator. Baudelaire's speaker appropriates and sharpens Poe's narrator's bitter emphasis on the king's love of "joking," carefully avoiding, for reasons of political censorship, a direct characterization of his monarch as "cruel," yet making clear that his narrow kingdom is a theater of sadistic entertainments. Baudelaire also borrows from "Hop-Frog" the latter's boorishly empty keyword, "capital": "notwithstanding the protuberance of his stomach and a constitutional swelling of the head, the king, by his whole court was accounted a capital figure": "there came into my mind a capital diversion," says Hop-Frog on conceiving of his revenge plan, disguised as a species of entertainment. "Capital!" roar the king and his counselors on hearing the details.[70] Perhaps because, like the phrase from Rousseau in "Rue Morgue," it remains an untranslatable irritant, the word is converted into the centerpiece of "Une mort héroïque."

Having condemned his clown (Fancioulle) to death following his role in a political conspiracy, the prince "voulait profiter de l'occasion pour faire une expérience psychologique d'un intérêt *capital*" (wanted to profit from the occasion to perform a psychological experiment of *capital* interest).[71] In other terms, he constrains Fancioulle to perform under the shadow of impending death. It is not entirely clear what happens during the performance or at its end: its quality is described entirely through the reactions of the narrator and the audience, which indicate a sublime, a perfect achievement, that mocks (literally or figuratively) the fatality framing it. During the spectacle the narrator sees the prince confer with a pageboy. Subsequently, a hiss sounds in the theater, and the clown falls dead on stage. Critics have wondered whether Fancioulle's art is considered inferior by Baudelaire since its exclusion of all awareness of death contradicts the account of comic art given in *De l'essence du rire*, where comedy is linked to human frailty and "fallenness."[72] Similarly, the intentionality and meaning of the connection between political sovereign and aesthetic event remains obscure. Was the prince provoked by the death-defying nature of the mime's absorption in his craft? How far and in what way can his death be considered part of the performance?

Poe's story is much less complex, even by the standards of his own aesthetic. It shows, unusually, the direct victory of the masochistic sufferer over his torturers. Hop-Frog's plan is to suggest that the king and his counselors dress up as orangutans. In the resulting confusion, he sets them on fire. The mention of the animal also found in "Rue Morgue"—and of the motif of animality in general (Hop Frog is also half-animal)—indicates the same displacement of malignant intention away from the central protagonist seen in most Poe stories, though occurring here in cruder outline. Baudelaire's poem, when the clown apparently dies and the king remains, his state of mind pondered by the equally enigmatic narrator, probes rather the outer limit of aesthetic sensation—since the interest of the scenario depends on a death taking place—and the limits of political authority, which seems evaded by aesthetic brilliance, even as it also depends on such brilliance for its own instantiation. Both tendencies are inimical to Sade, in whose texts the staging of libertine violence is only "aesthetic" in the Barthesian sense of reaching a sublime boredom, and for whom the consequent aggrandizement and inoculation against vulnerability is indispensable.

THE FINAL ANNIHILATION

Isidore Ducasse indirectly acknowledges Poe and Baudelaire as forebears, parodying them in *Poesies I,* the work that appears to throw out the post-Romantic literature of the nineteenth century in favor of a severe classicism, but that may rather seek to replace and substitute for it the comparably decadent strains of *Maldoror.*[73] *Maldoror* figures perversity in terms of discipleship: "tu me reconnaîtras comme ton disciple respectueux dans la perversité" (you will acknowledge me as your respectful disciple in perversity) the narrator decrees to his own shadow and mirror-image.[74] Baudelaire's reading of Poe is perhaps alluded to in the ultimate story of mentorship recounted by the poem: the meeting between Maldoror and the madman Aghone. Once the latter has conveyed the surreal history of his drunken, abusive father, the following reflections arise: "L'auditeur approuve dans son intérieur ce novel exemple apporté à l'appui de ses dégoûtants théories. Comme si, à cause d'un homme, jadis pris du vin, l'on était en droit d'accuser l'entière humanité. Telle est au moins la réflexion paradoxale qu'il cherche à introduire dans son esprit: mais elle ne peut en chasser les enseignements de la grave expérience" (the auditor inwardly approves this new instance of corroboration for revolting theories. As if, because of one man once under the influence of wine, one had the right to condemn all of humanity. At least that's the paradoxical reflection he tries to entertain: but it isn't able to dissipate the lessons of this serious situation).[75] In evoking the founding origin of Baudelairean perversity—the drunken state of the narrator of "The Black Cat"—and signaling its banality, or Baudelaire's doctrinal overprizing of an unremarkable anecdote, these sentences perform other work as well. Their sequence of cancellations and revisions exhibits a feature found throughout *Maldoror*: an apparent inability to decide whether man is naturally good or evil—or a constant circling around this question.

Due to these vacillations Lautréamont might—if we accept a claim made by Maurice Blanchot[76]—be considered more sentimental than Sade, who aims rather at an interested neutralization of cruelty, which he deems nothing other than *"l'énergie de l'homme* que la civilisation n'a point encore corrompue"* (the energy of man not yet corrupted by civilization) or *"une des branches de la sensibilité"* (one of the branches of sensibility).[77] Such axioms, like the determining role of the libertine in the scenarios of torture, confirm and consolidate libertine power, only inflicting the experience of threat and mystification on the victim. Sade's political treatise "Français, encore un effort si vous voulez être républicains" follows the same logic. Adopting the slogans of the French revolution, it institutionalizes libertine right, turning all frameworks of regulation toward the implementation of a reduction of others to a condition of equivalence. As we have seen, Baudelaire's verbal tableaux do not follow such a rigid epistemological program, leaving the play of positioning between victim and perpetrator open, though always turning on a question of sadistic calculation and reversal. Lautréamont performs several operations. He revises and interrogates the Sadean project, exposes the stakes of Baudelaire's prose poems, and reveals the influence of Poe.

As Maldoror's reaction to Aghone's story indicates, Lautréamont dramatizes the process of making statements about human moral character. The process appears interrogative and open-ended—since the narrator seems to disagree with his protagonist's conclusion, or the protagonist hesitates and reflects—but has in fact been decided in advance. Lautréamont thereby infects the Sadean commitment to decisive cynical statement with a certain disorientation. However, he preserves its finality and malignancy. Indeed, the sham questioning of cynicism only exacerbates the crime Maldoror is about to perpetrate, just in the way that Sade's libertines' false promises achieve the corruption of victims before their deaths. Contrary, therefore, to Blanchot's belief in Lautréamont's sentimentalism, the poet radicalizes the potential of the statement by making it into a malignant act: the true meaning of his resolution "je fais servir mon génie à peindre les délices de la cruauté" (I dedicate my genius to painting the delights of cruelty).[78] Throughout, *Maldoror* elaborates acts that are inextricable from statements, or which statements ostensibly cover up and obscure. By means of this revision of Sade, Lautréamont pushes to a more extreme point the ambiguous status of injurious acts in Baudelaire's prose poems. There, the issue of how far art requires the specter of violence for its impact remains a question—in Lautréamont, murder is always already perpetrated, or phantasmally ongoing. The decisive factor in this confluence between Sade and Baudelaire is Poe because of the incongruity between statement and happening presented in his model of the perverse.

Maldoror pursues many ways of posing the interchangeability of statements and acts. A comic summing up of the oscillation between them occurs in Maldoror's encounter with the typical object of his lethal intrigues, a young boy, on a park bench, where he endangers the physical well-bring of his victim not with violence but only with misanthropic doctrines.[79] The poem also undermines the temporal tangibility of acts: past violence is dramatically absorbed into metamorphosis (the two victims of Maldoror who become a spider; the abused boy transformed into a swan) or reported through layerings of testimony (infamously, the letter in which a woman reports the killing and dismemberment of her daughter; additionally, the recounting of numerous sufferings as stories or anecdotes).[80] *Maldoror*'s most important dissociation, between its narrator and its main character, contributes significantly to the telescoping of time, abolishing linear life story and identifying this personage with his fictional series of male victims in a manner that converts the trajectory of innocence outraged into a kind of virtual biography, an infinitely repeating cycle.[81] Perhaps more than any other nineteenth-century work, *Maldoror* is obsessed with its effect on the reader, often theorizing this effect rather than fashioning the devices to produce it, as in the opening sequence, where, through the image of a flock of birds wary at the approach of a storm, the cautious, reasonable reader is asked not to peruse the verses at all.[82]

The true meaning of the obfuscation between statement and act is found in the perverse workings of a rhetorical figure that was of fundamental importance for Baudelaire and that also carries within it the moral thematics of the similarity between the self and fellow human beings, along with the incommensurability that dominates the general structure of Poe's narratives of the perverse. Lautréamont already reveals an interest in the arbitrary capacities of the gesture of comparison (the connector "comme") in incidental remarks that assert the force of the poet's power of intervention, if not the associational potential, that Baudelaire inscribes in the sensuous musings of his "Correspondances."[83] "J'aime cette comparaison" (I like this comparison) announces the narrator, as he likens the ocean to "un immense bleu, appliqué sur le corps de la terre" (an immense blue, applied to the body of the earth), a line that is no discovery or illumination of resemblance, but rather the very painting of characteristics themselves.[84] Concomitantly, Lautréamont dispatches trite or standard similes, as when Maldoror finds himself in a mock-scene from *Hamlet,* where a gravedigger compares scattered tombs to "les fleurs dans une prairie" (flowers on a prairie)—"comparaison qui manque de vérité" (a comparison that lacks truth"—or when the narrator declares his intention of composing "une strophe sérieuse et froide" (a cold and serious verse), but declares (since he is not about to die): "Écartons en conséquence tout idée de comparaison avec le cygne au moment où son existence s'envole" (consequently, let us avoid any idea of comparison with the swan at the moment of his expiration).[85]

The longest rumination on comparison—and one that highlights its centrality in the rhetorical gamut of the poem—occurs in the second stanza of the fourth canto. In his hesitant, yet panicky, breathless style, the narrator introduces "deux piliers" (two pillars) "qu'il n'était pas difficile et encore moins impossible de prendre pour des baobabs" (which it was not difficult and even less impossible to take for two baobab trees) and which were "plus grands que deux épingles" (bigger than two pins) and which he then specifies abruptly to be "deux tours énormes" (two enormous towers) (159). He becomes lost in the trivial complications generated by the unnecessarily graduated comparison (two baobabs do not resemble two pins, but it is not that a baobob differs so much from a pillar, etc.), such that the alignment between the objects is abandoned, and the figure of comparison itself pinpointed as an inevitable and regressive (since it may violate precision) product of books, the influence of one's peers ("semblables"), or habit. By the end of the stanza, however, the narrator returns to his contorted simile, with a typically perverse compaction of preference and fact, saying that "tous les goûts sont das la nature" (all tastes have their basis in nature) and that his likening of the pillars to pins was based on the laws of geometrical optics.[86] It can easily be seen that the comparison on which Lautréamont dwells is an unremarkable one, not worth its problematization, and that his disquisition is concerned not with the arbitrariness, conventionality, or residually inventive capacities of poetic rhetoric, but with the articulation of an essentially "dead" statement perversely reanimated through mere speech. The framing of the comparison indicates the import of this "deadness": the "two towers" invoked prefigure the gallows that open the next stanza, and the ending, where the narrator suggests he will not walk in the valley of the towers again, links him to the wolf reluctant to linger near the gallows-site at the conclusion of the subsequent vignette.[87]

This peculiar relation between the two stanzas, where the non-event of the first seems the rhetorical backdrop to the second (in which a man is tortured by his wife and mother), reveals the strange significance of defunct tropological pyrotechnics; they accompany, almost as voiceover, a scenario of human expiration or near-expiration. Repeatedly in the poem, the narrative contorts itself pedantically over the spectacle of a dead or near-dead object, reveling both in the inevitability of its demise and the piquancy of a sign of life. The link between actual death and rhetorical nullity is clearest in the sixth stanza of canto five, where the narrator ("Silence!") draws our attention to the progress of a funeral cortège. His long comparison between the face of the child appearing in the open coffin and the beauty of a swallow's flight and, then, a lily's piercing of water's surface—again punctuated and halted by reflections on poetic legitimacy—not only violates the standard similes thrown out elsewhere (of graves to flowers, poets to swans) but suggests violence and malignancy underneath the figure. This time, he says, no one will be able to recognize the "connection" ("rapport") between the terms of the comparison, a failure precipitated by "l'inamovible situation d'un manque de repentir, touchant l'ignorance volontaire dans laquelle on croupit" (the stubborn fact of a lack of remorse regarding the ignorance in which we fester).[88] Since such ignorance, earlier in the stanza, was connected to the mystery of death and its suddenness or unexpectedness (in which the narrator also dramatizes himself as being caught up, happy to be able to live from one sentence to the next), the figure of the dead child is based on a murder that it does not reveal. Maldoror lurks ominously around the scene, and the narrator protests that his comparison only imports a "calm majesty" commonly recognizable and perfectly proper to literary efforts at estrangement and renewal of the everyday.

Lautréamont's use of comparison explains otherwise obscure (and to date unremarked) comments in Walter Benjamin's essay on surrealism. Benjamin condemns as "scurrilous" Ducasse's attempt (in a letter to his publisher) to place himself within a literary tradition (one that includes Baudelaire). Noting that the surrealist effort to provide a political "curriculum vitae" for Ducasse failed, Benjamin argues that the kernel of "evil" in Ducasse's work is only a political force in the sense that it clears away "moral dilettantism." Otherwise, it must be recognized that Ducasse offers an aesthetic based on "hate" ("haß") and "die Tiefe Poescher Gedanken."[89] Benjamin can only be referring here to Poe's "Philosophy of Composition." The reference is paradoxical in that Poe precisely argues for the creation of aesthetic effects through superficial yet, as it were, grave means: the resonance of "The Raven"'s hollow refrain lies in the allusion to a dead girl.[90] Lautréamont obviously literalizes and maliciously flaunts this structural dependency of art on death. In doing so, he at once radicalizes and closes down Baudelaire's exploration of the relationship between the effectiveness of art and the spectacle of murder. Both developments transfer to the aesthetic realm the concerns of Sadean libertinage, which only repeats and accumulates tableaux in order to confirm a certain relation of power.

Poe's "philosophy" of "The Raven" could also be applied to his "perverse" prose works, since, in them, producing dead bodies is the driving purpose of storytelling, though in a profane manner, generating not melancholic longing, but rather a sense of escape from destruction or guilt, as well as an enjoyment of violence without consequences. The deeper, unrecognized "tradition" into which Benjamin inserts Lautréamont includes not only—in fact—Baudelaire, but also the range of formative nineteenth-century American literature contemporary to Poe, where killing is ignored, disavowed, but primary to the fabrication of narrative. In the report on the French literary scene written in 1940, Benjamin reviews Gaston Bachelard's study of *Maldoror* and remarks that Bachelard's delineation of the characteristics of the poem's aggression—imaginary action; avoidance of contest with equals; menaces, deception, and vengefulness—transmits the very contours of "Hitlerism."[91] Of course, Benjamin's conclusion concerns an extrapolation from Lautréamont within a new context; it addresses the idea of his aesthetics become a politics. What the observation discloses is the uneasy positioning of the boundary between aesthetics and politics in the case of the "perverse": through this motif, American literature shows the reverse-image of a murderous history; Baudelaire continually presses the sensationalism of the prose poem toward the shock-effect of actual killing, while Lautréamont makes literature no more or less than just this virtual achievement. The journey of the "perverse" suggests that the career of American influences in French poetics goes beyond the transfer of Cooper's prairies and Poe's ratiocination to the Parisian urban wilderness, to encompass a gesture that queries the very ends of literature itself.

CHAPTER TWO

"Some Things Which Could Never Have Happened"

Near the close of the letter to Nathaniel Hawthorne dated 13 August 1852, which details the set of anecdotally recounted events later known among scholars as "The Story of Agatha,"[1] offering them as the basis for a new literary work, Herman Melville gives the following description of the development of fiction from biographical foundation: "You have a skeleton of actual reality to build about with fulness & veins & beauty."[2] The effort of persuasion informing his equation between skeleton and textual framework, in seeking to overcome the metaphor's "deadness" by envisaging the labor and the appealing results of imaginative embellishment, strangely accentuates this very quality—in part because of the inherently paradoxical nature of the catachresis involved—evoking an artificial, almost lurid corporeality. In 1855, communication with Hawthorne having lapsed into silence,[3] the elements of the trope reappear, this time starkly literalized and dramatically reversed: "Benito Cereno" (1855) "builds about" a source account of slave-ship revolt (and the ship in question) an actual skeleton, and organizes plot around the permanently unsolved mystery of its vanished flesh.[4]

Critics who remark on the novella's echo of the letter assume that the figurehead fulfills Melville's earlier model of fiction's evolution from preexisting record, and are concerned only with whether it constitutes a legitimate instance of authorial license—a racist slander or the emblem of an abolitionist, anti-imperialist aesthetic design.[5] Wider and more recent interpretation has largely sidelined or obscured the skeleton's Gothic sensationalism, dedicating itself instead to the explication of allusions that confirm the narrative's inextricability from "actual reality" of historical and political consequence. It is my contention that the tale's reversal of the metaphor outlines the anatomy of its form, revealing it to be a self-demolishing fiction that overturns the teleology of plot and the protocols of allegory, simultaneously with the ideal of sympathetic, collaborative alliance undergirding the "Agatha" project. A reading of this process lays bare the story's politics of affect and their predication on features needlessly marginalized by criticism's historicist commitments—contrived visual theatricality[6] and insinuated "cruelty"—along with the attachments that have inspired a recurring tendency, throughout the story's reception history, to cover its fleshless structure with an edifying "veins and fullness."

The rhetorical genealogy of the "Agatha" skeleton and the literary gift it embodies parallels the alleged origins of "Benito Cereno"'s figurehead, being composed of a series of cannibalistic metaphors traceable in preceding letters to Hawthorne. Caleb Crain argues that these flesh-eating tropes disclose an overwhelmingly powerful, even disorienting physical passion,[7] but such an emphasis on the force and immediacy of desire discounts a striking contextual factor: the ways in which they are prefaced, bracketed, or entangled with paeans to Hawthorne's popular success and emergent cultural importance. Melville's confused and, as Crain reads it, coaxingly reproachful claim that "the cultivation of the brain eats out the heart" succeeds a mention of seeing Hawthorne's stories in *Holden's Dollar Magazine,* which occasions an hypothesis about his formidable effect on "the tribe of 'general readers'" and is followed by a surreally metonymic reflection (glimpses of a portrait of "N. H.," advertisements for and "flattering . . . allusions" to him during a "four-and-twenty hours" visit to New York) on his ubiquitous authorial presence in the quotidian landscape.[8]

Similarly, a postscript where Melville styles himself as the comically cannibalistic little boy in *The House of the Seven Gables* (1851) ends a missive which cites that novel in the manner of a publisher's list and then posits the title of a review-essay perhaps redolent of his own struggle with the difficulty of pleasing an extensive audience: "Hawthorne: A Problem."[9] Depicting Melville as a voracious character inside Hawthorne's novel, the postscript itself shows that his devouring language encompasses the pursuit of an imminent, potentially usurpatory share in his friend's literary industry, also conveyed

by the wish to fill him with "a specimen mouthful" of *The Whale*.[10]
The cannibalism metaphors' libidinal verve therefore denotes something more closely associated with the phenomenon than desire, if
still not wholly separable from the latter: identification,[11] absorbing
or striving to become another, or in this case an implied assimilation
of Hawthorne's literary endeavors to Melville's, driven in part by an
avid interest in the secret of reconciling artistic ambitiousness with
critical acclaim and public appreciation.

Hawthorne's praise for *Moby-Dick* (1851) seems to appease this
consuming urgency, since the famous communication of November
1851 regards (and professes to value) his reaction as transcendent
of physical being and need, surplus to the "reward" of "supper" at
the end of a "hard day's work," a rejection of the book's "imperfect
body" in favor of its "soul," and, most important, the occasion for
a spiritualized, abstract cannibalism, wherein both writers are eaten
together in a version of Eucharistic sacrifice.[12] Yet in the aftermath
of *Moby-Dick*'s disappointing reception and prior to *Pierre*'s publication (1852), Melville's fascination with Hawthorne's writerly lot
resurfaces, pervading a note that lightheartedly but insistently charts
the vocally and typographically public omnipresence of his sur-
name.[13] "Agatha"'s skeleton—to which this last letter, with its lack
of metaphorical cannibalistic activity, is a transition—represents, I
would suggest, a renewed, strategic attempt, undertaken once the
failure of *Pierre* was becoming evident, to consolidate the identificatory orientation toward Hawthorne, with its entwinement of ardor
and ambition, superseding the reckless indulgence of physical appetite
with the artificial "building" of a body, and in so doing substituting
for anxious awareness of public taste a calculatedly productive, practical scheme of quasi collaboration.

Focused on whether, when, or in what form Melville eventually
completed the story himself,[14] critics have not explored the reasons for
the decision to bestow it on his correspondent, taking at face value his
"plump" assertion that he thought Hawthorne "would make a better
hand" of the reported material;[15] judging the letters to be a sign of his
continuing concern, after *Pierre*, with questions of popular appeal,[16]
or, on a less optimistic note, of an inability, as Hershel Parker has
argued, to tell anyone "that he could not pursue this darkly fascinat-
ing topic while in such pain from the reviews."[17] The terms of the
plan and its rhetorical antecedents indicate that it is governed by an
aim hinted at in Parker's observation: the temporary displacement

of the question of authorly successfulness onto—and its working-out within—the safety of the private realm (a refuge from public hostility, misunderstanding, and indifference), through the bid to become, if only imaginatively and fleetingly, an originator and facilitator of Hawthorne's at that stage more widely acceptable brand of literary creativity. Examination of relationships between "Agatha"'s thematic matter and Melville's own typical concerns and later fiction forgets that it is meant to be compelling to another writer and appears intended to draw Hawthorne closer, challenging him to replicate the initial "sympathetic" reaction to the real-life chronicle; to share, significantly for two men left fatherless in childhood, compassion for the abandoned heroine and curiosity about her "latitudinarian" deserter, and to picture an archetypally benevolent father, whose function is to safeguard others from suffering.[18] "Agatha"'s skeleton and its surrounds, in short, replace apparent declarations of amorous and aspirational longing with the corpus of an identificatory union, which is also the "body" of a conjointly built literary work.

As Melville's comparatively unexuberant last known letter to Hawthorne tells us, the reciprocal generation of "Agatha" did not take place.[19] Whether or not Hawthorne received the idea with a mere "polite interest,"[20] his inability or unwillingness to bring it to fruition may be attributable to lack of need for the cooperative compact Melville sought, resulting precisely from prior success in the "vein" (as the 13 August letter puts it) typified by the tale, and a nascent preoccupation with a different strand of public life.[21] The end of the exchange is concurrent with the beginning of a new phase in Melville's career, involving magazine writing and an augmentation of the propensity, discernible to critics in his concern with "Agatha"'s passive endurance and in the nature of her reincarnation as The Encantadas' "Chola widow," to feign affinity with while undermining his readership's cherished assumptions.[22] Coded memorializations of the faded friendship with Hawthorne are also evident in the surreptitiously iconoclastic works of this period: "Benito Cereno," seen as exemplary of their duplicitous strategies,[23] has been thought to incorporate such a feature only in an incidental or ancillary fashion, despite its diverse catalogue of disappeared, obstructed, failed, and sham homosocial bonds.[24] I want to propose that the story's reversal of the 1852 metaphor, contrary to exclusive stress on Melville's inward turn or prevailing worldly engagement, confers a shape on biographical disillusion (and the professional dilemmas bound up with it), which provides the apparatus for a political critique.[25] The fleshless figurehead marks the overthrow of the hopes inscribed within "Agatha"'s skeleton, reintroducing, as ambiguous menace, its cannibalistic prehistory (the "things which could never have happened" in which Cereno, certain chimerical clues apprise us, may have inadvertently participated). At the same time, it "unbuilds" the two things signified by the metaphor (sympathetic identification and fiction), dislocating their tenacious interdependence.

"Benito Cereno"'s assault on identification is hardly a new motif in its critical history, which has returned repeatedly to the inviting snares and subtly self-condemning characteristics of its most prominent (Delano's) perspective. What has been neglected is that the story achieves this objective using its central fabricated device to dismantle fictional form in a way that prompts readers to complete it with their sympathies, as if in covert and coercive reenactment of the "Agatha" proposal. Not only does the skeleton's missing flesh, and the nonrepresentation of the act that removed it, solicit and render phantasmal racist antipathy (designating the unincluded "veins and fullness" of a nullified sensationalist plot), it operates in tandem with other purposely tantalizing "absences" that ultimately void prospective readerly affiliations: the skeletal Cereno himself and the visible, diverse, but inaccessible African population inhabiting the *San Dominick*'s skeletal edifice, whose launch from "Ezekiel's Valley of Dry Bones,"[26] refers to the hidden outline of their unportrayed anterior circumstances. These positions' evacuation depends for its significance on the skeleton's acquired function as—more than an emblem of New World colonialism or an isolated "reversal" in the connotations of "white" and "black"[27]—a prop in a parodic staging of "white" racial identification, which retrospectively overhauls the narrative, glossing the malaise of a seemingly sterile allegory and transfiguring the pattern of individual encounters.[28]

The omitted cannibalism and the figurehead's meaning transfer the cruelty associated with "savagery" to sympathy itself, forcing empathetic interactions between whites to act out their racial underpinnings by becoming unintentional inflictions of pain. Encapsulatory concreteness is thereby given to the defining American contrast, remarked on but considered coincidental by Alexis de Tocqueville, between a generalized "sympathy" pervading civic existence (produced by the leveling, in a "democratic" culture, of feudalized social hierarchy) and the "dreadful miseries" and "very cruel punishments" inflicted on those excluded from citizenship, African slaves.[29] An inversion of the priority of interpretation over image in the skeleton's deployment performs a further theoretical simulation, dramatizing the dependency of "white" sympathy for slaves on spectacle, and its disengagement from and unrecognized complicity with the causes of the suffering to which it responds. The "reversals" propagated by the presiding fictional object, then, schematize the preconditions and repudiate the aesthetics of the shifts of position conceived by abolitionist, sentimental literature, which allow and encourage readers to identify with or vicariously inhabit an "experience" of slave suffering.

Continuing critical reluctance to grapple with the totalized nature of this breaking down of sympathetic identification can be ascribed to the residual survival in American criticism of a nineteenth-century attachment to its autonomous value as a political resource. Traces of an esteem for the independent efficacy and primary political importance of sympathy are evident even in pessimistic, demystifying readings concerned to point out that "Benito Cereno" adduces no clear victimized party or justified cause to endorse, only an impression of suspension, homogeneity, and equivalence. Such preoccupation with the impossibility of identification shares in the ambivalence manifested by a broader investigation of the nineteenth-century culture of sentiment, which, although offering a dissection of its corruptions, compromises, and dangers (most notably its promotion of aesthetic enjoyment over knowledge of and remedies for the causes of suffering), nevertheless concentrates on the problem of refining sympathetic response or refuses to contemplate the kind of trenchant condemnation sustained in Melville's tale.[30] "Benito Cereno"'s narrative skeleton and missing flesh, however, ensure that all identificatory gestures, including melancholic fixation on the failure or irrelevance of any, will be obliged to add "veins and fullness" to its form, and, as a result, to construct themselves as fictional inventions, decorative adornments obfuscating the structural actuality of the racialized culture it exposes. The novella's reception history, a move from a concern with "evil" to a focus on slavery (and latterly, political stagnation), can also be read as a sequence of identificatory choices, each of which entails building flesh about the work, with the result that later interpretative contributions sometimes uncomfortably resemble those of earlier, ostensibly far less enlightened critical moments. In what follows I seek to trace the stripping down of identification and fictional plot brought about by the figurehead, through those acts of formal and sympathetic completion that it both invites and undercuts.

VEINING AND FLESHING

Readings that canonize Cereno and equate Babo with "evil" produce (not surprisingly) the most unquestioning completion of the fiction with identification, apparently filling in the horror of cannibalism while concealing it and the skeleton in vague praise for Melville's meditation on "the foulness and cruelty of man" and refusal to "spare us the sickening cruelty of the original mutiny."[31] These solemn, squeamish assessments allow celebration of a "beautiful design," but leave unresolved one niggling puzzle, which symptomatically reemerges in later arguments: the apparent "unity" of symbol and concept or material phenomenon: "when one tries to translate [a given symbol] into anything other than itself, one is bound to tell some lies."[32] Conversely, critics who decline to accept the political difficulties created by such conclusions contest admiration for "beautiful" fiction with an emphasis on the ugly "fact" of the skeleton's presence and on the facts of history.

Sidney Kaplan asserts, "The fact is that Melville's intention must be determined mainly by what he did with his plot, how he veined and fleshed it"; "to the source account Melville adds a strong hint that Aranda's skeleton has been cannibalistically prepared"; "the image of Melville as subtle abolitionist in *Benito Cereno* may be a construction of generous wish rather than hard fact."[33] F. O. Matthiessen reminds his readers that "although the Negroes were savagely vindictive and drove a terror of blackness into Cereno's heart, the fact remains that they were slaves and that evil had thus originally been done to them."[34] Yet as Kaplan's phrase "veining and fleshing" suggests, and as more recent reiterations of his objection verify, accentuation of the "factual" in protest against the fiction and support of the slaves' position generates "fictions" that the tale itself excludes, either supplying the event of flesh stripping ("[the rebels] take [Aranda's] body below decks, where they remove every bit of his flesh"),[35] or hallucinating the actual occurrence of a cannibalistic act ("This unspeakable experience is perhaps the most sinister scene Melville devises to illustrate the Africans' brutish propensities").[36] An indirect proof of the correlation between these additions to "Benito Cereno" and the divergent identificatory adherences inspiring them can be found in the singular perspective of one earlier analysis: Newton Arvin, unmoved by the plight, merit, or moral profundity of specific parties in the drama, neither finds significant fictional development upon the source nor adds to the fiction contrivances of his own, implying that Melville, "too tired to rewrite" the original "drearily prosaic" Deposition, made no changes to it whatsoever.[37]

The now largely uncontested perception of "Benito Cereno" as an antislavery work has followed from a different kind of critical building or fleshing, which, aiming to substantiate an identification with the rebels, inserts into the narrative "gaps" not visions of cannibalism but "historical knowledge" and aspects of "other works by Melville" to produce "a sympathetic reading" of their cause.[38] The weaving of such a reading, charged with foregrounding the revolt's origins, seems to laud a banal and homogenized elucidation of the story's allegory, ascribing the same recurring meaning to all prominent symbols and vignettes: "slavery itself."[39] It also scrupulously evades the complex play of the visible and the invisible molded around absent cannibalism and the alternately veiled and uncovered skeleton. Carolyn L. Karcher declares:

> Personally, I find Babo on the whole a favorable portrayal of a black rebel, despite the fearsomeness with which he is tinged in his role as white America's nemesis; Babo's cruelty—to the extent that it strikes us as peculiarly savage—is never actually visible to us, except possibly in the shaving scene, where it takes the form of psychological torture rather than physical brutality.[40]

Although she points out that the chronicling of events refuses to "flesh out" the cliché of African "savagery," Karcher's "personal" testimony ignores the inaccessibility of Babo's consciousness—and therefore the want of a basis for her own sympathetic identification, which she uses to annul the two "gaps" simultaneously, disregarding a possible analogical relationship between the rebel leader's near-invisible "psychological cruelty" and the conjuring tricks of the tale's own form. Other expectations of grounding such an identificatory commitment by means of "sympathy" and "historical knowledge" are similarly emptied out by absence. Condemnation of Delano's inability to recognize that a slave revolt has taken place (because he thinks the blacks are "too stupid" for the undertaking) indirectly endorses, given that the African protagonists are accorded no interiority, an opposite but twin nineteenth-century emphasis on slaves' latent "treacherousness,"[41] as do eager acclamations—which override Melville's depiction of the blacks through the lens of white stereotyping—of the uprising's portrayal as a celebration of indomitable humanity.[42]

The determination to infuse the tale with "sympathetic" judgment
and a sharper cognizance of historical causality and conflict treats the
skeleton figurehead—in an echo of Karcher's idea that "cruelty," to be
relevant to the reckonings of sympathy, must be "visible"—as the sign of
an *act*, one that should be considered "proportionate" (despite changes
to the source undermining this conclusion and its literalist orientation)
"to the cruelty of Don Benito and Aranda themselves."[43] Reinscriptions
of it within the literal cycle of historical oppression and resistance negate
and unravel Melville's use of the addition to condense in fictional synthesis the ideological prerequisites of actual events, laid out in his narrator's
deliberate survey of the ship's mysterious canvas-wrapped hull, the slogan beneath this, the craft's name, and its status as a kind of hearse and a
charnel-house from which liberation from slavery will have to proceed.[44]

One approach draws on elements from Melville's source to classify the skeleton as a "symbolic reflection" of concrete violent acts
by whites, proposing that "strip[ping] the flesh off Aranda's body"
points to the Spaniards' mutilation of the Africans' flesh after the
ship's retaking in the real-life Delano's recollections.[45] Another relegates its appearance to fleeting quotation, hastily shifting attention
onto retaliatory white violence: "Not only does the *San Dominick*
have 'death for the figurehead, in a human skeleton; chalky comment on the chalked words below, '*Follow your Leader*,' it also has
death for its avenging angel—death in the form of a fleshed-out whiteness sent by Delano through the agency of his first mate."[46] A further
maneuver dissolves the remains altogether by converting them first
into a metaphor for cause and effect—stealthily "re-inserting" the
obvious reasons for the rebellion—and then into an abstract emblem
of "the work as a whole."[47] Though resulting from a temporary phase
of critical labor that sought to rescue the novella's complexity from
easy dismissal and reactionary appropriation, these conceptions of
the figurehead have established minimization of its pivotal presence
as a guiding presupposition. A recent discussion of "gothic" antisentimentality fails to mention the skeleton at all,[48] while an argument dealing with "an ideologically charged occlusion of the body"
cites only the written words on which its white visual appearance
"comments," glancing at the purport of questionable cannibalism in
a pun: "Authority, under the rubric 'leadership,' is indeed one of the
more gnawed-over problematics . . . in Melville's tale, which returns

repeatedly to the larger implications of the injunction 'follow your leader' painted onto the hull of the *San Dominick*."[49]

The project of adding the "veins and fullness" of history to "Benito Cereno" for the purposes of achieving an unambiguous (readerly and authorly) identification with the "slave cause" has more recently competed with (and perhaps in part given rise to) the articulation of a sense of flat textual uniformity and a lack of substantiation for identificatory sympathy. Maurice Lee wryly surveys the interminable critical deciphering of "locks, knots, masks, tableaus," proposing that Melville, drawing on Niccolò Machiavelli and Bernard Mandeville, shows "revolution and counterrevolution" to be equally repressive of speech,[50] while Eric J. Sundquist names the extreme, sometimes overtly "ridiculous," proximity of symbol to signified "tautology," linking the paralysis it creates to a deadlocked "suspension of commanding authorities."[51] Though these claims challenge the sanguinity of "sympathetic readings," their willingness to accept the filled-in narrative (Sundquist's category of "tautology" lavishly renovates but does not explain a previous critical worry about the near-"unity" of symbol and literal referent) and even to pursue the work of "building about" (Lee perseveres with the questionable labor of allegorical decoding) indicates a continued defense of sympathetic identification as the ideal vehicle of political redress.

Lee blocks out the skeleton figurehead's transfiguration of identificatory gestures, omitting its "speech," its "chalky comment" on the phrase "follow your leader," when he cites the first mate's quotation of the slogan (during the *San Dominick*'s recapture) to demonstrate that commanders and rebels use the same language.[52] Invoking the connotations given to the skeleton on its initial unveiling (recounted in the Deposition), the "comment" shows that the words were never a revolutionary rallying cry, but rather were part of a negative staging of white racial identification, whose link with "death," forged in that scenario, the mate's repetition blithely embraces. Like some previous approaches, Lee's expunges the critical force of the skeleton's theatrical role by categorizing it as the sign of an actual act, inherent in the basis of a connection between "Benito Cereno" and the *History of Florence* (1520–25): Machiavelli's mention of "a disinterment, a tyrant who is cannibalized, a man who kills a prince then displays his head on a stick in the piazza."[53] His exposition of Melville's version of the last of these incidents, the public display of Babo's severed head, bolsters simplification of the story's ruseful interference with intentions and outcomes, essentially inverting the conclusions—and circuitously paying tribute to the values of—readings that champion the primacy of "sympathy": "rather than style Babo's 'hive of subtlety' an alien African mind, we should note that in 'Benito Cereno' no one understands anyone and that Babo's hive most likely points to Bernard Mandeville's *Fable of the Bees* (1714)—a cynical work of political philosophy in the tradition of Machiavelli and Hobbes."[54]

Sundquist produces a parallel tactic for neutralizing the story's interference with and sadistic redirection of its readers' (and protagonists') sympathies: fleshing out a fourth position alongside the triumvirate of characters who harbor the sources of "suspended" commanding authority, "the reader" whose strained, confused state, "turn[ing] in the half embrace of Melville's painfully revealed figures," resembles "Benito Cereno, 'painfully turning in the half embrace of his servant' and master Babo" or, when caught in "the precarious standoff" caused by "the interrupted function of the comic," "a kind of enslavement or tormented constraint."[55] Though potentially an acknowledgment of "Benito Cereno"'s covert operations against its interpreters, this afflicted figure, imagined as an embodied addition to the narrative ("turning" in Babo's arms), in fact manages, in a uniquely complex evasion, to preempt and resist its attack on identification, acting as a repository for melancholic devotion to sympathy's political value. "Torment" and "enslavement" are in themselves hyperbolic names for the readerly condition, and their relevance here seems temporally unlocatable, since they are applied to a static dilemma and not to the retrospective alterations wrought on the reader's sympathies. Sundquist's concentrated emphasis on an existential interpretative stalemate suggests that readerly "suffering" here stands for the predicament, in a landscape peopled by inaccessible protagonists, "suspended" authority, of being denied a legitimate and progressive identificatory fraternity, while at the same time creating a kind of identification *out of* that prohibition, one that is beyond the reach of the story's machinations and critique, secure in an abstract "innocent" victimhood—linked with "enslavement" in general as opposed to Babo in particular, and with the apparently more profound, melancholic Cereno in preference to the much-excoriated, shallow Delano.

A SKELETON OF ACTUAL REALITY

The structure that underlies, and that is covered over by, critical identifications or the "flesh" they add—whether hallucinations of cannibalism, declarations of "sympathy," "historical knowledge," the anguished reader—can only be unveiled by an examination of the moment when its actual skeleton is first introduced:

> . . . during the three days which followed, the deponent, uncertain what fate had befallen the remains of Don Alexandro, frequently asked the negro Babo where they were, and, if still on board, whether they were to be preserved for interment ashore, entreating him so to order it; that the negro Babo answered nothing till the fourth day, when at sunrise, the deponent coming on deck, the negro Babo showed him a skeleton, which had been substituted for the ship's proper figure-head, the image of Christopher Colon, the discoverer of the New World; that the negro Babo asked him whose skeleton that was, and whether, from its whiteness, he should not think it a white's; that, upon his covering his face, the negro Babo, coming close, said words to this effect: 'Keep faith with the blacks from here to Senegal, or you shall in spirit, as now in body, follow your leader,' pointing to the prow; * * * that the same morning the negro Babo took by succession each Spaniard forward, and asked him whose skeleton that was, and whether, from its whiteness, he should not think it a white's; that, each Spaniard covered his face; that then to each the negro Babo repeated the words in the first place said to the deponent.[56]

Analyses of this scene, despite praising its "extraordinary" power[57] and Babo's "wickedly ironic remarks,"[58] have avoided deciphering its progress with the help of various strategies of filling in or completion. Sundquist smooths over the chronicle's gap by wondering if "the preparation [of Aranda's corpse] may [have involved] methods vaguely comparable to those that R. S. Rattray recorded in the case of Ashanti kings," eventually betraying a historicist disorientation in the face of the omission's function: "Aranda, of course, is not likely to have been done the honor of a king."[59] The precise "effects" of Babo's display are also occluded by their conflation with hidden and/or notional sources of menace or other narrative episodes: Sundquist assimilates it not only to phantasmagoric cannibalism but also to the skeleton's unveiling during the *San Dominick*'s capture and concealed presence during preceding events: "the imagined ritual rises into the form of Aranda's skeleton, only to be shrouded in canvas and held from view until the moment of climactic revelation; in the meantime, its work of terror goes on."[60]

Geoffrey Sanborn, though recognizing the wholly theatrical status of the skipped-over cannibalism, screens his eyes like the Spaniards—experiencing only Babo's voice—to contend that the figurehead merges with the image of the slave-leader's head on a pole in the piazza, so that the "shadow" over Cereno is "'the negro' *as projected in the skeleton*"[61]—a conclusion that elides and participates in the Captain's later refusal (affirmed by his last words) to confront the enacted "reversal." Even interpretations confined to the scene proper build its skeletal delineation into a finished summary, apprehending in the exhibited remains an "emblem" of the murderousness of white imperial and colonial power in the New World; observing vaguely that Babo "explains that the figurehead is literally the leader of the slavers and what it means,"[62] or stating that, in the association of death with "whiteness," he undermines racism "by pointing to the universality of death."[63]

Rather than "literally" "explaining" anything, however, putting forward an all-encompassing "emblem" or symbol or declaring a "universal" truth, Babo's object-lesson fashions a spurious process of identification, positing an equation—between "white" skin and "white" bones—which seems literal, yet which because of its false *non*universal, exclusive implication, rests on an unadmitted symbolic underpinning. His tableau, reversing the privileged, ideological associations of racial "whiteness," not only parodies the logic of racial identification itself—the endowment of "literal" appearances with symbolically loaded overtones—but also makes the skeleton into a prop for staging, in marionette movements and dreamlike, abstracted space, the nightmare version of something that need never physically "happen" in order to have the force of actuality: a scene of "interpellation" or imposition of identity, specifically, the "moment in America" that Toni Morrison considers to have been recognized in *Moby-Dick*, "when whiteness became ideology."[64]

The rhetoric and action of this performance recast the language and encounters of the antecedent text as a reflection of its terms, "unbuilding" their contribution to the teleology of plot and political conspiracy. Investigation of this retrospective alteration has been prohibited by criticism's commitment to treating "Benito Cereno" as a test of its identificatory impulses. Robert S. Levine rules out scrutiny of the rebel leader's interrogative mode on the grounds that this would accomplish an "act of domestication and containment that [would make] the 'lividly vindictive' Babo rather too much like us," condemning arguments governed by revisionary knowledge as precipitate dissolutions of the lure of Delano's perspective.[65] The Deposition as a whole has been dismissed as a "lock[ing] up" of the revolt's import, and seen as noteworthy chiefly for its ellipses, which are thought to divulge the chauvinistic nature of "official history" and to require the insertion of a more well-informed and "sympathetic" reading.[66] Such views take the narrator's conspicuously tentative hypothetical suggestion that the document provides the "key" to the *San Dominick*'s hull merely for a warning about empirical and political unreliability, when it may instead alert us to the thorough reordering achieved by its presiding fictional invention.

UNBUILDING ALLEGORY

Babo's use of the skeleton to dramatize the terroristical rationale of racial identification creates a "tautological" structure (already inherent in his device, which is at once an actual dead body's remnant and a hackneyed symbol of Death), which advances it as the "key" to the claustrophobic overcloseness between literal and symbolic planes permeating the already elaborated allegory and puzzled over by critical argument as productive of, variously, "lies," uniformity, futility, even a sense of the "ridiculous."[67] With Aranda's remains as "figure-head" for this allegorical dysfunction, its "wasteful" detail,[68] and the disproportion and asymmetry in the correspondence between its symbols and referents, can be seen to imitate, on the level of form, the coercive "allegorical" foundation of racial identification exposed in the Deposition's vignette. The resonance between the two elevates the skeleton figurehead into the orchestrating source of a radical disintegration within the fiction, its self-reflexive intensification and disruption of its own participation in a wider racialized imaginary. One minutely laborious early passage overtly thematizes the evolution of "Benito Cereno"'s language from a reluctance to endorse (and the pressures exerted by) a rule of correspondence, kinship, or similitude establishing allegorical inference:

> With no small interest, Captain Delano continued to watch [the ship]—a proceeding not much facilitated by the vapors partly mantling the hull, through which the far matin light from her cabin streamed equivocally enough; much like the sun—by this time hemisphered on the rim of the horizon, and apparently, in company with the strange ship, entering the harbor—which, wimpled by the same low, creeping clouds, showed not unlike a Lima intriguante's one sinister eye peering across the Plaza from the Indian loop-hole of her dusk *saya-y-manta*.[69]

This sentence, moving from a mere comparison to an extended simile, strives painstakingly to generate a visual apprehension of incipient allegorical interest, but its use of negatives to specify all measurements and degrees renders the extent or even the tenability of the specified "likenesses" doubtful.

The phrases "no small" and "not much," which, while opposite in their quantifications, are mutually contaminated by a shared form, destabilize the later expressions of "likeness": "much like" being undercut by the negative association in the earlier "much" of "not much," and "not unlike" by the "not" of that same pairing. With this spread of interlinked negations, the passage almost gives the impression of having assembled a phantom, contrary phrase: "not much like." A further unspoken negation of comparison lurks behind it: "much like the sun" inevitably recalls the "nothing like the sun" of Shakespeare's Sonnet 130: "My mistress' eyes are nothing like the sun," an intertextual inversion all the more thoroughly pertinent in the (shadowed) light of the Lima intriguante's eye. (The borrowing of the figure of the intriguante from another simile in Melville's work might in itself be said to enfeeble her illuminative capacities.)[70] Developing a propositional yet self-canceling momentum, the line surpasses deadlocks of "tautology" or "similitude," since the narrator's style, crafted by the competing pressure of uncertain "likenesses," constantly alerts us to their deceptiveness and asymmetry, anticipating the self-consciously dubious resemblances critically at play in Babo's theater.

If the involutions of "Benito Cereno"'s first section seem only a formal analogy for the Deposition sequence divorced from its political content, we need only note the contrast between stylistic reticence about "likeness" and the adept facility for racially charged allegorizing exhibited by the Captain-protagonists. Delano resolves to excuse Cereno's hauteur by recalling how "peculiar natures" hardened by suffering "as if forced to black bread themselves . . . deemed it but equity that each person coming nigh them should, indirectly, by some slight or affront, be made to partake of their fare."[71] Those critics committed to "providing" sympathy for the slaves consider Delano's reasoning—along with other suspiciously bland morsels of wisdom on human nature expounded by characters and narrator—mobile in application, citing it to exonerate the rebels' actions: they also were "forced to black bread."[72] But the essence of Delano's thought lies precisely in its lack of universalizing reach, in the fact that it cements white social sympathy via an allegorical denigration of "blackness." This is driven home by his encounter, a few moments later, with the haggard Spanish sailor stirring tar. The narrative voice cautions against hasty judgment, producing a neutral, indecisive version of the "black bread" theory: "since, as intense heat and cold, though unlike, produce like sensations, so innocence and guilt, when, through casual association with mental pain, stamping any visible impress, use one seal—a hacked one."[73] Nevertheless, the American ("not again that this reflection occurred to Captain Delano at the time. . . . Rather another idea . . . ") sees only blackness (the tar) and recoils with an expeditious moralizing flourish: "If, indeed, there be any wickedness on board this ship, thought Captain Delano, be sure that man there has fouled his hand in it, even as now he fouls it in the pitch."[74]

Severing the grip of the reader's identification with the American Captain has concentrated on pinpointing his telltale racist assumptions, their subordination to Gothic and sentimental modes of perception and subtle but discernible divergence from the omniscient perspective.[75] The two moments of evaluation mentioned here show that Delano's benevolence derives its language and direction from an evaluative and, in this narrative, racially weighted white/black opposition, which is queried by the ambiguous, noncommittal, elusive character of the broader allegory in which it is embedded. That stylistic slipperiness delivers a comparable rebuke to the racialized rigidity of Cereno's mentality, contained in his response to the question, "what has cast such a shadow upon you?"[76] Early champions of Cereno are keen to point out that, since the two speak in Spanish, his answer, "the negro," also means simply "blackness" or metaphysical "evil,"[77] accepting a dubious "tautology" that overlooks the Spaniard's own spurious translation: having seen a display of the horror of "whiteness," he reacts with a demonization of "blackness," so confined within the identity and interests of his race that, when shown its true color, he sees only the Other. Unlike Cereno's last words or Delano's inferences, the rhetoric of the narrative's descriptions bears the imprint of the skeleton figurehead, compromising the basis of the identifications mocked by its apparition and utilization.

UNBUILDING FICTION

Just as the theatrical interlude in the Deposition unravels the informing source of the dual and contradictory capacities of "Benito Cereno"'s allegory (the overproximity and ostentation that has both generated and confounded hermeneutic activity), it exposes the inner workings of the preceding narrative action as a process not primarily of multiplying clues about a slave revolt or prophesying postbellum racial polarization, but of soliciting and destroying identifications. In addition to diagnosing a corruption permeating allegorical language, the meanings Babo derives from the skeleton, coupled with the elision of cannibalism or flesh stripping, construct a dexterous ideological contraption that adulterates intentions and visual appearances, transforming solidarity into oppression and sympathy into cruelty. Because of powerful expectations centering on the ethical importance and aesthetic indispensability of "sympathy," the narrative's designs on its characters also implicate critical responses, provoking readings that dissociate individual scenes from their almost mechanical retrospective rearrangement according to the terms of the Deposition episode, or that absorb them into decontextualized theoretical abstractions. Both maneuvers result from treating the action as though it offered a static depiction of the essence of real-historical political conflict, as if it were not a synthetic, critical, fictional experiment, and more particularly one that "unbuilds" fiction, along with the sympathetic responses presumed to be constitutive of its substantiality.

Reading "backward," the first instance of this immanent "unbuilding" occurs in the two separate sightings of the skeleton recounted in the battle for the *San Dominick*'s recapture. Delano's crew is goaded by a spectacle that may have prompted Matthiessen's damningly qualified praise of the story as "pictorially and theatrically effective":[78]

> With creaking masts, she came heavily round to the wind; the prow slowly swinging, into view of the boats, its skeleton gleaming in the horizontal moonlight, and casting a gigantic ribbed shadow upon the water. One extended arm of the ghost seemed beckoning the whites to avenge it.
> "Follow your leader!" cried the mate; and, one on each bow, the boats boarded.[79]

The triumphalist partisanship apparently saturating these lines is complicated by an immediately preceding depiction of the figurehead's emergence: "the fag-end [of 'the ship's cut cable'], in lashing out, whipped away the canvas shroud about the beak, suddenly revealing, as the bleached hull swung round towards the open ocean, death for the figure-head, in a human skeleton; chalky comment on the chalked words below, '*Follow your leader.*'"[80] Here, as Sanborn observes, we descry the allegorical signification of the object before encountering the object itself, as well as, Robert Kiely notes, an

impossible relationship between written words and "inarticulate figure."[81] However both critics' theorizations of this reversal, rounding
it into finished abstractions (Kiely perceives "a display of the susceptibility of language to obliteration," while Sanborn sees a dislocation between body and soul or essence that denotes a larger voiding
of identities' substance),[82] ignore its encrypted connection with the
Deposition sequence and with the skeleton's other, more incendiary
manifestation.

The strange privileging of symbol over object, of figure over words,
is nothing other than a fossilization of the meanings bestowed on
the skeleton by Babo's theatrical performance. Its "chalky comment"
refers to the interpretation given to its "color," which has made it, in
conjunction with its dissociation from an individual body, a sign that,
instead of denoting the destruction of identities or a neutral, incontest-
able philosophical truth, terroristically imposes a politically "actual"
facsimile of "white" identification. Through this link to the Deposition, the skeleton's "first" appearance unpacks, in a two-pronged retrospective movement, its second: Delano's first mate's rallying shout,
his apparently heroic "answer" to the skeleton's seeming "call" for
revenge, is recast as a response to a (demystified) instance of interpellation, a willing pledge of allegiance to "whiteness," now visually but
(ironically) imperceptibly construed as equivalent to murderousness,
death. With such a chain of retrospective reverberation and juxtaposition, "Benito Cereno" neither merely imitates the "pictorial" or "theatrical" features of popular fiction nor creates historical significance
in spite of them; it devises a deft mechanism of political "commentary" from their elementary parts.

Even when it is hidden from sight, the figurehead continues to
revise the alliances and sympathies of characters according to the
contours of the Deposition episode, making its presence felt when
Delano—bearing out Tocqueville's theory of American social interaction—proffers a soothing identification with Cereno's miseries:

> "Pardon me," said Captain Delano lowly, "but I think that, by a sym-
> pathetic experience, I conjecture, Don Benito, what it is that gives
> the keener edge to your grief. It was once my hard fortune to lose at
> sea a dear friend, my own brother, then supercargo. Assured of the
> welfare of his spirit, its departure I could have borne like a man; but
> that honest eye, that honest hand—both of which had so often met
> mine—and that warm heart; all, all—like scraps to the dogs—to
> throw all to the sharks! It was then I vowed never to have for fellow-
> voyager a man I loved, unless, unbeknown to him, I had provided

> every requisite, in case of a fatality, for embalming his mortal part
> for interment on shore. Were your friend's remains now on board this
> ship, Don Benito, not thus strangely would the mention of his name
> affect you."[83]

Delano's rhapsodically graphic lament over his brother's dismemberment and devouring brings to mind, critics have noted, Aranda's possible end. Yet their subsequent deductions have either been literal (William B. Dillingham argues that it merely reminds Cereno of his prospective punishment in case of noncooperation with the rebels),[84] or abstracted from the narrative's temporalities: Sanborn attributes Cereno's swoon to an intuition that "after suffering the mutilation and likely disposal of parts that Delano unthinkingly describes, Aranda's remains can no longer serve as an assurance of 'the welfare of his spirit,'"[85] but designate a general erasure of identity's substance. What is most important about the scene, however, is that it constitutes the only portrayal of the supposed stripping and consumption of Aranda's flesh: the hypothetical act of "cruelty" that disgusted earlier readers is conveyed solely by means of an expression of sympathy, an irony that sums up the mutation of plot into an enforced performance and undermining of identifications. The narrative "gap," the unrepresented cannibalism, brings out the racial origins of Delano's "sympathy" by lending it an inadvertent sadism, suffusing it, in artificial miniature, with an allusion to the oppressions and abuses of white colonial domination.

This vignette's shape and implications situate the characters of Delano and Cereno—contrary to established fleshed-out views of them—as adjuncts, even effects of the figurehead's centrality, serving principally to facilitate and reinforce its impact. Levine's argument that, since breaking our trust in Delano has become a taken-for-granted move, "the reverse is in order: We need temporarily to relinquish our political right-mindedness and . . . *begin* by considering the grip of the reader's initial identification with the captain,"[86] which clouds Delano's already existing subjection to a decisive "reversal"— in the fate of "whiteness"—that precipitates an invisible internal mobilization of the narrative against him, dramatizing the architectonics of his beneficent impulses (their complicity with institutionalized hierarchy and cruelty) and his own obliviousness (framed as quintessentially "American") to their place in a regime of systemic division, coercion, and injury. While Delano's function is to act as the reversal's unknowing target, co-opted into a demonstration of his sympathies' actual form, Cereno's is to be a figure utterly identified with "whiteness" who *suffers* its change in fortune, becoming more and more like the skeleton itself, "eaten" away (in another displaced version of Aranda's doom) by Delano's unintended consolidation of his newly aversive identity. Cereno's reducibility to his identification is clear in the unremitting persistence and end result of his suffering (he "does indeed" "follow his leader"), and its distinctly untragic timber, which underlines, ridicules, and mercilessly thwarts his expectation of a natural racial fellowship with Delano.

The otherwise unaccountable synonymy between Cereno's name and the title encapsulates at once the vacuousness, the "fictionality" of his identificatory attachment, his indissociability from this fiction, and, finally, the tale's status as a narrative dedicated to disassembling both its own fiction and the structure of identification— all three suppositions are entwined when it is confirmed, "pass[ing] over the worst" (the presumable act of cannibalism, or missing racist "plot"), that Cereno really was only a "paper" Captain.[87] His role as a narrative "gap" that, like the absent cannibalism, traces the empty form of an identification and solicits readerly sympathies in its turn is borne out by the durability of his appeal—consistently eclipsing that of Delano—as a putative locus of knowledge and insight. Recent readings credit him with "some awareness that the institution of slavery is less a matter of law than of . . . cruelly coercive and disproportionate power";[88] a "recognition of the significance of 'the negro' which Melville encourages us to share";[89] and a conviction that "one would finally have to believe 'the Negro' not human—incapable even of memory—to imagine slaves might live unprotestingly with their enslavement or let it pass unrevenged."[90] Comparison between these claims and the Captain's sparse, enigmatic pronouncements show that they add abundant flesh to his emaciated outline: Cereno makes no mention of slavery; his reference to the "Negro," like his shouted identification of the anonymous skeleton *as* Aranda, may be read as a rejection of the general political "actuality" that has been paraded before him, while the idea that he poignantly applies his criterion for humanness (memory) to the Africans is undermined by a wider proliferation of bland, promiscuously supple "universalizing" statements and an ostentatiously cautious treatment of correspondence and similarity.[91] Positive extrapolations from Cereno's words are therefore grounded in an undeclared belief in the promissory value of his suffering itself as a sign of profundity and guarantor of truth, an assumption specifically interrogated by "Benito Cereno" the story, which dislocates a postulated alignment between visible suffering, sympathetic identification, political judgment, and reformation.

Such an agenda on the part of the narrative appears more obviously problematic in the case of the third character in the triumvirate—and in regard to the population for which, with the help of a concentration on an all-absorbing triad of power, he tends distortingly to become the substitutive sign—because it threatens to conjure away the reality of the suffering caused by slavery and dilute its relevance to the self-perception of contemporary and subsequent historical moments. The relation between the logic of the skeleton figurehead and another, generally overlooked scene following the much-analyzed shaving episode (whose status as a displaced version of Aranda's fate and a transposition of "white" identification and sympathy into averseness and unintended sadism needs no elucidation) introduces a means of describing the action's approach to this question precluded by an avoidance of "retrospective" interpretation. When Babo steps on deck with a cut on his cheek exclaiming that Cereno inflicted it in punishment, Delano remarks (inwardly), "This slavery breeds ugly passions in man.—Poor fellow!"[92] He just misses the chance to "speak in sympathy to the negro" before the latter reenters the cuddy. Adopting a tactic that recalls the widespread critical focus on the slogan beneath the skeleton in preference to its visual materialization, what investigations there are of this incident privilege Delano's unspoken words above Babo's manufactured wound, abstracting them from the exchange and using them to reinsert the causes of the rebellion, hailing their validity as a general statement about the behavior of slave masters.

Alternatively, a choice considered truer to the "context," critics deem his response an unwitting allusion to the "ugly passions" bred by slavery in the slaves themselves. As with the decoding of the first mate's cry during the San Dominick's recapture, however, the explanatory "context" of the plot's occurrences and its parodic simulation of the wider ideological and material contingencies of New World slavery is provided by the Deposition episode and the figurehead's inversions, which, far from encouraging the discovery of any profundity in Delano's conveniently portable phrase, render Babo's originless, theatrical, visually manifested injury a "comment" on the hollowness of the American Captain's sympathy and political reasoning, their dependency on the aesthetic stimulation of a "scene of suffering."

In the shape of its satiric treatment of Delano, the scene reveals the two main features of Babo's role: the complete unavailability of his consciousness (another narrative "gap," functioning differently from that surrounding Cereno) or the omission of any recorded, "authentic" expression of his intentions; and his orchestration of the action's various tableaux. Understanding Delano's words as an evocation of the rebel leader's "ugly passions" represents one prominent critical mode of dealing with his opacity, shared in by Karcher's "personal" testimony: that of fleshing out absent interiority and thus building grounds for an identification. More sophisticated readings recognize Babo's link with the author-function, but that assessment leads, like Kiely's remark on the figurehead's "comment," to a general, abstract truth about the operation of language,[93] or indirectly furnishes proof of a laudable identificatory alignment: Melville's "approval" of the rebel leader,[94] his abandonment of an earlier, exploitative "ethnic ventriloquism" for a less condescending solidarity with "ethnic" characters as "underwriters of his own literary plotting, inscrutable icons of his will to create."[95] Babo's surrogate authorial power, coupled with his inaccessibility, warrant a less celebratory conclusion, and a fuller appreciation of the story's political dilemma and formal machinations, its total confinement within and simultaneous critique of a stultifying white/black American racial division and hierarchy. His introduction of the central fictional device, the skeleton figurehead, announces the purpose and strategy of the narrative: a use of the degraded term in the hierarchy, "blackness" (whose stereotypical "essence" it evacuates), to reflect "whiteness" back to itself, exposing its undeclared, pivotal centrality in the determination of sympathy and racialization of social sentiment—including, in the scene with the cut cheek, cross-racial sympathy—while suggesting that such a "reflection" could never be recognized or accepted. Even readings that do not attempt to flesh out Babo's absent character and that apprehend a version of its ultimate significance forgo an account of the precise workings of his agency within the narrative's composition and under the auspices of its main prop, drawing either a homogenizing, suprapolitical inference comparable to Cereno's and Delano's dubious commonplaces ("the appearance of substance is always an illusion,")[96] or simply noting that his feigned obedience purges slavery of its supporting ideology.[97]

The thoroughness as well as the design of "Benito Cereno"'s dismantling of "whiteness" are hinted at by the figurehead's allusion to the 1852 letter and "unbuilding" of what that trope denotes, an identificatory bond and the fashioning of a work of fiction. One might see the skeleton's link to a private exchange as an indication that its undermining of characters' and readers' identifications emanates from an atavistic revenge for the failure of a personal "sympathy" (sought as compensation for professional isolation) to provide the refuge demanded from it—a possibility raised by the relish with which the narrator, echoing Babo's laughter at Delano's remark about the Spanish flag, dispatches Cereno to the doldrums of his "white" identity.[98] According to such an argument, the skeleton's (re)appearance on the initiative of a slave-rebellion leader would constitute an exploitation of questions of race and slavery more profound than any "magazinish" sensationalism, serving ultimately to create an aggrandizingly politically charged image—the executed Babo's "unabashed" presence before "the whites"—of a disparaged author's unrelenting challenge to his public. Attributing Melville's critique to an individual disaffection would also affirm the primacy of identification as the foundation of political judgment and exonerate the various efforts to add flesh to the skeleton and text (whether in order to supply sympathy or pay tribute to it as a resource that has been repudiated or disabled), of a common collusion with the polarized structure that he mimics and internally subverts. The tale's formal reversal of the terms of the letter's metaphor, however, and its recasting of them as the blueprint for a narrative's unfolding and immanent undoing and for a systematic disruption of fraternal feeling and transparent communication, demonstrate that it converts the collapse of a particular identification into a reflection on a wider system of public and social sympathy and on the doubtful desirability of identification's importance as an autonomous political value. The Deposition sequence, with its "missing" cannibalism, both brings about and foregrounds this transition from the biographical to the political, since Babo "shows" Cereno what may be the skeletal remnant of a departed friend, transformed into an anonymous emblem for the affective dysfunctions of a polity.

CHAPTER THREE

Murder and "Point of View"

In *Henry James Goes to Paris*, Peter Brooks argues that James's stay in Paris in 1875–76 eventually played a decisive role in shaping the style of his late works, even though at the time James condemned French literature as "unclean," "intolerably unclean," and of "monstrous uncleanness."[1] Brooks repeats that the late works stage "a kind of return of the repressed" whereby James "appears to reach back . . . to the lesson of Flaubert [and] to what he picked up in the city that was beginning to invent modernism," "to reach back to the kind of perspectivism that he had learned from Flaubert and others," and to "discover some of the radical issues in perspective that we associate with modernity in French painting and with the later work of Flaubert," absorbing "without full acknowledgement, no doubt without full awareness, Flaubert's lessons on perspective."[2] This loosely psychoanalytic explanation expresses the difficulty of appropriately specifying French influence on James given his immersion in French language and culture, his squeamish response to its most enduring literary productions, and the fact that his own literary medium was a dispossessed transatlantic English.

The difficulty has attracted a variety of resolutions. One has been to show how the extensive use of French and references to French literary texts in James's novels tends to open a wider horizon of moral awareness than their protagonists seem to embody, thereby treating such traces as a talismanic counter to James's own critical conservatism.[3] A second has been to assert James's conformity to a French narrative model: David Gervais argues that James's creation of dialogue that shares the intricate style of his narrative voice can be seen as an implementation—through a reverse method—of the principle of seamless formal unity that was the goal of Flaubertian free indirect discourse.[4] Brooks (in another study) situates James within the tradition of Balzacian melodrama, although he notes that James's reliance on this genre's division between public veneer and hidden background has American roots as the secularization of a puritan obsession with the "secret" of sexuality.[5] Finally, Philip Grover holds Flaubert and James to a common standard—the nonmodern paradigm of tragedy—with their inevitable failure to meet it perhaps also another indication of the challenge of aligning their work.[6]

"Perspectivism"—the repudiation of a "direct presentation of the story" in favor of "the play of interpretative consciousness on the action"[7]—may also be too general a means of effecting a rapprochement between James and Flaubert, since it mischaracterizes their respective narrative methods and ultimately weights ethical conscientiousness disproportionately on James's side. Brooks argues that James's complaint—articulated as late as 1902—that Flaubert was unaware of having "missed" the opportunity to represent Madame Arnoux, Frédéric's love object in L'Éducation sentimentale, "as well as he could"[8] misunderstands Flaubert's aim, which was precisely that of restricting her portrayal to "what Frédéric sees and believes" such that we "can never tell" what her character "is 'objectively' like."[9] However, this précis overlooks the way in which Madame Arnoux is shown responding to—and thereby inadvertently blemishing—Frédéric's romantic idealization of her, a development that epitomizes Flaubert's presentation of characters as competing, occasionally complementary, centers of narcissistic projection. Omniscient interventions also ensure that the errors generated by such projections do not go unchecked: for instance, when Frédéric encounters Madame Dambreuse, the remark that aristocratic training can lend the effect of natural grace.

The contrapuntal shifts between subjective delusion and external fact in Madame Bovary are well known, having led even to the view that the arrangement of circumstances expresses a hidden authorial savagery toward the protagonist, a natural suspicion given Flaubert's idea of the novelist: "comme Dieu dans la creation, invisible et tout-puissant" (invisible and all-powerful, like God in creation).[10] In Salammbô, the agnostic panorama of religious belief and cultural practice is capable of suddenly turning upon itself and citing gods as determinative of the action, violently confusing belief and external forces in a manner that renders novelistic decision—like the biases of idols—literally unpredictable. Brooks's sense that Bouvard and Pécuchet are "not given a chance to be anything more than what is needed for Flaubert's demonstrative project" and so "don't matter in themselves"[11]—his speculation as to why James dismissed their adventures—seems to disregard Flaubert's goal in this text: exploding both the meaningfulness of a concept of individual personality and the effectiveness of objective knowledge.

Because Flaubert's "perspectivism" offers a more diverse or violently transformative interplay between objective fact and subjective consciousness than the term suggests, James's misunderstanding of the French writer's aims may not have the ethical significance Brooks attributes to it. The same may also be true of James's perennial habit of contrasting Flaubert's choice of limited novelistic personnel with Balzac's willingness to respect the "liberty of the subject," to give characters "the long rope" for "acting themselves out," to indulge a "joy" "in their communicated and exhibited movement, in their standing on their feet and going of themselves"[12]—a judgment that for Brooks is "at once technical and somehow moral" in keeping with the stigmatization of "manipulators" in James's own plots.[13] Such an assessment parallels the early critical view that James's primary narrative strategy involved the representation of "point of view," a phrase that implies the equal weighting of distinctive outlooks in an aesthetic akin to political liberalism, and that helped enshrine "the appreciation of alterity" as a "categorical assumption" at the core of Anglo-American novel theory.[14]

Although it is easy to assume that the claims of Percy Lubbock's inaugural theorization of "point of view" have been supplanted by the insights of poststructuralism and skeptical critiques of Lubbock's popularizing proselytism, the subterranean contribution of Lubbock's formulations to the view of James as an ethically committed novelist of perspectival divergence should not be underestimated, especially given their long period of unchallenged privilege—and even critical prestige—as a means of access to the complexity of the prefaces.[15] Lubbock's distortions have less to do with an insufficient distinction between perceiver and narrator than with a diminution of the strangeness of Jamesian technique and the identification of James's achievement as the portrayal of consciousness.[16] Posthumously flattering his subject's wish for success as a playwright, Lubbock asks us to imagine "point of view" by "suppos[ing] that instead of a man upon the stage, concealing and betraying his thought, we watch the thought itself, the hidden thing, as it twists to and fro in his brain— watch it without any other aid to understanding but such as its own manner of bearing may supply."[17]

For James, however, the choice of characterological "center" is a merely instrumental way of illuminating whatever is being unfolded by the fiction: "the most polished of possible mirrors of the subject."[18] Furthermore, his "preference" for "'seeing my story' through the opportunity and the sensibility of some more or less detached, some not strictly involved, though thoroughly interested and intelligent, witness and reporter, some person who contributes to the case mainly a certain amount of criticism and interpretation of it" blurs the positions of author and fictional observer. A reference to the "shorter tales" also erases the specificity of "first person" recitation, since these tales rely either on anonymous protagonist-narrators or omniscient tellers who say "I": "an unnamed, unintroduced and (save by right of intrinsic wit) unwarranted participant, the impersonal author's concrete deputy or delegate, a convenient substitute or apologist for the creative power otherwise so veiled and disembodied."[19] Even the straightforward statement that the works range themselves "not as my own impersonal account of the affair in hand, but as my account of somebody's impression of it" contains a curious superfluous doubling, with the proprietary specificity of "my own" antithetical to the authorial tradition of the "impersonal."

Moreover, James also appears to agree with Max Beerbohm's slapstick lampooning of his narrative method as one that involves physically keeping characters company throughout their experiences,[20] a method that also entails, as Brooks puts it, a license to speak "over and beyond" them.[21] James describes the process of evoking a given consciousness as "track[ing] my uncontrollable footsteps, left and right . . . while they take their quick turn, even on stealthiest tiptoe, toward the point of view that . . . will give me most instead of least to answer for." The Preface to *The Golden Bowl* affirms the triumphant consistency of the approach by picturing the author "rub[ing] shoulders and conversing with the persons engaged in the struggle."[22] The sense that "point of view" creates a kind of physical doubling or shadowing of the character by the author is further borne out by James's account of the stirrings of inspiration for *The American* and *The Princess Casamassima*. In the one case he occupied two locations that proved important for his future wealthy hero: an American "horse car," where the idea first appeared; and "the cold shadow of the Arc de Triomphe," where it crystallized.[23] In the other he was walking, like the impoverished Hyacinth, around London;[24] in both, he felt the outsider status their two stories would resolve in kindred ways.

Furthermore, what renders an ethical valorization of "point of view" difficult is not merely the ambiguous mode of speech it entails, but also what James calls "the subject." By bringing this term closer to its psychoanalytic meaning, we can identify one aspect of its Jamesian sense as the configuration of personages typically appearing in his fictions. His first novel, *Watch and Ward*, establishes the foundational elements of the pattern, but not, as has been claimed, because of its "courtship-and-marriage motif,"[25] or indeed in spite of its throwback eighteenth-century trope, the disillusioned "philosopher" who educates a girl-child to become his wife. All of James's novels depict a child or child-figure cut loose from the parental relation and in search of, or taken up by, a mentor or guardian. This guardian is not simply a disinterested—or filially loved—protector, advisor, or patron; in later, more devastating instances he or she becomes a sexual rival or betrayer. For example, Roland Mallett is both Roderick Hudson's real love object and the obstacle to his winning Christina Light; as the Princess Casamassima, she in turn becomes (in this viral epic of mentorship) at once Hyacinth's competitor for Paul Muniment and the focus of his aspirational desire. James's detachment of the "child" from an original parental relation also allows adult sexual betrayals to carry the force of a "primal scene" involving the traumatic discovery of parental sexuality, as in Isabel Archer's detection of her counselor and exemplar Madame Merle's true identity, or Milly Theale's discovery that Kate Croy and Merton Densher, who have encroached on the prerogatives and proximity of older and allied mentors and guardians, are a couple.

In a contrary dynamic that suggests that the ideal intimate relation is between mentor and ward, the guardian is "betrayed" by the child, as in Verena Tarrant's abandonment of Olive Chancellor for Basil Ransom, or the reverse-experience of a primal scene in *The Ambassadors*, where Lambert Strether, stepfather-to-be and patronage-emissary, apprehends the sexual nature of his charge's Parisian allegiance. The period of transition to James's late work involves literalizing, almost practical, experiments in his fundamental scheme. The deciphering activity of the telegraph girl in "In the Cage," for example, can be seen as a technological version of the interpretative conjectures of the child in *What Maisie Knew* concerning the sexual alliances of her parents. In *The Turn of the Screw*, ghosts allow a reflexive enactment of the guardianship drama: the governess simultaneously interrogates the potential sexual errancy of her pupils, her predecessor, her fantasy (and nightmare) love-object, and herself—all with the help of a "mother"-figure who may be her own projection or conspiring in the management of revelation and concealment.

The completeness and finish of the final three novels (in contrast to the fatalities or banal futures in earlier plots) consist in their vindication of the betrayed mentor and traumatized child. Strether cancels the effective force of his weary domestic commitments in response to Chad's formalistic fidelity, Milly voluntarily performs the function (benefactress) that was to have been imposed on her by deception, and Maggie Verver deploys the power of patronage, as well as the presumption of innocence, to nullify the adultery between stepmother and husband. Each of the "intense *perceivers*" in James's list of those he foregrounds by means of the technique of "point of view" belongs to this configuration and plays one or more of the roles of mentor, love-object, and child.[26] James's valedictory description of his works as an "uncanny brood" with "wizened faces" that need to be tidied up before making their descent like "awkward infant[s] from the nursery to the drawing room under the kind appeal of enquiring, possibly interested visitors"[27] also implies all of these roles: the "children" are preternaturally mature and about to encounter the resurgence of the repressed; James performs the role of guardian. The scenario itself, echoing the spatial and moral conceit of *The Awkward Age*, gestures toward the presence not only of receptive readers but also of a Vanderbank or love-object around which the relation between mentor and child coalesces, or which it already contains.

The manner in which James speaks about particular characters also makes clear that "point of view" is not a device for facilitating the representation of distinctive individualities. For example, the prefatory matter of "In the Cage" describes an author fretting about his tendency to "imput[e] to too many others, left and right, the critical impulse and the acuter vision," to "read rank subtleties into simple souls."[28] James's approach becomes in this instance a kind of palimpsestic overwriting of the meager and inexpressive contents of working-class consciousness, an undertaking regrettably but unavoidably distorting in its sophistication. A related self-defensive acknowledgment appears when James recalls "a reproach [regarding *The Turn of the Screw*] made me by a reader capable evidently, for the time, of some attention, but not quite capable of enough, who complained that I hadn't sufficiently 'characterised' my young woman engaged in her labyrinth; hadn't endowed her with signs and marks, features and humours." James's response, a striking echo of Miles's fate and the "impression" made on Douglas ("one's artistic, one's ironic heart shook almost to breaking"), is that the writer must "choose among" his difficulties, and the fleshing out of character had in this case a low importance relative to other imperatives.[29] The condescending tone hints that the complaining reader, like the character under discussion, was a woman, both deprived by the author of a kind of mental completeness ("not capable of enough"). That James should be her victim, have his heart "shaken" by her comment in the way that evokes Miles dying in the governess's arms and Douglas (clearly in some way a charge or protégé or object of interest to the first narrator) succumbing to the impact of her experience, intimates that idiosyncrasy of "character" has been sacrificed to the eternal, if virulently supple, Jamesian triad of mentor, ward, and the desired ideal of their shared creation. His resistance to the demand for "marks, features and humours" in the female protagonist confirms a wider sense that his heroines are "far more intelligible as Jamesian alter egos"[30] than as women faced with a determinate set of circumstances and conditions.

THE MIDDLE YEARS

I want to suggest here an alternative conception of the relation between French literary influence and the forging of James's late style. Brooks quotes the title of the 1876 review "Charles de Bernard and Gustave Flaubert" as proof of James's earlier relegation of Flaubert to minor status.[31] The piece, however, is a tripartite study of Orléanist, Second Empire, and contemporary French literature, with the brothers Edmond and Jules de Goncourt ending the sequence. James seems always to have thought of the Goncourts alongside Flaubert, and near the end of his life he fondly remembers his youthful Paris sojourn as "a golden blur of old-time Flaubertianism and Goncourtism,"[32] both influences together composing for him something like a beloved, well-worn ragtime melody. In 1884, embarking on the undertakings whose failure would fire the shaping of his final works, he praises the brothers alongside Alphonse Daudet and Émile Zola:

"They do the only kind of work, today, that I respect."[33] The omission of the Goncourts from James's later reflections on Flaubert, furthermore, may have mostly to do with the greater penetration of the latter into the modernist circles of the English-speaking world, since James, although tepidly corrective of middlebrow Anglophone theories of the novel (Walter Besant's), was never a determined champion of the neglected or marginal.

Although the 1876 essay fully displays the prudish prurience Brooks identifies in the letters from Paris of this period, its repeated consideration of the Goncourts' *Soeur Philomène* suggests a different and more serious objection to the aesthetics of the "little band of the out-and-out realists"[34]: for "all its perfection of manner," the work gives James "an impression of something I can find no other name for than cruelty."[35] His refusal to specify the sources of this quality is one of several elisions in James's account of the novel. Apart from melodramatically indexing her situation as that of having "fall[en] in love" with a house surgeon, James's summary does not mention the main protagonist; in fact, he seems to confuse her with the male hero when he notes the "great skill" it required "to interest us in the comings and goings of a simple and ignorant man, around the sickbeds of a roomful of paupers."[36] The Goncourts, however, do not present the surgeon Barnier as an "ignorant man" (he debates religion with atheistic vehemence and is expected to surpass everyone else on the qualifying exams), while they go to some lengths to emphasize that Philomène is both ignorant and unintelligent, if distinguished by an extreme spiritual intensity. Neither do they show Barnier typically doing the rounds of sickbeds—the novel follows the rhythm of Philomène's movements in this regard. James's final stricture, on what "art" should and shouldn't represent, seems completely to absorb her, and her habitual action, into a general condemnation of the Goncourts' project: "When she means to overhaul the baser forms of suffering and the meaner forms of vice, to turn over and over again the thousand indecencies and impurities of life, she seems base and hungry, starving, desperate."[37]

While his vocabulary may suggest otherwise, James's objection is less to the novel's subject matter than to the manner of the Goncourts' treatment. His oversimplification of Philomène's biography, and his sense that the novel as a whole can, in form and content, be reduced to her movements, reveals that he does not wish to scrutinize its details and structure. Philomène "falls in love" more than once.

Rather than being a romantic heroine, she resembles the ambiguously "spinsterish" figures of James's middle period, whose thwarted or unfulfilled desires are a doomed recapitulation of maternal attachment. She idolizes Henry, the spoiled son of the bourgeois household in which she grew up. The nature of her attachment to Barnier is made clear through her theft, after his death, of the lock of hair meant for his mother.[38] The Goncourts' method of representing these successive attachments does not mimic the repeated "turning over" of ailing bodies; it recalls instead the action of the implement at the center of the novel, the surgeon's knife: the narrative cuts brusquely away from the scene in which Philomène communicates to Henry her resolution to take holy orders; it splices the burgeoning of Philomène's love for Barnier between abrupt vignettes involving raucous dialogue and medical grotesquery, only returning to a dream-sequence in which its sensual dimension is revealed, in order to meld together the plot's denouement.[39] This sharp treatment of sentiment complements the summary disposal of important characters: Philomène's childhood friend Cécile, for example.[40]

The methods and effects of the novel are perhaps best epitomized when Philomène sings holy orisons over the cries of Barnier's former sweetheart, who is dying following his amputation of her breast.[41] The contrapuntal clash between the two voices seems at once to sound the hopelessness of their incompatible longings, mock the fate of the mutilated woman, and expose the pious, dutiful Philomène as atavistically jealous. The "cruelty" James identifies in the novel therefore describes its formal reinforcement, or perhaps *en*forcement, of the disappointments, frailty, and destruction of its characters. His refusal to analyze this impression marks out the as-yet empty arena of his own interest in the perpetual preparedness and yearning for romance and incident, yet permanent exclusion from both, of figures like Philomène. Unlike the narrators of the two Parisian "rafinées" he criticizes, his narratives from the 1890s both share and accompany the passions of his female protagonists on their asymptotic flights and make (in contrast to Philomène's disgraceful orisons) individual merit a running and complex theme. His attack on the Goncourts' "cruelty" is in this sense a stronger articulation of his objections to *Madame Bovary*, which he excoriates as crudely punitive and skewed in its choice of an unworthy protagonist. In essence, then, the fiction of the 1890s presents James's version of the female figure dismantled by French realism and naturalism. As such, it demonstrates the nature of his decisive difference from this aesthetic, the forging of a style in reaction to it, and the ethical conundrums that this style, together with his condemnation of French "cruelty," conceals.

As Brooks observes, "no biographer has or probably ever will 'explain'" how James made the extraordinary transition from the late-Victorian novelist he was in the 1880s to the intricate modernist "master" he became in the early twentieth century.[42] Recent novelizations of James's life have followed Leon Edel's lead in identifying the disastrous opening night of *Guy Domville* as the low point that shaped the making of that formidable eminence.[43] Edel proposes an astonishing trajectory for James's gradual recovery from this disappointment; if the death by drowning of a baby girl in *The Other House*, the second novel James wrote following the opening-night fiasco, recalls the "subacqueous" feeling he claimed to have experienced during the humiliating experience of being booed on stage,[44] baby Effie, herself, marks in Edel's view the beginning of a series of female children who mature successively with each novel from the middle period: "murdered at four; she is resurrected at five (*What Maisie Knew*, 1897) and we leave her at seven or eight, or perhaps a bit older. Flora is eight (*The Turn of the Screw*, 1898) and the one little boy in the series, Miles, is ten. . . . Then we arrive at . . . the adolescence of an unnamed girl in a branch post office ("In the Cage," 1898.) Little Aggie, in the next novel is sixteen, and Nanda Brookenham, eighteen when the story begins (*The Awkward Age,* 1899)."[45] This predominantly female series attests to James's childhood instinct that he had to relinquish masculine assertiveness in order to avoid futile struggles against his domineering father,[46] and to his belief, expressed in the Preface to *What Maisie Knew*, in the superior intellectual receptivity of little girls.[47]

However, there are anomalies and omissions in this important account of James's "middle years." The most obvious example of the former is the incongruous male child in the series. Alongside these sequentially sprouting girl-children, James also concentrates on a particular kind of female character: impoverished in circumstances, sensitive in intelligence, and with the prospect of some dramatic improvement in fortune that is never achieved, in part because of a heightened identification with the state of expectation and passive attendance characteristic of romance, a state that never corresponds to the demands of reality. The mild, imaginative, and artistic Fleda Vetch of *The Spoils of Poynton* thus displays affinities with the daydreaming career-governess of *The Turn of the Screw*, and even, since all three are loosely arraigned by critics under the appellation "spinster," with *Maisie*'s incongruously passionate and indispensably prominent Mrs. Wix.[48]

The Spoils of Poynton was the first novel James wrote after *Guy Domville*, and his account of its origins emphasizes that Fleda was its pivotal invention, the crucial addition to the "germ" or "particle" of inspiration provided by the real-life story of a mother and son at loggerheads over the furniture of an inherited home. The rapidly spreading "virus of suggestion" and James's wish not to hear any more of the familial anecdote underline Fleda's function: to introduce the motif of mentorship and surrogate filiation, with its multicellular possibilities of attachment and devastation.[49] *Spoils*, furthermore, contains another complication for Edel's picture of the unconscious *Bildungsroman* effecting James's psychical renewal: the "things" ultimately destroyed by the feud seem to occupy a place analogous to that of the murdered child Effie, making the first element in the series identified by Edel not a female infant, but works of art. The status of these works of art as substitute progeny, prized above a natural son or the recruited prospective daughter groomed to ensure their recovery, also links them to a recurring minor motif in James's work: the mysterious death of a male child, which signals both familial prohibition of an unacceptable sexuality and the "price" exacted by the sublimation necessary for aesthetic creation. After playing a decisive role in "Owen Wingrave" and "The Pupil," this motif reappears in *The Turn of the Screw*. Its scenario having been sketched five days after the opening night of *Guy Domville*[50]—on the very evening when James experienced his "subacqueous" feeling—*The Turn of the Screw* includes all three elements noted above: the marginal, desiring, and frustrated heroine, hopelessly anticipating, like James the would-be playwright, recognition and spectacular elevation in the world; the killed, but not unmistakably murdered, male child, who represents the paradox of James's cultural removal and escape; and the transitional little girl, clandestinely advancing James's regeneration.

The tale's incorporation of all these elements (all characteristics of the middle phase), together with its unparalleled—in the Jamesian œuvre—critical and popular success, suggests that it provides an important key to the psychological underpinnings of Jamesian plotting. It also brings together James's two failed attempts at popularity, *Guy Domville* (1895) and *The Other House* (1896), juxtaposing them

within its structure and drawing out the hidden meaning of these otherwise superficial or crass bids for public attention. It is difficult not to
be pained by the contortions that went into the making of *Guy Domville*—not only the play's lack of subtlety but also the historical and
confessionally alien setting required plausibly to embody the Jamesian
theme of male renunciation and retreat. James's letter to his theatrical producer, protesting against the demand for a happy (matrimo-
nial) ending, indicates his misplaced faith in the direct popular appeal
of this theme: "Domville throwing up his priesthood to take posses-
sion of his place in the world [finds] that he [is] only to make himself
happy at the expense of others . . . in the face of this reality—ugly and
cruel—[he] turns back again to his old ideal."[51] A letter to William
James following the humiliating first-night curtain call even suggests
that James identified with Domville's gesture: condemning the booing
audience's "savagery of disappointment" that "one wasn't the *same*
as everything else they had ever seen. . . . I saw they couldn't care
one straw for a damned young last-century English Catholic [who]
acted . . . from remote and romantic motives."[52] In contrast, James
from the beginning repudiated and disowned *The Other House* as an
act of vengeance directed at the bad taste of the public: "If that's what
the idiots want, I can give them their bellyful."[53]

Indeed, the story, uniquely violent within the Jamesian oeuvre, seems
"irrational and uncontrolled," lacking authorial "understand[ing] or
command" of its subject-matter, an "Ibsen play without his morality—or his insight."[54] Because *The Other House* aggressively supplies
what *Guy Domville* presumably lacked, the works may be seen as
counterparts. On the one hand, Guy Domville, the literary brother
of, at either end of James's "uncanny brood," Christopher Newman
and Lambert Strether, enacts the gesture of withdrawal from marriage and from worldly involvement that has increasingly been read
as the securing of an unspoken homosexual possibility. On the other
hand, *The Other House* presents the osteology of James's usual model
of heterosexual relations. As Hugh Stevens points out (*contra* Eve
Sedgwick's critique of the "erotic triangle" as an expression of patriarchal proprietorship), this model is not a ritualized, bonding com-
petition between two men for an objectified woman, but "figure[s]
two women as rivals for a man."[55] The dynamic is no less destructive,
in that it shows one of the women attempting to expand her social
possibilities by using the other "as an object of exchange." However,
in the fiction of these exploratory years James extends this dyadic

stand-off into a phantasmal multiplicity of competing females: the avid lady telegraphers of "In the Cage" chasing after likely romantic loves; the at least four (but only one viable) admirers of Sir Claude who precipitate the progress of *What Maisie Knew*. *The Other House* inaugurates the phantasm in a scene between Mrs. Beever, presiding genius or matriarchal strategist of the plot, and the village Doctor, associated with the law and its discretionary prerogatives. She shows him the doll she has bought to give as a birthday present to Effie, daughter of Tony Bream, who is the son of her dead husband's business partner and whose wife died at Effie's birth. The doctor (and the narrator) creepily appraise the qualities of the doll and confuse her with a living female: "The young lady was sumptuous and ample; he took her in his hands with reverence: 'she's splendid—she's positively human! I feel like a Turkish pasha investing in a beautiful Circassian." "Warned" by Mrs. Beever that the doll will be "no less than the fourth" the child will receive that day, the Doctor then rehashes his orientalist quip: "It's a regular slave-market—a perfect harem!"[56]

The numerous dolls in this strange scene, unusual for James in providing a frozen allegory of the narrative in which it is placed, stand for the array of women who position themselves to attain the eternal devotion of Tony Bream: his dead wife, who enjoins him not to marry again while Effie is alive; Jean Martle, Mrs. Beever's preferred bride for her own son; and Rose Arminger, "insanely" in love with Tony, who eventually kills Effie, at once violating and obeying his wife's decree. That Effie is plied with dolls seems to insist that she will in the future join the general assembly of female sexual equivalence. In an almost shockingly flat irony, both the occasion of the gift (her own birthday and the day of her mother's death) and the doll mark this position as itself indistinguishable from death or nonbeing. In this symbolic economy Rose's murder of Effie then becomes the fulfillment of what Effie was always destined to be, even though it is at the same time a violent rebellion on Rose's part against her own equivalent status. Like the efforts of other James heroines to turn a rival into an object of use, Rose's act simply reinforces the structure it seeks to evade, and the "harem" vignette perhaps explains why her legal culpability attracts no justiciary or cathartic requital: the conceit the novel relies on is in some sense taken as a literal truth, or as a sensational laying-bare of actual social relations, which the crime does no more than secondarily (if emphatically) confirm.

The Turn of the Screw combines the narrative tendencies of *Guy Domville* and *The Other House*. Its frame text pointedly evolves toward—and states its preference for—all-male company and focuses on two figures about whom nothing is known other than what is revealed through their interaction over the succeeding tale. The tale proper reiterates the fate of Rose Arminger: a woman deprived of her object of romantic desire is led to kill a child, although the event is not construed as a literal killing, since there is no judicial or even clarificatory aftermath implied by the ending. Nor is there an explanation of how the event could be overcome in order to make possible later events recounted in the frame. The frame, therefore, does not function as an explanatory real-world context for the ending (the typical gambit of such narrative openings), but as part of the cycle of storytelling (now fully enclosed). The woman's story is also bequeathed like an article of inheritance between the two frame characters, again indicating that the child's killing is not a literal crime, but a somehow treasured symbolic event, and that the tale expresses the otherwise unspoken truth of these characters. In its invention of a smoothly efficient hinge between the preoccupations of James's most public self-assertions, as well as a means of exorcising the burdens that inhibited his enjoyment of the fruits of his artistic labors (the purchase of Lamb House, presumably as an answer to the haunted "other house" of childhood), *The Turn of the Screw* constructs a specifically Jamesian mythology of sexual development, one that anticipates yet modifies Freud's theory of the evolution of homosexuality.

Freud sketches the following outline of the psychical etiology of the orientation: "der bis dahin intensive an die Mutter fixierte junge Mann einige Jahre nach abgelaufener Pubertät eine Wendung vornimmt, sich selbst mit der Mutter identifiziert und nach Liebesobjekten ausschaut, in denen er sich selbst widerfinden kann, die er dann lieben möchte, wie die Mutter ihn geliebt hat" (the young man, intensely fixated on his mother until this point, undertakes a change of course a few years after puberty, identifying himself with his mother and looking for love objects in which he can find himself again, and that he can love just as his mother loved him). A notable feature of this process is the need for love objects "[die] das Alter haben müssen, in dem bei ihm die Umwandlung erfolgt ist" (which must be the same age as he was when this transformation took place), a narcissistic choice influenced to varying degrees by the need to remain "faithful" to the mother and by the high value set on the male sexual organ.[57] The definitive pretensions of Freud's theory have of course been challenged; its usefulness here depends on its emergence from, and progression beyond, the nineteenth-century discourses of homosexuality with which James was familiar. For example, Freud's use of the word "turn" ("Wendung," as opposed to the cognate "inversion" or the earlier "konträre Sexualempfindung")[58] recalls the transformative importance of that noun-verb throughout James's works: as the valedictory repudiation of marriage and sullying worldly antagonism; as the unwieldy, sometimes nonsensically violent "gothic" plot twist borrowed from Balzacian romance and ultimately integrated into the triumphant, yet silent, psychological table-turning of the last novels.

The structure of *The Turn of the Screw* revises Freud's blueprint in two significant ways. In its air of being a secret code for which there is no definite deciphering, it creates only allusive invocations of the positions referred to by Freud, an allusiveness that is also in keeping with James's consistent transfer of the parental relation to the more ambiguous one of wardship and guardianship. An eroticized alignment to a younger alter-ego is evident in the exchanges between Douglas and the first narrator, whose interaction seems asymmetrical (given the intense interest the "I" trains on Douglas, and the authority the latter apparently attributes to that "I"). However, Douglas dies first, suggesting that they are close in age (or that the asymmetry is reversed). Both the first narrator and Douglas therefore occupy the same position, one relative to an erotic formation, rather than within it. More obviously, the governess, as a caretaker of orphaned children, is a substitute mother. The central difference from the Freudian schema in this case is that the amorous intensity of the "motherly" focus on the male child evolves from her deprivation of, and disillusionment with, the adult male object of her desire. (The final scene has the governess seem to "rescue" the young Miles from the contaminating "horror" represented at that moment by both the master and Peter Quint.) That the effect of her concentrated solicitude also appears murderous or crippling, but in a manner that preserves it as precious and undeniable—and so like the anguished "change to something queer" and dramatic "loss of consciousness" that constituted for James the origin of his artistic commitment[59]—suggests that the story is a parable of sublimation rather than of "homosexual orientation" as such.

That this "parable" fundamentally subtends the stylistic mechanism of "point of view" is indicated by the fact that it shares the characteristics of "psychoanalytic allegory" with E.T.A. Hoffmann's "The Sandman," a text that likewise elaborates a homosexual formation encoded through heterosexual development.[60] Whereas traditional allegory (as Hegel argues) personifies abstractions, robbing concrete individuality of subjectivity in order to achieve universality,[61] the "uncanny," I suggest, unleashes unconscious desire into the external world in a manner that makes it difficult to tell which events are the result of a subjective propulsion and which of external physical laws or phenomena. "The Sandman" achieves this undecidability by distinguishing three levels: the remembered childhood "horror" that is, in its concealment of some unconscious repressed, continuous with nightmare and fable; a set of actual relationships that in their own strange contingency and relation to the experiences elaborated, appear less and less so; and a mechanical device (the doll Olimpia), whose function it is to uncover the meaning of the unconscious repressed and, in its violent collapse, to dismantle the "reality" of the relationships. In *The Turn of the Screw* these three levels are mediated by a narrative voice that is closely connected to the apparently all-male company who hear the governess's testimony. Hoffmann's narrator both vouchsafes and—in his arbitrary anonymity—undermines any sense of the internal reality of the story he is recounting. He seems to invoke another story that he would like to tell, a story that has possessed him and to which his "friends" have challenged him to give utterance.[62] In "The Sandman," furthermore, "friends" always refers to a male collectivity that indeed facilitates the action, moving Nathanael's belongings to the room where he can see Olimpia after his previous student lodgings, in a kind of fateful psychical synchronicity, have burned down during the period of his reconciliation with Clara.

The pivotal role of such "friends," the desired addressees of an untold story (an audience that potentially includes the reader, if he knows how to understand the code) as well as the mysterious stagehands of events, gestures toward a point beyond the motifs of castration and narcissism that Freud locates in Hoffman's text.[63] According to Freud, Nathanael is overcome by a threatening father whom he distinguishes in fantasy from his actual father, and whose menace he can only attempt to annul through adoration of his injured self. The narrator's enthusiasm for an unspeakable alternative articulates an affirmative version of this diagnosis of damage and failure—namely, a homosexual formation that here can only be expressed through successive destruction of heterosexual ideals ranging from the model of the sensible wife (who may have been given all her ideas by a male counterpart, a scientist, or philosopher) to the idealized woman of

courtly love (the love-object become "Thing")[64] to, finally, the hearth
of reproductive domesticity glimpsed in the tableau of Clara's family life: "das ruhige häusliche Glück . . . das ihr der im Innern zeris-
sene Nathanael niemals hätte gewähren koennen" (the calm domestic
happiness . . . that Nathanael, inwardly torn apart, could never have
given her).

An implicitly male collectivity also appears in the frame narrative
of *The Turn of the Screw*, performing the contradictory role of veri-
fying the ensuing document and hinting at an untold alternative or
undecipherable significance. At first glance, the governess's history
seems not to contain the other decisive element relied on by "The
Sandman": a technological artifice that deconstructs unconscious
horror, the complement, in the plot, of narrative demystification. In
his preface to the *New York Edition*, James jokes about the aesthetically unserviceable nature of the modern ghost, who does not even
move much or surface often, acknowledging that Peter Quint and
Miss Jessel "are not 'ghosts' at all, as we now know the ghost, but
goblins, elves, imps, demons as loosely constructed as those of the
old trials for witchcraft."[65] However, this claim ignores the fact that
the ghosts behave much as the "phantasms" investigated by the Victorian Society for Psychical Research (of which William James was a
member);[66] never speaking or attacking, but merely coming into view
occasionally and in a manner almost compatible with their being continuing coresidents of Bly, whose fate and character have been misre-
ported by its housekeeper. Elsewhere in the preface, defending himself
from a reader's allegation that he failed to give the governess a fully
fleshed-out identity, James admits the distinction between "her crys-
talline record of so many intense anomalies and obscurities" and "her
explanation of them, a different matter."[67] What James occludes is
that it is in the governess's "explanations," rather than in any activity
or even appearance of the ghosts themselves, that the effect of "caus-
ing the situation to reek with an air of Evil" resides. If one recalls that
James in another preface alludes to "the small recording governess"[68]
as though his narrator were a machine, a mechanical amanuensis,
it also becomes clear that the ghosts themselves are a technological component, a hobby-horse of nineteenth-century experimental
science, who require for their impact an interpretation supplied by
a recording device, a systematic generator of "explanation," which
adds the supposition of their "evil" in a tale whose significance James
summed up as "a very mechanical matter."[69] "The Sandman" and

the psychoanalytic allegory of which it is paradigmatic demonstrate that the meaning of this technological element, as well as the reason for its emergence in a discussion of the governess's "character," is the dismantling of the dynamics that have gone into the making of the "subject." In Hoffmann's story, the tawdry device of the doll suggests that all amorous infatuation is narcissistic, the love-object (like the self) a mere product of all that has been projected onto it, so that fleshly humanity is reduced to formula and system. Any reading of *The Turn of the Screw* cannot fail to notice the way in which the action is assembled through the interplay between visual manifestations and explanation or interpretation. Neither aspect is self-sufficient, and the "device" or the "technological" consists in their separation and incremental conjoining. In keeping with the mechanical quality attributed to the governess's writing, it is as if we are watching the story being built, and this in turn renders its provocation of tried-and-tested reflexes of response self-referential. Indeed, a mechanical reference appears in its title, and a "turn" is noted at almost every development of the action.

In the automated nature of the reaction it elicits from the reader, the governess's document can be understood as a mobilization of the unconscious drive. The trajectory of her testimony also follows the logic of the drive. According to Lacan, the drive performs a *tour* ("turn" or, resonantly, "trick") around its lost object,[70] seeking to recover an assumed state of original unity by incorporating this object, whatever mutilations or misrecognitions may occur in the process. My argument is that the governess's document dramatizes the trauma underlying the narcissism of the frame. The relation between the two sections of text is at the same time the connection between the defining stylistic method of James's fiction and his recurrent thematic preoccupations. The frame's homoerotic mutual appreciation presents us with the epitome of "point of view"—the narrative absorption of an alternate "perspective"—while the document, the arc of the drive, traverses the usual components of Jamesian plot, namely, the collision between the "family romance" motif of patronage and the childhood experience of the "primal scene." Parsing the psychical form of the tale reveals why it has been difficult both to treat it conclusively as the portrayal of a "character" (insane or "agreeable") and to explain the function of its notorious apparitions. Like the mechanical doll of "The Sandman," the pseudo-technological apparatus of *The Turn of the Screw* gestures toward a more banal chronicle of the difficulties of the subject's formation: uneventfulness, nothingness, and perhaps indifference and abuse. By doing so, it shows the kind of "cruelty" Jamesian narrative embodies, but which is too easily overlooked if one takes at face value his condemnation of the "cruelty" in the Goncourts. Rather than systematically "cutting off" characters from their wishes or illusions (as Flaubert does also), Jamesian narrative, as anatomized by *The Turn of the Screw*, indulges desire while simultaneously making clear its subordination to trauma.

THE TURNS OF THE DRIVE

Despite Bruce Robbins's early reminder that "sexual or literary ambiguity" should not be "elevated into an abstract principle,"[71] there has been little attempt to explore the relevance for actual bodies and concrete relationships of Shoshana Felman's now-canonical, rhetorically exhaustive Lacanian reading of *The Turn of the Screw*. In a maneuver typical of her argument, Felman accepts the identity between the dynamic of "transference" (or the attribution of knowledge to the other) and love and proposes that the elliptical dialogue of the frame presents us with "a series of pairs or *couples*: the governess and Douglas and the first-person narrator" or "a double love-relation, between the narrator and Douglas, and between Douglas and the governess."[72] However, the transferential mobility of the exchanges seems instead to be a means of converting the encounter between the governess and her employer into a vehicle for expressing an erotic alignment between Douglas and the first narrator. Douglas's "laugh" in response to the narrator's conclusion—"I see. She was in love," itself a rejoinder to his own solicitation: "you'll easily judge . . . *you* will"—suggests that he receives the anticipated answer in the form of an unexpectedly direct come-on or reminder.[73] His stress on the past tense may register a change in his own sentiments toward his addressee, or perhaps their relegation to a former time: "Yes, she was in love. That is she *had* been."[74] "It *was* the beauty of it,"[75] he emphasizes again, when the narrator insists on "the beauty" of the governess's succumbing after one interview to "the seduction exercised by the beautiful young man." Felman's assertion that "Douglas had been secretly in love with [the governess], even though she was ten years his senior"[76] seems to participate in the projections staged by the conversations, since she summarizes (and reconciles) a disagreement between the only actual couple present in the party: the husband thinks the infatuation, because of the age-difference, improbable; the wife regards it as all the more likely.

While the frame creates a dialogic imitation of "transference" that enables a homosexual relation to be evoked through reference to a prototypical heterosexual romance, a homoerotic subtext emerges even more clearly when the exchanges disperse into an equally remarkable descriptive mode in which the narrator is the ventriloquist of Douglas's words. His comment on the governess's employer—"one could easily fix his type; it never, happily, dies out"[77]—could be an exact quotation from Douglas himself (as the latter again looks at or "fixes" the narrator) or a judgment of the narrator's own on both the speaker to whom he listened and the object of the discourse. Simultaneously encapsulating all of these positions, it expresses the two interlocutors' mutually approving assessment of one another, an assessment articulated through their shared appreciation of an imaginary ideal "type." Formally, the phrase and its conditions of origin achieve the *ne plus ultra* of "point of view": the narrative occupation of an alternate perspective from which it is nevertheless distinguishable. In addition, it establishes a definitive link between this technical strategy and a self-protective narcissism, an association confirmed by the deployment of the word "type" and its reverberations within the relayed description.

Lacan notes that the human species reproduces the "type," not the individual. He refers to the exemplar "horse" as a paradigm for species type.[78] John Carlos Rowe has noted a suspicious incongruity in the employer's application of the word "respectable" first to the former governess and then to the current membership of the household of Bly: "And there were further, a cook, a housemaid, a dairywoman, an old pony, an old groom and an old gardener, all likewise thoroughly respectable."[79] Rowe argues that the inapt inclusion of a horse in the list introduces a second connotation to the adjective—"usable" or "serviceable"—whose implied exploitative seigneurial license also snidely undermines its moral meaning in the case of the governess.[80] A query from the audience draws out this insinuation: "And what did the former governess die of? Of so much respectability?"[81] But it is unlikely that the word "respectable," in the sense of "serviceable," would ever be applied to a pony; in addition to the lurking gentleman's club joke, the incongruity is based on the more radical divergence between animal and human. Lacan proposes that acquiring knowledge of sexuality is traumatic for human beings because the reproduction of the "type" knells the negation and the death of the individual. Narcissism, the path by which human beings reach sexual seduction (their version of the "lure" in the animal world) is at the same time an imaginary denial of this fatal inevitability because it involves a fixation on the image of the self.[82] In the section of the frame text dealing with the master, everyone connected with him casually "dies," while he himself is eternal. The muted slander attaching to the former governess relegates the female to the merely animal fate of reproduction and death.

That the document following the frame text explores an inchoate arena of the psyche, both below and unconsolidated by the satisfactions of narcissism, is suggested by the way its female first-person voice is presented as a series of movements toward and recoiling from the external world that recall the amoeba organism Freud invokes to depict the libido and its earliest absorption of outside objects.[83] Her opening phrase—"I remember the whole beginning as a succession of flights and drops"—transforms words that denote shifts of physical matter, or the distances charted by them, into abbreviations for interior mood. The gloss on this phrase, "a little see-saw of the right throbs and the wrong," contracts the business of seeing and having seen her prospective employer into a swinging bar, which in turn conveys an internal vacillation, one where the lowered state, the "wrong" that clangs the end of the sentence, enfolds moral misalignment within spatial asymmetry. This depression converts the temporal duration of the first part of the governess's journey into a set of physical sensations at once internal and external, and it makes the vehicle by which she travels a proxy for her feelings: "In this state of mind I spent the long hours of bumping swinging coach." Likewise, the next conveyance, "a commodious fly," introduces the noun-form of her previous "flight," a mental transport repeated when, as the carriage approaches its destination, "my fortitude . . . took a flight," and the governess becomes indistinguishable from the carriage, referring to "the crunch of my wheels upon the gravel."[84]

The first "event" the governess confronts is neither the appearance of Quint nor the notice from Miles's school, but rather the effect of the decidedly abrupt note from the employer that encloses it: "This, I recognize, is from the head-master, and the head-master's an awful bore. Read him, please; deal with him; but mind you don't report. Not a word. I'm off!" Her account of her response—"I broke the seal with a great effort, so great a one that I was a long time coming to it"[85]—presents inaction in terms of action, leaving her devastation to be imputed by the implied reader, Douglas ("I saw it, and she saw I saw it"[86]). This unportrayed distress configures the governess's question to Mrs. Grose about Miles—"Is he really *bad*?"[87]—as a question about the "master" himself. Mrs. Grose thereby becomes—occupying a role brought especially to the fore in James's work of the 1890s and epitomized by *Maisie*'s Mrs. Wix—the agent of a kind of virtual initiation into knowledge of sexuality and the alliances and betrayals it enables. The housekeeper's "ambiguity" lies in a formal dramatics of instability. In a second exchange about the headmaster's letter, Mrs. Grose appears haughty and sophisticated—almost as if she were a speaking Miss Jessel—echoing, like a typical Jamesian personage of high good breeding, the exact grammatical outline of the governess's query: "Oh never known him [to be bad]—I don't pretend *that*."[88] At the same time, she overlooks the governess's choice of words ("contaminate"), and one wonders whether she later grasps the correct meaning of the word "infamous", or if the governess distorts matters in order to simplify them, for example, when she replaces "prevaricated" with "lied".

As a source of vital factual information, Mrs. Grose stands between the necessarily indispensable Mrs. Bread of *The American* and an even more earthily named successor, Fanny Assingham, of *The Golden Bowl*. In her occasional, incongruous sophistication and the uncertainty produced by her ignorance, she also recalls the volatility generated by a more sinister mother-substitute: Madame Merle of *The Portrait of a Lady*. Pericles Lewis has argued that *The Turn of the Screw* metaleptically combines the two "impulses" usually posed by James's ghost stories: an "eager[ness] to uncover hidden truths . . . heedless of consequences" and a belief in apparitions "desperate" for "confirmation . . . from others." Since only "partial confirmation" is furnished, and this by a believer who does not see, nothing slows the investigator's destructive "prosecutorial zeal."[89] In fact, the story multiplies and renders noxious all the positions composing the plot configuration of "point of view" in this experimental phase of its development as an aesthetic secularization of the religious concern with sexual "knowledge." In addition to Mrs. Grose's Janus-like nature, an errant adult couple is matched with a pair of children, and, most destabilizing of all, a heroine presides who is both innocent child-victim and adult-initiator.

The third important element in the master's letter is the phrase "I'm off!" Jamesian style often relies on the allusiveness created by phrases that seem poised between two kinds of parts of speech (in this case, an adjective—"off"—which, if followed by more precise information, would become a prepositional phrase). In *The Turn of the Screw* such allusiveness produces—like the multiplication of character function—a certain degree of toxicity. Attempts to reconstruct the "true" relations between characters have cited other ambiguous adjectives to establish kinship bonds: Rowe speculates that the use of the euphemism "lost" to describe the fate of both the master's younger brother and of Miss Jessel raises the possibility that the deceased were the (unmarried) parents of Miles and Flora.

As in "The Sandman," however, biological kinship cedes priority to psychical interconnection. The phrase "I'm off" connotes not only going away or imminent departure but also "relieved from duty" and so recalls Mrs. Grose's vague information that Miss Jessel "went off."[90] Coupled with the housekeeper's suggestion that Miss Jessel jealously looked at Flora, the little "princess of the blood," with eyes of "dislike" and was particular only "about some things,"[91] the connection could signal a refusal to do work, an abstention from pedagogical and nurturing tasks because of a morbid preoccupation with failed romance. In this regard, the echo resounded by "off" replaces a biological reference: Ned Lukacher assumes from Mrs. Grose's words that Miss Jessel "went off" to die giving birth to Quint's child,[92] an hypothesis never fleshed out by the housekeeper and that itself remains a grammatical allusion in Douglas's unfulfilled promise: "that will come out."[93] The phrase "I'm off" might also therefore function as an unconscious prompt to the present governess to abandon her duties—as she does soon after, leaving Flora in the schoolroom after only ten minutes the next day (although it is presented as a longer time) to consult Mrs. Grose. The ensuing narrative is strewn with innocuous, sometimes barely perceptible, hints of her delinquency: she is late to meet Miles; she does not play with Flora at the scene of Miss Jessel's first appearance. Throughout the narrative her stationary occupation of sewing is the main reference for the word "work": "my hypocrisy of 'work,'" she calls it in the final scene,[94] hiding in plain sight its status as a pretext. This scene also gives the second major meaning to the word: its association with the more grandiose undertaking of spiritual exorcism as "the demonstration of my work."[95] The association between "going off" and not working, sprung by the master's phrase and reverberating through the text, also resonates with the functioning of the unconscious drive, which comes to the fore when the constraints of the ego, with its socially induced awareness of responsibility, are weakened or lifted altogether.

In imitating the desire implied by the note (that of renouncing responsibility) and following merely the empty letter of its command ("don't report"), the governess "represses" not, as the "anti-appari-tional" critical lineage has in one way or another assumed, her "love" for the master, but his indifference toward her. The immediately suc-ceeding episode describes leisure hours spent enjoying "a sense of property," along with fantasies of the master's presence, the "kind light" of approval "in his handsome face."[96] Quint appears in the posi-tion occupied by the governess herself in these romantic and socially aspirational daydreams—namely, a princess high up in a tower, wait-ing to be rescued: "It was not at such an elevation that the figure I had so often invoked seemed most in place."[97] His alien features are the hallucinatory return of the intolerable indifference and a repelling image of the governess's own "self," since the structure of the vision recalls Lacan's model of the ego as a real content within an imaginary container,[98] in this case, the specter of the ominous "eccentric father" enclosed by a fairytale surround. The ensuing apparitional masquer-ade (deciphered with the help of Mrs. Grose) parades a relationship with the master marked, in its "horror," by the negation of this rela-tion or its impossibility on the conditions for which the governess must wish. The children's role is to embody an imaginary projection of these conditions and their decomposition: the identification with the "angelic" Flora degenerates into her rejection as a "chit";[99] the permanent attachment sought from Miles, which requires an elimina-tion of the sexual, culminates in being "alone" with nothing.[100]

That the governess's document enacts the traumatic underside of the narcissism celebrated in the frame is shown by the way the master's "liberality" becomes transformed into the "hound" Quint's despotic power over a household that included "several of . . . the half-dozen maids and men who were still of our small colony."[101] This polymorphous extension of the harem dreamt of in *The Other House* recalls in its almost comedic hyperbole the exultant inflation in "The Sandman" of those fictional or imaginary layers that obscure a banal and abusive reality. With Quint already established as the master's rural alter-ego, the chimera sensationalizes the latter's pos-sible seduction of the governess (and the threat to the individuality of the subject posed by sexuality itself) and both signals and denies the "horror" of such a seduction's nonoccurrence, while simultaneously distracting from and representing, through that very diversionary tactic, the hackneyed omnipotence of the proprietary exploitation of labor. In fulfilling, rather than rendering fully inconsequent, the governess's initial, callowly disingenuous "Oh I've no pretensions— to being the only one,"[102] the unthinkable scenario marks the inter- connection of sexual initiation and the concern with patronage as a potential liberation—here, as elsewhere, phantasmal—from pro- saic work. The reverse image relation between frame and document is also present in formal terms: just as the frame's dialogic elucida- tion of who loves whom disperses into a ventriloquized description of the eternally desired object, so Mrs. Grose's compelled communica- tion of vital facts to the governess becomes an implicit description of Quint's death: "the icy slope, the turn mistaken at night and in liquor, accounted for much . . . but there had been matters in his life . . . that would have accounted for a good deal more."[103] In other words, if the idealized gentleman-master is "happily" a "type that never dies out," Quint is one that, from the fused "point of view" of the two women, thankfully always does.

One obstacle to deciphering the "trauma" at the core of the docu- ment and to treating the governess as an individual "character" pos- sessing, in James's paraphrase of his dissatisfied reader, a "mystery" of her own, is that the content of the artless or unpremeditated dis- course she produces secretes the material of the Jamesian unconscious identified by Edel. Her insistent, uninhibited, self-focused chatter— "it was . . . over *my* life, *my* past and *my* friends alone that we could take anything like our ease"—raises the very topic it is designed to conceal: "the friends little children had lost."[104] It first provides a screen for the "more pains than one" caused by recent "disturbing letters from home" through indulgent reference to "many particu- lars of the whimsical bent of my father." More strikingly, accounts of "the smallest adventures . . . of my brothers and sisters"[105] seem at odds with the governess's introduction in the frame text as the "youngest of several daughters of a poor country parson,"[106] a detail that apparently attributes her innocence to membership of an all- female sibling household. Both references jar with an already pecu- liarly phrased use of the perfect tense when the Governess expresses sympathy with Flora's "idolatrous" attitude toward Miles: "I had had brothers myself."[107] Taken together, these inconsistencies allude to the subliminal presence of the familiar Jamesian motif of murdered little boys, here a kind of virtual series that makes the tale a psychical mine for "point of view," since the document progresses toward a further virtual killing—the governess, damaged by trauma, repeats this trauma—and enfolds this event within an account of the origins of stylistic technique (the frame's exclusive concern with "charm" and aesthetic effect).

The inclusion of a multiplied version of James's unconscious mythology concerning the origins of his artistic vocation also means that the governess's document constitutes something like a formal substantiation of the Lacanian revision (and augmentation) of Freud's theory of sublimation. Reminding us that Freud emphasizes the crucial importance of the aim of worldly success in the creative writer's successful transposition of private daydreams to public acceptability,[108] Lacan proposes that the phenomenon be thought of as the elevation of the object (or any possible object of satisfaction potentially obtained by means of aesthetic or intellectual endeavor) to the status of the "Thing" or the elusive source of a never-achievable and only putatively lost state of human completeness.[109] James presents us with a protagonist who longs for romance, for social elevation, for property, even—like her author—for success on the stage, in a narrative where the most prominently and vividly represented activity is that of writing itself. The conjunction between a protagonist who is not doing the work she is employed to do and the act of writing (in a tale that harbors the primary Jamesian myth) reveals not only the material and sexual objects for which sublimation substitutes isolated creative labor, but the reverse side of this commitment, or in Erich Fromm's terms the susceptibility to the stimulus of violence and cruelty that inevitably replaces the renunciations of work and effort.[110] The document scatters not only hints of derelictions of duty but also traces of bad temper (the "dropped" gloves on the dining-room floor), sudden punctuations of brutality (the children have "morally at any rate, nothing to whack!"), raising the suspicion that its lofty sentiments are a ruse of sadism.

The story foregrounds the question of "writing" not as the translation of all arrangements or physical and material bodies into configurations of rhetoric, but as an exhaustive exploration, the only such experiment in the Jamesian oeuvre, of the iterative nature of desire. When the children begin to speak at its mid-point, they talk in imitation of a language of amorous courtship for which no original model is provided—an omission that implies the universality of human participation in both the prompt given by speech to desire and the potential for (or inevitability of) untimely interference that this phenomenon involves (the governess pauses to muse about her approval of their endearments' "fond familiarity"[111]). When Mrs. Grose commiserates with her colleague's lament over the consequences of Flora's absorption of a more brutal version of this ill-befitting language—"she'll make me out to [her uncle] the lowest creature"—this is also the imitation of an unrepresented reiteration.[112] The most alarming resurgence of the signifier comes with Mrs. Grose's suggestion that Miles "stole letters!" at school. Its apparent groundlessness makes the inference an echo of the governess's concern with writing (literacy)—and not writing (noncommunication with and from her employer)—and modifies once and for all the reliability promised by the housekeeper's subordinate status and stolidity: the helpful suggestion is merely a dim reflection of her superior's mind, whose authority is by it reduced to the presumption of madness.

Necessarily, the text also features an allusion to the breakdown in the chain of reflection and imitation that preserves illusions of complementarity and autonomy in the workings of desire: an experience of the "real." Miles forlornly repeats that he found "nothing, nothing"[113] in the missive the governess supposedly penned for Harley Street, evoking a story not compassed by her narrative. By contrast, her own mood of jubilance and triumph ("and you found nothing!") expresses elation at managing to fulfill the "letter" of the master's command that she report "not a word." Neither repudiations nor adoptions (implicit and explicit) of Edmund Wilson's notorious interpretation of the tale recognize that the governess's "hysteria" conforms to Lacan's definition of the illness as an effort to "sustain the desire of the father,"[114] or that, as if in a mocking deployment by James of psychoanalytic diagnoses, the effort prohibits her from being a writer. The document is founded on two opposing but mutually supporting parameters: an injunction against communicating with the "master" and a continual address to Douglas, who is stationed—ten years younger and in almost parodic tribute to the repetition compulsion—in the permanently occupied place of substitute object. A single sentence encapsulates this interdependency and its meaning: "He [the children's uncle] never wrote to them—that may have been selfish, but it was part of the flattery of his trust of myself; for the way in which a man pays his highest tribute to a woman is apt to be but by the more festal celebration of one of the sacred laws of his comfort."[115] This extraordinary presentation of "nothing" as compliment, merriment, traditional marital coexistence—and not as an expression of bitter irony or psychotic delusion—also cannot logically be read as a statement by the character assumed to have written it. Instead, confiding with Douglas maintains the viability of the hopeless, unsatisfied desire animating the document, or perhaps lends an egoic superstructure to the willful, heedless drive that refuses to relinquish its wish.

With this structure, James figures a desire that remains unaware of its own doomed futility. The arrangement is more insidious than the direct, merciless dismantling of the prospects and aspirations of their female heroines by the Goncourts and Flaubert because the frame contains a secret, a joke, from which the governess is excluded. Her position is made clear by another anomaly in the superficial babble about "*my* life" that revives the central incongruity of the frame: she is "called upon to confirm the details already supplied as to the cleverness of the vicarage pony,"[116] forced to reiterate the human qualities of the animal, while the frame denies the animal, transitory nature of its human ideal. This closed, diametric relation between the document and its frame suggests a countervailing current in James's attentiveness to figures—especially, in these transitional years, female protagonists—whose longings are explored but never realized. That such a dilatory interest in the indulgence of desire has destructive underpinnings or origins is indicated by the clues to neglect and abuse scattered through the governess's document. The consequences of her implied obsession with unfulfilled romance are formally linked to the trauma hinted at in the frame (Douglas's "tapping" of his heart)[117] and in the preface, where James's own heart is "shaken" by the demand of his dissatisfied reader. It is this "trauma," according to the logic of the narrative, that gives rise to the mechanism of "point of view," the first-person "doubling" of a character's stance, an insulating narcissistic compensation and pleasure since the ideal love object, identified with the self, is enjoyed and preserved within its stylistic enmeshing. The Harley Street gentleman inaugurates a series of such fixed ideals: Sir Claude, Vanderbank, Merton Densher. *The Turn of the Screw* shows that "point of view" is not an ethical attentiveness to distinctive "perspectives." In laying bare the psychical skeleton of the technique, the story presents James's own version, or reassembling, of the "cruelty" he criticized in the French literature of the 1870s.

CHAPTER FOUR

The Marquis de Sade
in the Twentieth Century

A devastating coda ends one of the more unusual sections of Marcel Proust's *Du côté de chez Swann*. Having witnessed, from "Swann's path," Mlle Vinteuil profane the memory of her late father as part of a scene of seduction with her female lover, the narrator comments, "Perhaps she would not have thought of evil as a state so rare, so abnormal, so exotic, one in which it was so refreshing to sojourn, had she been able to discern in herself, as in everyone else, that indifference to the sufferings one causes which, whatever other names one gives it, is the most terrible and lasting form of cruelty."[1] The statement is not only a moral condemnation. Preceding reflections are preoccupied with the generic theatricality of sadism: "When we find in real life a desire for melodramatic effect, it is generally sadism that is responsible for it" (230; 136). The narrator regards sadism as a species of innocence incapable of disassociating evil from the sexual act and therefore dedicated to artificial, ritualized inflictions of humiliation. My argument here is that the kind of cruelty Proust juxtaposes to sadistic theatricality—permanent, ineluctable, despite being given other names—is one that reverberates throughout twentieth-century French aesthetics and philosophy, and that it is always formulated specifically with reference to (and in revision of) Sadean narrative features and conventions.

Like Antonin Artaud, who further refines and renders more abstract this concept of cruelty, Proust draws on it to formulate the terms of his own revolutionary literary undertaking. Mlle Vinteuil's ritual is not the only instance of sadistic theatricality in this section of *Du côté de chez Swann*. The segment is a virtual experiment in the close interrelationship between such staginess and cruel indifference. Organized sequentially through space rather than time (in the shape of a walk along "Swann's way"), the section is united thematically through the theme of filial piety (or its desecration). First, the narrator encounters Gilberte, attended by her mother and Charlus during Swann's absence, and is regretful at not having passionately insulted her in response to her disdain. Secondly, following the death of his aunt Léonie, he remarks to Françoise that he does not mourn Léonie because she was his aunt, but because she was a good woman. He admits that in making this comment he is adopting "the mean and narrow outlook of the pedant, whom those who are most contemptuous of him in the impartiality of their own minds are only too prone to emulate when they are obliged to play a part upon the vulgar stage of life" (217; 128). In each of these vignettes, sadistic theatricality and cruel indifference are inextricable and potentially causally reciprocal.

The position occupied by the narrator further complicates the interpretation of the section's explicit statements and conclusions. Watching Gilberte and Mlle Vinteuil from the path, the narrator is (the second time overtly) in the imaginary position of absent father, the figure prospectively injured by the presence of Charlus or by the lesbian seduction scene that involves his defilement as patriarch. Yet the narrator, later volumes reveal, is closely familiar with the hidden world and codes of the "vice," as he calls it, "which Nature herself has planted in the soul of a child—perhaps by no more than blending the virtues of its father and mother, as she might blend the color of its eyes" (208; 124). In its structuring and its syncopated replacement of real figures with fictional composites, *À la recherche* both conceals and exhibits the offence to bourgeois parental sensitivities constituted by this "vice." The entire work might be thought of for these purposes as a theatrical spectacle of dissimulation, informed by the detached coldness that punctuates the recording of Mlle Vinteuil's transgression. In the latter instance, as in the others that, later in the century, develop from and share fundamental elements of the narrator's final pronouncement, the phenomenon of cruelty is understood in a way that renders it the support of a whole aesthetic strategy.

Artaud's artistic innovations are generally not linked with Proust's. However, both authors participate in modernist tendency to "antitheatricality,"[2] one that is directly discernible in their invocations of Sade. Despite the absorption of Artaud's avant-gardist interventions into a broader understanding of modernism, and numerous commentaries glossing his use of the term "cruelty,"[3] the basic significance—and the peculiarity—of his choice of this term remain ungrasped. Artaud's deployment of the word proves to have much in common with the meanings bestowed upon it by Proust's narrator. His further refinement of Proust's definition resonates strongly in later twentieth-century readings of Sade by Pierre Klossowski, Maurice Blanchot, Simone de Beauvoir, and Georges Bataille. These readings also share Artaud's and Proust's aversion to the melodrama of sadism, or to a play-acted, ritualized enactment of profanation and taboo breaking. They participate in the fashioning of a distinctively twentieth-century concept of cruelty, distinguishing it from its philological associations with bloodshed and physical violence. The fundamental feature of their claims is an emphasis on abstraction, on cruelty as a totalized condition or imposition, which subordinates the perpetrator as well as the victim to its demands. With possibly the best-known French re-reading of Sade in the twentieth century, Lacan's notorious pairing of Sade's *La Philosophie dans le boudoir* with Immanuel Kant's *Kritik der praktischen Vernunft*, this minor tradition of Sadean exegesis comes to an end. Lacan is no less averse to the high-jinx of libertine pseudo rebellion than the predecessor-theorists he criticizes, but he challenges their valorization of an heroic Sade, their belief in the nobility and integrity of a commitment to defying the law. The concerns Lacan explores suggest the untenability of the concept of "cruelty" articulated by his colleagues. I draw on German philosophical instantiations of a Kantian Sade, or a Sadean Kant, to specify the historical exigencies underlying Lacan's interpretation and also to illuminate the particularity of the twentieth-century French engagement with Sade and the unusual redefinition of an at once "strange and familiar" concept that it involves.

ORIGINS OF ARTAUD'S "CRUELTY"

The importance of Friedrich Nietzsche as a progenitor of modernism has so long been accepted, also with regard to the demands in which he anticipates Artaud—a rejection of "naturalism," a wish that the theater return to an expression of "life"—that the relevance of his work for clarifying Artaud's selection of the term "cruelty" remains uninvestigated. Jacques Derrida's "Le théâtre de la cruauté et la cloture de la représentation" notes the affinity with Nietzsche's rejection of Aristotelian mimesis, and the affirmation of theater as "life" or "the non-representable origin of representation."[4] Nietzsche, however, does not use the word "cruelty" when describing the ideal (lost) theatrical experience of total participation in spectacle and performance, whereby the Ancient Greek public were possessed by a kind of ecstasy still susceptible to the incursion of pain, in the combination of primordial Dionysiac unleashing and Apollonian control achieved by tragedy. He does use the term when referring to "barbarian" or non-Greek upsurges of Dionysiac revelry, as if "cruelty" were characteristic of a disordered, primitive, not yet aesthetic contact with the sources of nature: "The wildest beasts of nature were unleashed here to the point of creating an abominable mixture of sensuality and cruelty which has always appeared to me as the true 'witches' brew.'"[5] In *Zur Genealogie der Moral*, cruelty is frequently mentioned as one of a number of expressions of untrammelled "life"—the joyful pleasure of the strong in the infliction of suffering on the weak—before it becomes stigmatized by Christian slave morality.[6] If Nietzsche's logic, and his theory of tragedy, can be a guide to Artaud's, then "cruelty" represents the rending of the Apollonian element or of the solace-giving imposition of beautifying form. In being assimilated to "life," Artaud's slogan suggests at the same time a conversion of the forces animating human life (whether natural or factitious) into a total, aversive subordination, a reduction of everything to the helpless condition of prey. The other affiliations for this development help to specify its significance, and its kinship with subsequent conceptions of "cruelty" in twentieth-century French philosophy.

Given his earlier involvement in their movement, the connotations of Artaud's terminology might be thought to bear the influence of the surrealists. One of their primary muses is Lautréamont and, more specifically, the epic poem *Maldoror,* which declares a passionate commitment to the following iniquitous project: "painting the delights of cruelty."[7] In addition, surrealist propaganda and filmic poetics are permeated by images of mutilation. We could call to mind the eerily procedural, melancholy-saturated tableau of the razoring of the woman's eye in *Un chien andalou*, or the stray remark "il y a un homme coupé en deux par la fenêtre" (a man is cut in two by the window) that suddenly surfaces in André Breton's first manifesto.[8] Yet these apparitions are more a demonstration of the sheer variety of associations that arise with openness to the unconscious, their juxtaposition of convention and anarchic power, and inevitable intimate connection with fragmentation. Artaud later accused the surrealists of having a single, shallow wish "to enjoy themselves on every occasion and through every pore."[9] Even were they interested in Lautréamont's probing of cruelty, the latter's initial emphasis on "delight" is far from Artaud's perspective on the term. Louis Aragon's "Lautréamont et nous," which describes his and André Breton's first encounters with *Maldoror* during their time as medical orderlies during World War I, suggests that they experienced the poem as a diversionary mirroring of the traumatic scenes surrounding them and not as a confirmation of the ineluctability of suffering.[10]

A telling sequence from Breton and Philippe Soupault's *Les Champs magnétiques* (1920) makes clear the disjunction from Artaud, even during the phases preparatory to the theater of cruelty. Combining the perambulatory fantastic with philosophical aphorism in the manner characteristic of Lautréamont, the text contains a section, "En 80 jours," the implicit theme of which is a man's wish to escape from the pull of memory. A policeman sees the man run out of a café, a notebook falls from his pocket, and the policeman reads the following lines written in crayon: "la rougeur des crépuscules ne peut effrayer que les mortels. J'ai préféré la cruauté" (the redness of twilight only frightens mortals. I preferred cruelty).[11] The subsequent lines offer an hallucinatory critique of modern life, before describing the absorption of the man into the built landscape the narrative delineates, into a "home." It is impossible to say what the words crayoned on the notebook precisely mean, but a comparison with Artaud's "Le Théâtre Alfred Jarry" sketches an alternate dream or associative configuration with respect to the word "cruelty." Artaud imagines the mobilization of a modern police force to deal with an unexpectedly banal matter—the prosecution of "un amas de femmes, seulement" (only a group of women)—and deems this balletic juxtaposition of forces "le théâtre idéal" (ideal theater): "For surely we are just as guilty as these women and just as cruel as these policemen."[12] Here Artaud anticipates his definition of cruelty in his later theatrical manifestos, as an external compulsion and a subjection to that constraint. Breton and Soupault's allusion to *Maldoror*, by contrast, preserves Lautréamont's stress on rebellion. The "policeman" suggests the constant yet nebulous pursuit of the criminal Maldoror, while the "preference" for cruelty and the reference to a natural formidableness (and implied violence) affirm the defiance of God that such criminality denotes in Lautréamont's poem. What for the surrealists is the trace of an influence, the crayoned expression of a tendency in the work of one of their favorite inspirers, becomes for Artaud a monolithic totality, an inescapable encapsulation of the whole of reality and the aesthetic it necessarily solicits.

Artaud's concept of cruelty has more in common with a text that deserves to be recognized as a manifesto of the modernist avant-garde, even though it has primarily a—hardly laudable—political agenda: Ernst Jünger's *Über den Schmerz* (1934). Jünger argues that modern individuals are incapable of tolerating pain. Their habituation to an ever-more anaesthetized existence means that the capacity to endure physical suffering—and even to decide in favor of death, where higher values are at stake—has disappeared. Concomitantly, modern life itself is increasingly "cruel," an accumulation of mechanisms of control and management, reflected in the monolithic apparatus of the contemporary city: "The spirit that has been gathering over our landscape for a hundred years is without doubt a cruel spirit."[13] Artaud similarly marks out a two-pronged vision. The theater, he proposes in the Alfred Jarry text, ought to afflict the spectator with pain: "Henceforth he will go to the theater the way he goes to the surgeon or the dentist. In the same state of mind—knowing, of course, that he will not die, but that it is a serious thing, and that he will not come out of it unscathed. . . . He must be totally convinced that we are capable of making him scream."[14] In the manifestos on the theater of cruelty, which do not shed the insistence on spectatorial ordeal, it becomes obvious that this experience of pain is at once the reflection and the hoped-for purgation of an external "cruel spirit" bringing "war, plague, famine, and slaughter": "I defy the spectator to whom violent scenes have transferred their blood . . . to indulge outside the theatre in ideas of war, rioting, or random murder."[15] Whereas Jünger's treatise recommends the bolstering of the modern mind and body to match the power of technological pressure, Artaud's proposals, centered on an aesthetic space, seem like the reenactment or reiteration of an external onslaught. His aesthetic resembles the processing of trauma through repetition. While Jünger readies the world for war, Artaud seeks its deferred accommodation (and future prevention).

Claims of historical resonance would be too broadly sketched here to hold interest in themselves, but it seems plausible that Proust, writing on the eve of World War I, puts paid to the formidableness of the Sadean tableau by placing it on the scales of overwhelming capacities for annihilation. Artaud shares Proust's emphasis on a permanence and ineluctability to cruelty, as well as his repudiation of physicality: "With that mania for deprecating everything that we all have today, as soon as I uttered the word 'cruelty' everyone immediately took it to mean 'blood.' But 'theater of cruelty' means a theater that is difficult and cruel above all for myself. And on the level of representation it is not a question of that cruelty which we can practice on each other by cutting up each other's bodies, by sawing away at our personal anatomies, or, like Assyrian emperors, by sending each other packages of human ears, noses, or neatly severed nostrils through the mail, but of that much more terrible and necessary cruelty which things can practice on us. We are not free. And the sky can still fall on our heads. And the theater has been created to teach us, first of all, that."[16] The main difference from Proust is the absence of importance accorded to relations between people. Artaud signals his awareness of the bold nature of this omission through the parodic analogy between Oriental extravagances and everyday barbarity. Permanence, terror, and demystificatory harshness belong to the subordinated position of humans with respect to the world, not to the mere indifferent continuance of interpersonal injury. Indeed, Artaud conceives of the torturer as subject to the cruelty he inflicts, as if cruelty transcended its own actualization: "Practicing cruelty involves a higher determination to which the executioner-tormenter is also subject and which he must be *resolved* to endure when the time comes."[17] It is this contention that forms the core of subsequent readings of Sade. Artaud's theory constitutes a bridge between their definitions of cruelty and Proust's, a nodal point in the transformative impact of historical catastrophe on a previously human-sized concept. Lacan's reading signals the inadequacy of these definitions against the backdrop of kinds of violation that surpass Sadean excesses and are travestied by the idea of a stoic, ascetic torturer. Interestingly, Lacan also restores a consciousness of Sadean theatricality. Like Proust, he finds it paltry in the shadow of its ostensible transgressive ambitions. But the tradition that follows from Artaud recuperates Sade for an ascetic concept of cruelty by repressing, not deriding, this theatrical element, neglecting it in favor of an attention to philosophical contradictions. A blueprint for its proceeding (rather than for any theatrical program) is found in a detail of Artaud's manifesto: the plan to stage: "A tale by the Marquis de Sade, in which the eroticism will be transposed, represented allegorically and clothed, resulting in a violent externalization of cruelty and a concealment of the rest."[18]

"CRUELTY IS NOTHING OTHER THAN—"

I begin with Maurice Blanchot's essay "La Raison de Sade" (1949) because it offers the clearest distillation of the transformation of the Sadean legacy after Artaud. Blanchot also links the two authors as paradigmatic of the subjective alienation from convention that gives rise to the elaboration of literature. The first important postwar work on Sade, Pierre Klossowski's *Sade mon prochain* (1947) is quoted by all later interventions and is the only one directly mentioned by Lacan. Blanchot's essay, however, is the unacknowledged primary interlocutor for "Kant avec Sade," and an examination of its conclusions, as of those proffered by contemporary works, reveals the peculiarities of a twentieth-century French concept of cruelty and its divergence from the actual structure of Sade's narratives. In Blanchot's case, the argument turns specifically on contradictory propositions, namely, the principle, "Everyone is allowed to do what he wants, nobody has any other law but his own pleasure."[19] Such license raises the classic Hobbesian conundrum of how safety can be secured in a world governed by the whim of the stronger. Even the stronger are subject to the hazards of the moment, in the absence of protective law. Blanchot concludes that libertine ambitions do not encompass survival as a value: "In truth, (Sade's) works are littered with the corpses of libertines cut down in their prime."[20] Neither are Sade's libertines bound to their victims in a practical way, relying on their existence as on a resource that feeds the endless pursuit of their crimes. In *Juliette*, Saint-Fond, obsessed with prolonging the tortures of his prey, is advised by Clarwil to accumulate new corpses instead of fixating on the same objects, and this principle Blanchot takes to be the governing ethos of libertine practice.[21] All victims are, like the inhabitants of Silling Castle, for the libertine dead in advance: they are "less than things, less than shadows. In tormenting and destroying them, it's not that the libertine extinguishes their lives; rather, he confirms their nothingness. It is their non-existence that he masters and from which he draws his greatest ecstasy."[22]

"Energy" rather than self-interest must be seen as the primary Sadean virtue. It trumps even the alternative ideological attitudes furnished by Enlightenment philosophy: militant atheism or valorization of nature. Fatal defaults on libertine commitment are attributable to lack of energy and not care for survival: for instance, Juliette's nervousness about a scheme to bring famine to two-thirds of France, or La

Durand's balking at the plan of unleashing plague in Venice. However, "energy" remains insufficient by itself. It requires mediation by "apathy" in order to maximize libertine atrocity, filtering through a necessary phase of "insensibility."[23] Blanchot finally offers the following definition of cruelty: "Cruelty is nothing but the negation of the self, carried so far that it transforms itself into a destructive explosion" ("la cruauté n'est que la négation de soi, portée si loin qu'elle se transforme en une explosion destructrice").[24] He does not mention that this definition mirrors Sade's own definitions of cruelty, and that it draws upon the reference to "energy" in the definition given by *La Philosophie dans le boudoir*: "Cruelty is nothing other than the energy of man not yet corrupted by civilization" ("la cruauté n'est autre chose que l'énergie de l'homme que la civilisation n'a point encore corrompue").[25] As this very grammatical form suggests, the slogan refashions and relativizes other more expected understandings of the phenomenon named.

Such processes of revision are fundamental to the Sadean dramatization of crime in general. Contrary to Blanchot's claims, self-negation or willingness to fall victim to the hazards of a life of crime is far from being a universal feature of Sade's novels. It overwhelmingly marks the careers of the female libertines of *Juliette*, but remains absent from the arrangements of the male protagonists of *Les 120 Journées*, bound by protective contract and kinship ties.[26] In the individual act of perfidy, self-interest may be an initial spur, erased through an interpretative dynamic that affirms pure gratuitous destructiveness. La Durand succeeds in persuading Juliette to kill Clairwil, on the grounds that the latter is threatening Juliette's life. When Juliette discovers that there was no conspiracy, and that La Durand simply wanted her for herself, she asks: "Pourquoi choisir ma main pour cela?" (Why choose my hand for that?). La Durand extols the greater villainy of deceiving those who are attached to one another into murderous betrayal, and Juliette avers: "I adore you so much that if this crime were to be done again, I would do it without any need for the motive you put forward."[27] The unmotivated expression of explosive "energy" is here merely a retrospective hypothesis. The sacrifice of Clarwil, proselyte of such purity, also undermines the absoluteness of this principle as the final truth of Sade's system.

Throughout the Sadean oeuvre, self-interest is deployed as a means of entrapping victims into collusion in their own fate. The tableaux that end the unfinished *Les 120 Journées* contain the repeated spectacle of anonymous libertine protagonists promising their prey survival if they betray or consent to the injury a relative or a beloved, only to use this complicity to execute (sometimes literally) the plan of destruction and, in the process, besmirch the value of bonds of blood and affection.[28] These tableaux, which are the distillation of all libertine activity, show that Sadean cruelty involves the duplicitous mobilization of ordinary human motives, not their transcendence; it seems important that the libertine figure is exempt from the vulnerability created by ties to others, which he mocks and manipulates. The contexts in which Sade defines cruelty reveal the significance of this fundamental gesture. *Juliette* proposes the grammatically similar formula "cruelty itself is nothing but one of the branches of sensibility" ("la cruauté n'est elle-même qu'une des branches de la sensibilité").[29] This counterpart "feminine" definition occurs in the vicinity of a speech by the libertine Belmor, on his election to the presidency of the Society of the Friends of Crime, which excoriates the emotion of love, with bitter emphasis, for the "cruel" sufferings it allows women to inflict on infatuated men. If we turn to *La Philosophie dans le boudoir*, and the treatise it contains, "Français, encore un effort si vous voulez être républicains," Sade's appropriation of a revolutionary agenda, the stakes of such a contradiction, between a condemnation of cruelty and a neutralization of it, emerge.

"Encore un effort" sketches a vision of the republican state in which the relation between public institutional organization and private life is reversed for the benefit of libertine pleasure. Sade expresses a horror (remarked on by all his twentieth-century commentators) at the practice of state execution, lamenting its cold-bloodedness and its calculative wastefulness, in contrast to murder committed out of individual passion. The treatise makes evident that libertine ideology fears above all the reduction—by the state or by another person—to a condition of abstract equivalence with others: a mere subject of the law, or a body not distinguished by reciprocation of an emotion—love—that depends on the elevation of another person to unique status. The whole of Sade's literary endeavors aims at an avoidance of this fate through its infliction on others, rather than at the achievement of a philosophical synthesis that is not simply a justification of libertine pleasure. Blanchot's interpretation overlooks the complicity inherent in Sadean cruelty and champions a heroic abnegation that is the fictional product of its trickery.

The resolution of Sade's contradictions pursued by Blanchot begins with Pierre Klossowski's work. Rather than focusing on antimonies (between self-interest and self-preservation) that would normally necessitate a social contract, Klossowski reads Sade as a synthesizer of developmental phases in eighteenth-century thought. Departing from an atheism that preserves the idea of a natural code of ethical responsibility among human beings, Sade turns to a simple reversal of this code (where cruelty is attractive because it is prohibited by nature and moral law) and then to "resentment," a belief in crime as justifiable vengeance on others for the suffering a criminal God has inflicted.[30] Finally, Sade arrives at the idea of a wholly impersonal, amoral, and intrinsically destructive universe, outlined by the Pope in *Juliette,* where crime (specifically, murder) forms part of a cyclical process of material transformation; man cannot commit any act that would outrage or violate natural cycles, and even his own destruction does not breach the natural order.[31] In offering this scheme, "Sade rises to the level of myth. The philosophy of his century did not suffice for him when it came to resolving the problem posed by cruelty, which he wanted . . . to *integrate* into a universal system in which it would be brought back to its pure state, rediscovering its cosmic function."[32]

If in the philosophical realm Sade achieves a "pure cruelty," or the discovery of a cosmic function for the phenomenon that also elevates it (as does Blanchot's definition) above any specific intrahuman relation or physical event, this is no less true, in Klossowski's argument, for Sade's analysis of politics. Klossowski believes that the promotion of the free reign of crime in the treatise "Encore un effort" exposes the hypocrisy of the revolution. He takes seriously the treatise-writer's disquieting question "isn't it because of murders that France is free today?"[33] With his rejection of the death penalty, Sade pinpoints the barbarity with which political ideals are implemented: "The collectivity, right or wrong, always sniffs out whatever endangers it, and it is for that reason that it is able to confuse, with the greatest security, cruelty and justice, without feeling the slightest remorse, the rites it tends to invent at the foot of the scaffold liberating it from the pure cruelty of which it knows how to distort the appearance and the effects."[34] As we have already seen, however, "Encore un effort," expropriating republican doxa for its own utopian schemes, is hardly an exemplar for the harmony of principle and recommended practice. Its attempted evasion of the abstract equivalence brought by citizenship encompasses both straightforwardly sexually interested institutional subversions (the universal prostitution of women) and parodic political arguments (parenting should be taken over by the state to prevent the dangerous outgrowth of idiosyncratic opinion that is a consequence of family life). Finally, the treatise even converts the state into a merely nominal political structure, with the stipulation that there should be no foreign wars, no quests to spread the ideology of republicanism.[35]

Nevertheless, just as attempts to harmonize Sade's opportunistic contradictions persist, so too does a tendency to credit him with the unveiling of political hypocrisy. Simone de Beauvoir's *Faut-il brûler Sade?* (1955),[36] though unlike the investigations of her contemporaries in a number of ways, also follows this trajectory. Adopting a more affective emphasis than other readings, she probes the reasons for Sade's repudiation of judicial execution: "What he demanded, essentially, from cruelty was that it disclose to him, as consciousness and freedom, and at the same time as flesh, discrete individuals along with his own existence; to judge, condemn or watch anonymous persons die at a distance—he rejected that. . . . When murder becomes constitutional, it is no longer anything but the odious expression of abstract principles: it becomes inhuman."[37] In an approach that combines psychological diagnosis with Blanchot's exploration of logical irreconcilability, she claims that Sade relied on cruelty to bridge an emotional distance from others, a project that necessarily foundered on the following impossibilities: "If he inflicts overly violent sufferings on himself, the subject falters, he capitulates, he loses his sovereignty; an excess of vileness brings a disgust that runs contrary to pleasure; cruelty is in practice difficult to effect except within very modest limits; and theoretically, it implies a contradiction that these two lines of text encapsulate: *The most divine attractions are nothing when submission and obedience do not offer them up to us,* and *it is necessary to violate the objects of one's desire; there is the more pleasure when it surrenders.* Where do we meet free slaves? It is necessary to be satisfied with compromises."[38]

Ultimately, however, Beauvoir's argument leaves behind these practical and existential difficulties—which contain within them the conundrum Blanchot investigates, concerning libertines' dependency on their victims—in favor of a political affirmation. She adopts Klossowski's interpretation of Sade's critique of the revolution and of political terror in the critique (supposedly derived from Sade): "Far from attenuating the cruelty of nature, society only knows how to exacerbate it by erecting scaffolds."[39] Like Blanchot and Klossowski,

she sees Sade's system develop in the direction of an active promotion
of total destruction, a goal she links with the endorsement of Sade's
rebuke to the petty and unacknowledged crime practiced by established orders of justice and control: "It is not contradictory that Sade,
while promoting crime, often expressed outrage about the injustice,
egoism and cruelty of humankind; there is nothing but contempt for
timid vices, unreflecting infamies that are limited to passive reflection
of the iniquity of nature; it is to avoid *being* evil in the manner of a
volcano or a policeman that it is necessary to *make oneself* criminal;
it is not a question of submitting oneself to the universe but of imitating it in free defiance."[40] The struggle to outdo and transcend both
social and natural cruelty becomes in Beauvoir's account a stringent,
self-imposed regime: "Cruelty appears in a new light: as an ascesis.
*Whoever knows how to harden themselves to the misfortunes of oth-
ers becomes inured to his own.* It is no longer towards agitation that
one must tend but *apathy.* Without a doubt, the apprentice libertine
has need of violent emotions to feel the truth of his singular existence;
but as soon as he has conquered this, the pure form of crime suffices
for him as a means of safeguarding it."[41] It is not difficult to detect
in this formulation an affinity with Blanchot's definition of cruelty
as the "negation of the self," and with his conception of the Sadean
system as a journey through apathy and indifference to an ultimate
destructiveness. What remains common to the three approaches, and
what links them to Artaud's vision of a cruel universe, is their inclusion of the perpetrator among the effects of the crimes he commits,
their image of an heroic Sade.

Georges Bataille's *L'Érotisme* (1957) coalesces Beauvoir and Blanchot's comments on Sade, while also looking forward, in its wider
exploration of transgression and the law, to Lacan. Throughout
Bataille's argument, Sade appears as the limit point of eroticism,
the accomplishment of murder and killing in fantasy that is the logical end-point, but also the dissolution, of untrammelled desire.[42] In
"L'homme souverain de Sade," Bataille appears to endorse Blanchot's
account of Sade's aim, that is, that he creates a form of sovereignty
that tramples on the rights of all others in the service of its own pleasure, transcending normal ties of interdependency, need, and love, by
cultivating an apathy severing the self from fellow human beings. He
quotes extensively Blanchot's passage on cruelty as the "negation of
the self." However, Bataille is more hesitant in his conclusions than
Blanchot, as his language suggests: "With regard to the principle of

the negation of others that Sade introduces, it is strange to perceive that at the pinnacle of this limitless negation of others is negation of self. In its essentials, the negation of others was an affirmation of the self, but it quickly appears that its limitless character, being pushed to the furthest possible extreme, beyond personal pleasure, becomes the quest for an unflinching sovereignty."[43] Bataille notes that real-historical sovereignty does not exist: the "lord" was always dependent on his followers and on their vicarious enjoyment of his rights. Sadean sovereignty is also an illusion, a fiction created for the benefit of readers, to show them how far absolute pursuit of pleasure may reach. Bataille's reformulation of Blanchot draws repeated attention to the surprising nature of this development: "What is remarkable is that Sade, starting out from a perfect faithlessness, leads nonetheless to rigor." Nevertheless he ultimately accepts Blanchot's claim, one that resonates through the other readers of Sade: that the libertine is negated along with his victim: "Personal pleasure does not count any more, only crime, and whether one becomes its victim is a matter of no account."[44]

In *L'Érotisme*'s next chapter, however, "Sade et l'homme normal," Bataille elaborates on the more skeptical elements of his interpretation of Blanchot (his emphasis on the fictionality of Sadean sovereignty), with reference to Beauvoir's view—correct, in his estimation—that Sade wishes to delineate erotic possibilities exhaustively without getting lost in them, without the oblivion characteristic of eroticism. Proof of this reluctance lies in the fact and content of the libertines' speeches. Their utterances are not the declarations of beings who have severed all ties to others and revel in the unbridled freedom of violence and violation. Such conduct would never be accompanied by anything other than silence, in keeping with its significance as an absolute rupture with the world of fellow humans. The speeches are attempts at justification, efforts at communication. Specifically, they are the utterances not of sovereign man but of a victim, and, yet more paradoxically, of a victim of *cruelty*: "His relations with other men were those of one devastated by a cruel punishment with the people who decided upon the punishment."[45] Bataille here seems to go beyond or discard the image of a heroic Sade elevated by the work of Blanchot, Klossowski, and Beauvoir, championing neither his political integrity nor the triumph of an ascesis or "negation of the self."

Common traits nonetheless persist between his conception of cruelty and theirs. First of all, his final thesis attests to an even more comprehensive rejection of Sadean theatricality than that implied by the efforts at reconciliation of divergent libertine views attempted in the essays of his predecessors. Bataille deems libertine pronouncements hopelessly incoherent, and an "interruption" of the vertiginous erotic quest the novels enact. Sade is also, in Bataille's ultimate depiction of him, a victim, if not a victim of the stringent demands of cruel action in Blanchot's, Artaud's, or Beauvoir's sense. Obfuscation of the repeated, contrived reduction of others to a condition of complicity with their own destruction persists. "Cruelty" remains one of the most ineffable categories in Bataille's study, even more so than "eroticism" itself. Given most extensive mention in a passage on warfare, it changes places in a series of definitions and specifications in such a way as to lose any essential quality other than that of the intention to transgress taboos, which it shares with eroticism: "Violence, which is not cruel in itself, is in its transgressiveness the deed of a being who *organizes* it. Cruelty is one of the forms of organized violence. It is not necessarily erotic, but it can move toward the other forms of violence that transgression organizes. Like cruelty, eroticism is mediated. Cruelty and eroticism are actualized by a spirit possessed of the determination to go beyond the limits of interdiction."[46] Furthermore, a cruelty associated with animals is mentioned alongside "a cruelty of which animals are incapable," yet the outer limit of physical warfare—never reached—is conceived of as animal cruelty. Bataille illustrates the cruelty of warfare through a long litany of quotations from Western observers of tribal African and Pacific-island practices.[47] His citation parallels the inclusion of the long passage from Blanchot on the negation of the self (these two are the only lengthy quotations in his text). It is as if cruelty is being circumscribed within formal limits and thereby preserves a certain mysteriousness. In this way, Bataille's argument also participates in the movement away from an association between cruelty and physical violence, toward the evocation of an abstraction that contains no distinct protagonists.

SADE "DEPUIS LA W.W.II"

Lacan's essay "Kant avec Sade" is notorious for the interlocutor it introduces to elucidate the Sadean oeuvre. Less widely recognized has been the iconoclastic attitude it adopts to an immediately preceding tradition of French Sadean exegesis. Bataille's homage to Sade the intrepid voyager across the limits of the erotic attracts mockery in a reference to "the sadists, a little bit hagiographical themselves."[48] More broadly, Lacan condemns "the invasion of pedantry that has weighed on French intellectual life since World War II."[49] Just as averse to the particularities of Sadean theatricality as his near-contemporaries—their peculiar neglect of the gymnastic details of organized libertine enjoyment—Lacan nevertheless does not attempt to ignore this feature. Of the Oedipally obsessed devices that end *La Philosophie dans le boudoir* he comments "of a treatise really about desire, there is little here, even nothing."[50]

This remark sums up the divergence between Lacan's argument and those of Blanchot, Klossowski, and Beauvoir. In the sketch of the Sadean phantasm that Lacan proposes, the libertine remains in a subordinated or "negated" position, but this is far from being a heroic or self-legislated role. Offering the formula $\$\lozenge a$ to illustrate the structural affinity between Kant and Sade, Lacan contends that the libertine is in the position of *objet petit a*, the sign for a putatively lost but in fact never existing state of satisfaction. Through his or her relentless activity of torture, violation, and murder, the libertine actually upholds the power of the external commands and interdictions that were formative in the shaping of—and that "split"—the subject because they are *internalized,* that is, external in origin. The *poinçon* $\lozenge$ denotes "désir de" or "desire for," to show that the phantasm seeks not pleasure or benefit from particular objects, but the maintenance of a structure: an hallucinatory and substitutive satisfaction derived from the preservation and reconfirmation of the subject's fractured relation to the law. To put it more simply, transgression must be reenacted and repeated to provide the assurance that such a relation exists. The formula also applies to Kant's moral law, since the subject there relinquishes all particular objects and attachments, but derives an unacknowledged satisfaction from upholding the law itself.

In elaborating this analysis, Lacan draws directly on elements of Sade's work discussed by Blanchot, as in the case of the imperative at the center of his discussion: "I have the right to enjoy your body, anyone can say to me, and I will exercise this right, without any limit to the exactions imposed by the capriciousness of my taste."[51] The contradictions expressed in this command are more intractable than those identified by Blanchot's attempt to resolve a Hobbesian conflict of interests, raising the impossibility of "reciprocity," a paradox already embodied by the way in which the command, in the form of a citation, slips from first to third person, while presumably articulating individual libertine wish. Lacan also mentions the case of Saint-Fond, schooled in "apathy" by Clairwil, taking his obsession with prolonging torture after death to be an instance of the "pulsion (demande) de mort" (drive [request] for death) and not an idiosyncrasy resolved by ideological synthesis.

It is in the examples Lacan juxtaposes to the stipulations of Kant and Sade that the inspiration for his critique of his contemporaries becomes evident. In illustration of the incipient presence of the *objet petit a* in the Kantian categorical imperative, he cites the saying from pèrc Ubu: "Long live Poland! Because without Poland, there wouldn't be any Poles."[52] That "Poland" should become the unacknowledged object of a German philosopher from a territory repeatedly carved out of periodically disappearing Polish lands suggests that Lacan's reference to "W.W.II" represents a more than merely temporal marker. Of yet greater explicitness in recent-historical import is the question Lacan asks with respect to Kant's conundrum concerning the giving of false witness at the request of a prince: "Ought he to say that the innocent one is a Jew, for example, if he actually is, before a tribunal—and we have seen this—that would find in that something to condemn."[53]

The allusion to a criminalization of Judaism reverberates with Lacan's comment on the discomfiture that ought to be caused by Sade's defense of "calumny": "But if you need a pretty strong stomach to follow Sade in his endorsement of calumny, the first article of morality to be instituted in the republic, one would have preferred that he spice it up after the manner of Renan." Omitting evidence of Ernest Renan's own anti-Semitism, he quotes two distinct segments from the *Vie de Jésus*, in which Renan discusses Jesus's fanaticism, his intolerance of ideological opposition—quintessential in a revolutionary leader and camouflaged in the Gospels by his treatment of (and identification with) the humble. Renan in fact argues that hyperbole and aggression in discussion are irreducibly "Semitic" characteristics, explaining why "subtle and refined works, for example, the dialogues of Plato, are altogether unknown to these peoples."[54] But Lacan focuses on Renan's wry observation concerning the historical good luck (or biblical distortion) generated by the absence of any law protecting the Pharisees from Jesus's rhetorical attacks: "Let us congratulate ourselves that Jesus encountered no law punishing insults against a particular class of citizens—the Pharisees would then have been inviolable."[55] Although Jesus's crucifixion was the ultimate result of the "hate" produced by the uncompromising nature of his challenge to the hypocrisy and faithlessness of orthodoxy, the longer-historical consequence was the disfigurement of the image of the Jew as such. Renan asserts that Jesus is not portrayed as a Jew and implies that his ridicule of the Pharisees weaves the fabric of later anti-Semitism. Part of the passage on this point quoted by Lacan runs as follows: "This Nessus-shirt of ridicule that the Jew, son of the Pharisees has dragged in tatters after him for eighteen centuries, it was Jesus who wove it with divine artifice. Masterpiece of sublime raillery, its characters are inscribed in a line of fire on the flesh of the hypocrite and the falsely pious. Incomparable features, worthy of a Son of God! Only a God knows how to kill like that."[56]

In citing Renan, Lacan criticizes his contemporaries' lack of imagination for at once extolling the impressiveness of Sadean crime and failing to realize the persistence of the most common injurious tactics. Implicit in the essay is the suggestion that readings of Sade are due to a failure to come to grips with historical lessons and betrayals, the novelties and the repetitions they contain. Nowhere does this become clearer than in Lacan's final (and closing) reference to French Sadean interpretation, his mention of the title of Pierre Klossowski's *Sade mon prochain*. Lacan repudiates the assimilation of Sade to a "Christian ethics": Sade "refuses to be my neighbor" because "he was not close enough to his own wickedness to recognize his neighbor in it." Proof of this attitude Lacan finds in the example discussed by Klossowski and Beauvoir: Sade's repudiation of the death penalty "which history, if not logic would suffice to prove, that it is one of the correlatives of Charity."[57] Lacan's remark shows that he interprets Sade's objection to judicial execution in a different way to Klossowski and Beauvoir. Rather than regarding Sade's view as an exposure of state hypocrisy, he sees it as a failure to realize that the law already contains all the violence to be expropriated from it by libertine whim. Secondly—a more sinister reading—his reference to "history" perhaps suggests that there are some crimes for which the death penalty may be a light punishment.

German instantiations (explicit or visible in retrospect) of the Kant and Sade pairing underline the nature of the critique of French concepts of "cruelty" that "Kant avec Sade" pursues. Published two years before Klossowski's study, Adorno and Horkheimer's *Dialektik der Aufklärung* fashions a very different perspective on the role of the perpetrator from that articulated by Blanchot and others. For Adorno and Horkheimer, Sadean cruelty is the persecution of those whose weaker position in a social order based on exploitation has relegated them to an association with nature deeply feared by the powerful, the latter having become alienated from any harmony with natural flourishing. This kind of cruelty emerges with the collapse of the cultural ornamentation or ideological reimagining of oppression (such as courtly love, or religious ritual): "To eradicate utterly the hated but overwhelming temptation to lapse back into nature—that is the cruelty which stems from failed civilization; it is barbarism, the other side of culture. . . . Women and Jews show visible evidence of not having ruled for thousands of years. They live, although they could be eliminated, and their fear and weakness, the greater affinity to nature produced in them by perennial oppression, is the element in which they live. In the strong, who pay for their strength with their strained remoteness from nature and must forever forbid themselves fear, this incites blind fury. They identify themselves with nature by calling forth from their victims, multiplied a thousandfold, the cry they may not utter themselves."[58] The libertine torturer, metonymic for the totalitarian order, is here also "oppressed," subordinated to a rigorous regime—negated, even strangely ascetic despite the voracious pursuit of forbidden pleasures—but he also occludes the sources of his malaise from himself. Equally important, the victim remains visible, as does the problem of complicity, the use of the characteristics of the physically weaker or politically marginal to promote or exacerbate a conversion into prey. Although Lacan would hardly be sympathetic to the commitments of Adorno and Horkheimer's analysis—"Kant avec Sade" contains the joke about capitalism, "the exploitation of man by man . . . And socialism? It's the opposite"—his focus on calumny as opposed to the sensational tortures and murders reconciled into abstract system by his predecessors, signals a sense of urgency regarding the distortion and defacement of identity, as a more thoroughgoing violation than attacks on taboo.

A text almost exactly contemporary with "Kant avec Sade" gives an even sharper exigency to this realization. Hannah Arendt's *Eichmann in Jerusalem: A Report on the Banality of Evil* can hardly be considered a theoretical contribution to the now inextricable, if still provocative, alignment of Kant with Sade, not only because it is in part a direct documentary confrontation with the historical catastrophe that drives the analysis of *Dialektik der Aufklärung* and which is only obliquely conjured in Lacan. However, the surprising appearance of Kant in the proceedings—when Eichmann declares he has always been a Kantian and gives an "approximately correct" definition of the categorical imperative[59]—has an uncomfortable resonance with Lacan's insinuation that the voice of conscience may not be distinguishable from an external decree, since in practice Eichmann never separated these two sources. Furthermore, although Arendt does not theorize the phenomenon in this manner, considering it rather evidence of Eichmann's "banality"—his (albeit terrifying) mediocrity or stupidity—his mode of speech embodies Lacan's description of the split between the subject of the utterance and the subject of the enunciation in the articulation of the law. Indicative of this are his final words, which pronounce in the first person the clichés invoked at funerals, without apparent awareness that "this was his own funeral."[60] Of course the slipperiness of Eichmann's speech may not point to the void Arendt assumes—she sees in it an absolute lack of the kind of educated reflective consciousness that could prevent instrumentalization by power. Instead, it may be a strategy of camouflage, an evasion of the question of ideological commitment. In either case, it opens a new problem of "evil," as a radical distortion of the possibility of communication and recognition, a stupefying disfigurement of intersubjective exchange and its conventional positioning relative to an external authority.

It seems neither a mere emanation of historical circumstances, nor purely a result of the interpretation (in the courtroom, and in Arendt's text) to which they are put, that the second major theme shaping the *Report* (its reception as well as its own discussion), is the question of complicity. Contrary to the attacks that followed her analysis, Arendt did not condemn victims of the Nazis for failing to rebel. She excoriates as "cruel and silly" the prosecutor's questions to this effect.[61] I mention this detail, and this emphasis, to indicate what may be at stake in Lacan's concern with calumny, misrepresentation, and the distortion of identity. It may be that, in the era of an emergent (and always inadequate) processing of the horrors of the war and the questions they pose, the essay "Kant avec Sade" forms part of a new conception of "evil," one attentive to its unimpressive (even typical) origins and constitution, but also to the radical devastation of its effects. By means of this focus, Lacan brings to an end a twentieth-century French lineage of thinking about cruelty—itself possibly overwhelmed and paralyzed by the prospect and aftermath of warfare—in which the perpetrator is the stoic hero, ready to become the instrument, and submit to the regime, of sufferings that would be inflicted even without his agency. Lacan may share the aversion to theatricality, which characterizes earlier encounters with Sade, whether negative (Proust's) or engaged in the attempt to fold his tableaux and dialogues into coherent abstractions. However, his approach opens the possibility of recognizing the importance of the enforcement and repeated enactment of complicity in Sade, however "banal" and predictable its intentions may be (the insulation of privi-lege and sovereignty, political and affective). It also reveals that the history of "cruelty" develops through the revision and rejection of the concept's original animal and physical connotations, without ever leaving them behind.

CHAPTER FIVE

American Cruelty

"Cruelty" acquired an unusually prominent place in public discourse following revelations concerning the use of torture in the "war on terror." Condemnations of a national "descent into cruelty,"[1] a journey "down a steepening path of cruelty,"[2] or the "shattering" of "a national consensus on cruelty"[3] were repeatedly heard. Such intonations show the force of the word, its association with moral corruption, as well as its relevance to judgments of legality. As a legal term, however, cruelty is considered less serious than torture. It is also specifically linked, in the American context, with the formulation in the Eighth Amendment to the Constitution, prohibiting "cruel and unusual" punishment. As Colin Dayan has demonstrated, the history of the Eighth Amendment's application has been fundamentally tainted by slavery—with potential determinations of what was "cruel" qualified by consensus on its necessary typicality—and the institution's continuing legacy in the Fourteenth Amendment, where it is retained as punishment for a crime.[4]

Theorizations of "cruelty" in American philosophy reflect this paradoxical and troubled history, showing a tendency to construct it as the negation or failure to recognize others' identity. Such a claim seeks to redress the wrongs of history, but remains complicit with a failure to conceive of cruelty as an effect of institutional or structural injustice, a deficiency that has resonances with the obfuscations that facilitate the prosecution of the "war on terror." The ruses of philosophy in this regard are in keeping with a long cultural genealogy of specifically American contradictions and aversions (both practical and conceptual) with respect to the category of cruelty. Firstly, and most strikingly, the rhetoric of national foundation assimilates slavery to English-imperial domination of the white-colonial population, as if to condemn the actual institution of slavery, even though it was perpetuated following independence. The Declaration of Independence rejects "cruelty and perfidy scarcely paralleled in the most barbarous ages," and in its draft versions implicitly equates chattel slavery with lack of political representation, holding the imperial power responsible for the introduction of the practice of maintaining persons as property.[5] Secondly, the United States, as is well known, was at the forefront of the reform of practices and regimes of punishment at the end of the eighteenth century and the beginning of the nineteenth. But the most exemplary innovation in this process, one that excluded all physical chastisement—namely, absolute solitary confinement— was repeatedly denounced even by well-disposed commentators and investigators.[6] Charles Dickens, even before detailing his encounters with prisoners and his attempt to imagine his way into their mentality and experience, famously denounced the practice as "cruel and wrong" although "in its intention" doubtless "kind, humane, and meant for reformation."[7]

With regard to the functioning of executive power, a condemnation of European despotism sits uneasily alongside a defense of the helpful benignity of absolute presidential authority. Alexander Hamilton urged federal unity under the constitution on the grounds that "ambitious, vindictive and rapacious" human nature will otherwise produce contests between the states of the kind whose "cruelty and inhumanity" the European powers furnish a cautionary spectacle.[8] When justifying the actual apparatus of American sovereignty, he reverts to a "reasonable foundation of confidence" on the "portion of virtue and honor among mankind." This "confidence" is to be the basis of a trust in the exercise even of arbitrary and exceptional prerogative, such as the granting of presidential pardons, which, in an allusion to the vanguard progress of the United States in the reform of punishment, ought to be endorsed, lest justice "wear a countenance too sanguinary and cruel."[9]

Above all, and most relevantly for the creation and expansion of the United States as a territory and for critiques of its recent-historical role, we see the continual conflict between claims of democratic benefit and the actual methods used to secure land and hegemony. As Amy Kaplan has recently pointed out, critiques of US imperialism in the

nineteenth century tended to confirm the official narrative of eman-
cipatory intention by condemning particular enterprises as contrary
to, in the phrase she quotes from Mark Twain, "the regular *American
game.*"[10] To note the consolidatory effect of humanitarian critique is
not to mark the unusualness of the functioning of American power,
but rather the peculiar strength of a particular aspect of its ideology—one evident in the debates on the torture policy—namely, the
need to believe in or fabricate its essential benignity. The literary heri-
tage addressed in this book already symptomatizes such a tendency.

The repeated, compulsive precipitation of anonymous corpses in
Edgar Allan Poe's narratives—only named a kind of "cruelty" by foreign readers—attests to the imprinting of American literary gesture
with the unacknowledged systematicity of genocide and population
clearance. Herman Melville's "Benito Cereno," a pivotal text in its
encapsulation of mid-century narratives of slave rebellion and of the
transfer of Spanish seaborne dominance to North American ascen-
dency, registers the corrosive effects of a predication of political community on race. In the story, which is at once Melville's revenge on
and regalement of popular taste, sympathy between whites becomes
an expression of "cruelty," in conformity with the logic by which
"whiteness" and full membership of the polity are coterminous, to
the exclusion of others.

Henry James, a writer exemplary for his engagement with foreign
literatures and cultures, and one who traverses the evolution from
late nineteenth-century realism to the innovations of the modern,
expressed unease with the "cruelty" meted out by French naturalis-
tic narrative. Informed by a professed concern with the integrity of
characters' individuality, and affiliation to a representational method
that involved sympathetic tracking of their hopes and desires, James's
aversion constitutes an earlier instance of the association between
cruelty and a failure of recognition characteristic of American philosophy. However, James's narratives betray a curious symptom,
one that links him to a motif in American literature stretching back
beyond Poe to Brockden Brown, namely, the occurrence of a killing for which no agency is claimed or discernible. In James's work
this feature exposes the cancellations and curtailments that actually
attend the indulgence of characters' dreams and desires, revealing the
explicit distaste expressed for cruelty to be a matter of cultural piety
and affiliation. American philosophy bears the legacy of these contradictions and declared ideals, producing an understanding of the

category of cruelty that is quite as far from its original philological association with bloodshed as that seen in French philosophy. The entwinements and divergences between these two developments chart the forging of a specifically modern interpretation of the term.

"CRUELTY" AND "TORTURE"

The documentation, defense, and critique of the torture policy in the "war on terror" (such of it as lies in the public domain at least) gives a telling guide to the meaning and stakes of the invocation of cruelty as a legal term. At opposed ends of the spectrum of political interests we see, on the one hand, an attempt to avoid any substantive terminology whatsoever and, on the other, an acceptance of the idea of a continuity between "other cruel, inhuman and degrading treatment or punishment" and "torture" (the two themes of the 1987 UN Convention Against Torture) such that making distinctions between these categories should be considered irrelevant for humanitarian concern. US army and government investigations, the Church Report on Guantanamo (2004), and the Fay/Jones investigation (2005) of the treatment of detainees in Iraq lean on the indefinite capaciousness of the designation "abuse."[11] The wording of the Schmidt Report of April–June 2005 suggests that it is deployed precisely in order to evade and fragment the prohibition against CID treatment outlawed by the Geneva Conventions and by the CAT. The report claims to have found only one case of "degrading and abusive treatment," which "did not rise to the level of inhumane treatment."[12] If "abuse" carries the political advantage of remaining at once vague and indicative of standards that may have been violated, psychological vocabulary can also assist obfuscation. The Schlesinger panel to review operations at Abu Ghraib resorts to psychoanalytic terminology, condemning the "purposeless sadism," "deviant behavior," and opportunistic venting of "latent sadistic urges" on the part of a few individuals.[13] It includes in its appendix the Stanford prison experiment of 1971, as if the results of a contrived exercise were more telling than its own real-life object, a maneuver that treats research not as guide but as substitute, pretending that the conditions under examination resemble those in a laboratory, isolated from cause and context.[14] In contrast with approaches designed to protect policy while lending the impression of regulative oversight, independent assessments, such as the 2007 International Red Cross Report on the treatment of "high-value" CIA detainees

treat "torture" and "cruel, inhuman and degrading treatment" func-
tionally and morally equivalent.[15]

The notorious "torture memos," however, go to considerable trouble to distinguish between "cruel, inhuman and degrading treatment"
and "torture," with the implication that the former might indeed be
being practiced, but need not meet with serious legal sanction. In addition to this introduction of a clear hierarchy in the practices prohibited
by the CAT, the memos stipulate a geopolitical limitation on its application, reiterating the caveat submitted by the United States at the
time of its ratification, namely, that Article 16 of the CAT ("each State
Party shall undertake to prevent in any territory under its jurisdiction
other acts of cruel, inhuman or degrading treatment or punishment
which do not amount to torture as defined in article 1")[16] means "the
cruel, unusual, and inhumane treatment or punishment prohibited
by the Fifth, Eighth and/or Fourteenth Amendments to the Constitution of the United States."[17] Such a stipulation renders domestic case
law on these Amendments, detailed by three of the memos, relevant
to the interpretation of Article 16. Nevertheless, geopolitical circum-
scription turns out to be further limited by function, in the case of the
Eighth Amendment prohibition of "cruel and unusual" punishment,
because of the claim that it protects "persons upon whom criminal
sanctions have been imposed," not those incarcerated during a war,
who will be "released at the end of the conflict."[18]

Within the discussion of Eighth Amendment case law, and the exigencies of national security, the memos show a dramatic reversal of
the relation between institutions or state apparatuses and individuals. As Dayan has pointed out, case law on the Eighth has tended
increasingly (under a conservative Supreme Court consolidated since
the 1980s) to emphasize the requirement of intention or deliberate
malice—rather than the criterion of institutional neglect or systemic
inadequacy of basic care or provision of resources for prisoners—
in making its assessment of prison conditions.[19] The overwhelming
asymmetrical nature of the memos' juxtaposition of individual with
institutional power is evident in its use of a "self-defense" argument
to justify the use of force against detained "enemy combatants," suggesting that the interrogator is in the position of a nation or group of
people potentially imminently subject to terrorist attack, an attack
of which knowledge is possibly harbored by the detainee.[20] Analysis
is scarcely needed to note the conversion of persons into metonyms
for entire apparatuses here, a maneuver that negates the specific

circumstances of constraint and prerogative determining the positions of the two parties confronting one another in the situation of interrogation. Construction of the individual as a creature at the mercy of the state is implicitly suggested by the most notorious element of the first torture memo, the use of a reference to a statute on health benefits to arrive at a definition of torture. The body of the citizen in a state of collapse, requiring the care of the state for ordinary survival, is identified with the body of the incarcerated subject afflicted with torture, a parallel that inadvertently implies a limitation of the state's responsibilities to the most extreme exigency.

Once reference to the case history of the Eighth Amendment drops out of the memos, a wholly new strategy emerges that nevertheless retains stark links with the terms of the central debate in the philosophy of jurisprudence concerning the interpretation of the amendment. Stephen Bradbury's memos of 2005 condemn torture unreservedly (citing the replacement memo for the policy dated December 2004, released in response to public outcry), but go on to detail techniques including varieties of controlled assault, sleep deprivation of more than forty-eight hours, cramped confinement, and waterboarding. Bradbury's third memo, which was prompted by the prospect that Congress would move to close the ambiguity covering Article 14 of CAT's protection of aliens held abroad, repeats the opinion that the Eighth is applicable only once "there has been a formal adjudication of guilt,"[21] while the relevance of the Fifth (concerning due process) is—although analyzed in more detail—rejected as not applying to detainees held in locations situated within other nations' jurisdiction.

Bradbury's reliance on the attemptedly face-saving memo of December 2004 indicates the fate of "cruelty" in the evolution of the torture policy. The replacement memo does not detail the case history on the Eighth Amendment, as if not wishing to risk provoking awareness of the suffering caused by the methods pursued in interrogation. David Cole notes the "almost verbatim" dependency of Bradbury's argument on this earlier document (omitting these sections in his collection of the policy defenses), but in doing so overlooks Bradbury's expansion on the 2004 memo's reference to John Langbein's *Torture and the Law of Proof*.[22] Bradbury quotes Langbein's explanation that torture was "generally intended to cause extreme pain while not killing the person being questioned"—by quoting the historian's catalogue of the commonest devices "strappado, rack, thumbscrews, legscrews."[23] Essentially, Bradbury's approach sanctions extreme techniques implemented with "careful screening, limits, and medical monitoring"[24] while excising any possible names (whether "cruel and unusual," "cruel, inhuman and degrading" or "torture") that could be applied to these. In addition, his reference to historical methods of torture amounts to a caricature of an "originalist" interpretation of the Eighth Amendment, which (for example) might contend that it does not prohibit the death penalty but rather the punishments considered "cruel" at the time of the passing of the Bill of Rights.[25] The kinds of injuries excluded by the Amendment are crudely evoked in the objections of one contemporary representative: "Villains often deserve whipping, or having their ears cut off."[26]

The themes raised by the memos on the torture policy reveal the precarious and unwieldy status of "cruel" as a legal adjective. It extends beyond types of behavior to engage questions of civic inclusion, given the incessant return of controversies concerning the interpretation of international treaties according to domestic law, and the cancellation of these domestic provisions for persons classified as enemies, yet not entitled to the protections putatively accorded enemy combatants in wartime. Where the meaning of domestic provisions are explored, questions of "intention" or deliberate purpose arise, in such a way as to dissolve the actuality of institutions and their systemic operation. Finally, we can discern an erasure of "cruel" as a term, which was always implied in its subjection to a hierarchy in which "torture" is considered the most serious, or pinnacle category. Such an erasure attests precisely to the paradoxical status of "cruel" as an incendiary moral designation, and its comparative weakness as a judgment incurring punitive sanction. The very use of the term in a rights provision that pertains to punishment already suggests its potentially archaic, unstable quality.

The tradition of interpretation of the Eighth Amendment does however contain traces of an alternative understanding to that chronicled in the earlier memos' catalogue of its case history, or in the originalism crudely travestied by Bradbury's interventions. A central case in its elaboration is the ruling *Furman v. Georgia* of 1972, which temporarily rendered the death penalty unconstitutional. The concurring opinions in this ruling clearly embody the kind of jurisprudence recently advocated by Stephen Breyer and Ronald Dworkin in their opposition to originalism. Breyer opposes the use of "past historical fact" to determine the meaning of constitutional provisions, pointing out that there was no perceived incompatibility, in the eighteenth

century, between flogging as a routine punishment in the American
navy, and the Eighth Amendment.[27] Dworkin argues that the term
"cruel" was chosen precisely for its elastic historical mutability; in
contrast, the specification of the age of persons qualified for presidential office (for example) was not meant to leave room for interpretative flexibility.[28] The governing principle for such an interpretative
approach as that represented by Dworkin and Breyer appears in an
observation articulated by an earlier Eighth Amendment case, *Trop
v. Dulles*, in 1958 (quoted in *Furman v. Georgia* by Justice William
J. Brennan), which formulated the elegant and wide-ranging, if of
course also contentious claim that understanding of the constitution
should reflect "the evolving standards of decency that mark the progress of a maturing society."[29]

Brennan argues that the kinds of punishments characteristic—like
those evoked in Langbein's description—of medieval and early modern torture ("the rack, the thumbscrew, the iron boot, the stretching
of the limbs and the like")[30] were not just outlawed or condemned by
the framers and their contemporaries because they inflicted extreme
suffering, but because "they treat members of the human race as
nonhumans, as objects to be toyed with and discarded."[31] In Brennan's view, the death penalty can also be viewed as such a relation
of objectification and expurgation. His definition is also applicable
to the cataloguing and fragmentation of the body that takes place in
Bradbury's litany of CIA methods; even though the emphasis is on
preservation, medical supervision, and safety, there is no sense of an
individual or discrete bodily entity, who might experience all these
assaults and forms of endurance along a continuum (if interrupted,
regimented) of consciousness and time. Although the aim of such
treatment is (at least ostensibly) not frivolous, and killing not the purpose, the relation of objectification obtains. The definition of cruelty
as an objectification that negates the sensory actuality of consciousness, arbitrarily inflicting experiences from outside, unfortunately
relies on a more ambiguous element in the interpretative conclusions
of the ruling, and in the wording of the amendment itself.

Both William O. Douglas and Thurgood Marshall are in their
concurring opinions rightly preoccupied with an overriding theme:
the disproportionate infliction of the death penalty on citizens who
are black males. Their interpretation concentrates more on persons
and the identities of particular groups than on terminology. Brennan
compares the founders' democratic and religious sensibility to that of

their puritan ancestors—victims of the "bloody assizes" during the Restoration period—and compares the latter in turn to those disproportionately targeted by the death penalty: the poor, and the African American population. His conclusion aligns the intentions of the framers with a sympathy for the latter group: "Those who wrote the Eighth Amendment knew what price their forbears had paid for a system based—not on equal justice, but on discrimination. In those days the target was not the blacks or the poor, but the dissenters, those who opposed absolutism in government, who struggled for a parliamentary regime, and who opposed governments' recurring efforts to foist a particular religion on the people."[32]

Marshall's concurring opinion queries this precise historical derivation and thereby also the import of the amendment's formulation. He notes that the "bloody assizes" may have been less important than once thought in influencing the wording of the English Bill of Rights, since its initial phraseology "prohibited 'illegal' punishments, but a later draft referred to the infliction by James II of 'illegal and cruel' punishments, and it declared 'cruel and unusual' punishments to be prohibited." Marshall concludes that the use of the word 'unusual' in the final draft is "inadvertent."[33] He later adds to this reminder the observation that "there is nothing in the history of the Eighth Amendment to give flesh to its intended meaning," as an "innovative punishment" would not necessarily be unconstitutional.[34] His discussion of the meaning of the word "cruel" is more conclusive and systematic, deeming it to have included, in the American context, a prohibition not only against—as in the English case—punishments not authorized by statute or disproportionate to the crime, but also torture, excessive punishments, and those not "necessary" if replaceable by a humane alternative.[35] His culminating argument, however, returns to a focus on persons and groups, contending that if the public were informed and aware that "the burden of capital punishment" fell overwhelmingly on "the underprivileged" and the black male population, they would surely reject it.[36] What is most rhetorically noteworthy about the combination of Douglas's and Marshall's reasoning is that although the word "unusual" is marginalized, it effectively comes to define the word "cruel," since the emphasis of the judgment is on exceptionality, exclusion, and arbitrariness. Like the nineteenth-century case history invoked by Dayan, the judgment attests to the distortion of the Eighth by the institution of slavery, but in a countervailing sense. Rather than "cruel" punishments receiving authorization because they are in practice "usual," it pinpoints the "unusualness," the arbitrary exceptionalism of racial discrimination and seeks to abate it. Through such a maneuver, cruelty comes close to being assimilated to the negation or nonrecognition of identity, and a solution is discovered in empathetic solidarity.

In this, *Furman* shares profound affinities with the conceptualization of cruelty in American philosophy, where the phenomenon is defined by a failure to "notice" others' affliction (or is only mitigated by such noticing). It might be said that the Supreme Court ruling proposes a legal solution for a social problem and seeks to correct an entrenched historical division with a curb on its most extreme expression, and with a transformation of sensibility. Philosophical discussions prioritize the gesture of recognition over any acknowledgment of the structural causes of suffering. There is a continuity between these positions and a more radical critique of the "war on terror," which reduces invasion and occupation to an affective insufficiency. The crisis precipitated by the advent of a justification of torture raises the question not only of what a progressive jurisprudence can and should in future oppose to such a development, but of how the reflexes of philosophy and theory contribute to the culture that made it possible.

"CRUELTY" AND AMERICAN PHILOSOPHY

An argument that most centrally integrates a concern with "cruelty" into the worldview of recent American philosophy is offered by Richard Rorty's *Contingency, Irony, and Solidarity*. One sign of this integration is Rorty's guiding slogan, "for a liberal," "cruelty is the worst thing we do,"[37] which is borrowed from another philosopher, Judith Shklar, and significantly generalizes her approach. Shklar's more frequently repeated formulation is that liberals should "put cruelty first" among the vices—a reconceptualization of the Aristotelian ethical hierarchy.[38] Although Rorty's reformulation is meant to articulate his goal of championing the importance of avoiding cruelty without recourse to ontological justifications, its adaptation from Shklar suggests that it also rests upon her historical claims. Shklar believes that liberalism's significance lies in its contribution to a marked progress away from cruelty. She points out that nascent liberal thought (such as that of Montaigne) is conceived in reaction to the gratuitous corporeal horrors of the religious wars of the sixteenth and seventeenth

centuries.[39] This claim ignores the lack of ethical or moral significance in some protoliberal rejections of torture and sanguinary chastisement; their emphasis on the productive use-value of human bodies
and equal concern with property as well as sovereignty.[40] (Signs of
such utilitarian calculation are already incipient in the views on cruelty expressed by the philosophical enemy cited in her overview: the
supposed defender of state persecution, Machiavelli.)[41] Shklar goes
so far as to attribute the abolition of slavery in the United States to
the influence of liberalism's moral force, ignoring the significance of
the long lapse of time between the country's political foundation as
the first formally liberal polity and this event,[42] in addition to the
evident structural symbiosis between its social and constitutional
architecture and the phenomenon of racism, or as Pierre Rosanvallon has described this form of prejudice, one of the "pathologies" of
equality.[43]

Although he repudiates any narrative of progress or even sequen-
tial causal development, Rorty's conception of cruelty conceals and
seeks to redress a historical burden: the institutionalized racial antithesis that long disfigured and in *Furman v. Georgia* becomes the primary concern of Eighth Amendment interpretation. Like Shklar,
Rorty sees literature rather than philosophy as the true locus of explorations of cruelty, encompassing novels that "help us see how social
practices which we have taken for granted have made us cruel," and
those which show us "the ways in which particular sorts of people are
cruel to other particular sorts of people."[44] Taking Nabokov as a case
study of the latter, he turns this writer's aestheticism against itself: the
man who was haunted by "the fear of being, or having been, cruel,"
and who turned away from the spectacle of torture and pain, is in
Rorty's account an ethical artist who encourages and tests attention
to signals of distress behind the obscuring prisms of linguistic virtu-
osity, self-preoccupation and indifference. The detail of the "Barber
of Kassbeam" in *Lolita,* which Nabokov declares in his afterword
to have cost "a month of work" encapsulates not only the fastidi-
ousness of the writer lavish in his concern for minor characters and
vignettes, but an interest in moral blindness: the barber chatters to
Humbert about his "baseball playing son," who, Humbert eventually
realizes, has been "dead for the last thirty years."[45] Rorty proposes
that the afterword is Nabokov's way of "tell[ing] us what we have
missed," namely, an instance of the primary example of human pain
throughout his oeuvre: the death of a child.[46] To notice the barber's

disavowed grief is to absorb the ethical lesson derivable from literature and relevant to all human interaction: the imperative of "noticing" the suffering of others, with "cruelty" itself being defined as a fatal incuriosity, a culpable paucity of attention rather than a direct violence or malignancy.[47]

Whether Rorty is right about Nabokov's inadvertent moral instructiveness, "cruelty" in this formulation is a mere by-product of "searches for autonomy" or "the pursuit of aesthetic bliss."[48] This claim plays a pivotal role in Rorty's larger argument, which is essentially a redrawing of the boundaries between "public" and "private" in the tradition of Kant's "Beantwortung der Frage: Was ist Aufklärung?" In his reading of a literary text, which explores his first category of theme, "social practices" "which have made us cruel," Orwell's *1984*, Rorty highlights the contention central to his overall thesis, that even "public" or nonintimate cruelty is the result of the illegitimate extension of what ought to be a "private" quest for autonomy. (Rorty apprehends that quest in the artistry with which the figure of O'Brien shatters Winston's personality.)[49] Concomitantly, the reform of social institutions and practices, or as Rorty more comprehensively puts it, the diminishing of cruelty,[50] should be furthered by the refining of what is fundamentally (though it is not named as such), a "private" principle, the emotional capacity to achieve a "sympathetic identification" with those who do not possess a set of beliefs or "final vocabulary" identical to our own.[51] In other words, reform will be furthered through acquisition of the skill of "noticing" promoted by Nabokov's pitting of the reader's perceptiveness against the self-absorption of aesthete protagonists.

Rorty's scheme for enlightenment is undermined not only by the fact that it inverts the relation—rather than reconceiving the boundary—between the two spheres of life, but also by the fact that his recommendation that the search for "autonomy" be kept "private" would erase or nullify the philosophical work he surveys. That of Nietzsche, for instance, is implicitly propelled by the ambition to transform a wider world.[52] In the case of Heidegger, the problem seems not so much the dangerous expansion of an individual philosophical endeavor, as the willing adherence to a persecutory public discourse in its pursuit.[53] With Freud, Rorty finds a rich mine of explanation for "why our ability to love is restricted to some very particular shapes and sizes and colors of people, things, or ideas" but not a key to the origin and manifestation of collective vicissitudes of

feeling and obsession.[54] Anthropological extrapolations from psychoanalysis, which include attempts to illuminate the adaptive origins
and depredations of "cruelty," he rejects as having no value.[55] Rorty
approves Michel Foucault's efforts to draw attention to the histories
of the marginal and the stigmatized, but disagrees with his negative
assessment of social progress.[56] This judgment ignores the fact that
Foucault specifically denounces as "cruel" (it is only a deprecatory
qualifying adjective in his evocation of early modern torture) the
methods of incarceration and surveillance characteristic of modernity.[57] In other words, Foucault sees the institutions of the modern
public sphere already pervaded by the feature Rorty associates only
with the dangerous generalization of private whim.

Discussing Derrida, Rorty commends in "Envois" an exercise in
philosophical discourse that amounts to a kind of game of self-under-
standing.[58] But his admiration of this as an exemplary instance of
"privatized" autonomy-seeking overlooks the way in which the play
of misappropriation through which Derrida queries a "communica-
tive action" model of exchange could be humiliating to interlocutors.[59] Such experimentation also keeps in permanent suspension the
possibility of reaching agreement on matters of mutual or public concern. In a complementary example, Rorty justifies Proust's objectification of the personages that people his novels as a marginal and
reduced soul asserting itself through the scrutiny and evocation of
social superiors or overpowering influences.[60] Never mind that the
novels objectify affective experience itself as a solipsistic illusion, rendering concrete others mere equivalents in a series.[61] Proust's theoretical ambitions challenge the very notion of what it means for an
experience to be "private" or "individual."

It is clear from the cancellation of philosophy effected by Rorty's
reconfiguration of public and private, as well as the unacknowledged
expansion of what is essentially a "private" impulse, the cultivation
and proffering of "sympathy," into the public sphere, that the main
consequence of his schema is the deflection of attention from the social
and institutional causes of "cruelty" themselves. In this, it shares a
history with the paradoxical status of the Eighth Amendment's wording, capable of being interpreted for the purposes of simply consolidating a *status quo* and negated when deployed to achieve the high
ideals it might otherwise be considered to embody. Like the racial
hierarchy that beset the amendment's application—in each of his
temporal phases—Rorty's proposals foreground a dyadic structure

marked by privilege and pity, whether they evoke readers' awareness of a protagonist's indifference toward his victims, or the struggles of the conscientious citizen to recognize and empathize with the suffering of those whose experience may be different from her own. Finally, his argument participates in the imaginary erasure of "cruelty" from American soil, eviscerating its meaning in the very process of recommending its avoidance. The approach of a philosopher closer to Shklar's neo-Aristotelianism, Martha Nussbaum, shows a further step in this trajectory of reasoning.

LITERARY CRUELTY

Also turning to literature for a treatment of ethical themes neglected in her discipline, Nussbaum regards the cultivation of sympathetic, identificatory feeling as an end itself, the ramifications of which need not affect the outcome of decision making. Her presentation of this view demonstrates that her emphasis on the importance of an attuned sensibility overlooks the preconditions of choice, the institutional, social, and political determinants that make it possible in the first place. Nussbaum argues that in Truman's decision "to bomb Hiroshima," "it matters deeply whether the bombing is to be treated simply as the winning alternative, or, in addition, as a course of action that overrides a genuine moral value" or "whether Truman takes this course with unswerving confidence in his own powers of reason, or with reluctance, remorse."[62] The same claim is made with regard to the denouement of Henry James's *The Golden Bowl*, where Maggie Verver conceals her knowledge of the affair between her husband, an impoverished Italian prince, and her strikingly beautiful friend, Charlotte Stant, who is also the wife of her wealthy father.

Nussbaum approves of Maggie's maneuvers to engineer the departure of Charlotte and the rescue of her marriage: "If love of your husband requires hurting and lying to Charlotte, then do these cruel things, making the better choice. But never cease, all the while, to be richly conscious of Charlotte's pain and to bear, in imagination and feeling, the full burden of your guilt as the cause of that pain."[63] The imperative is also put in general terms: "In this world . . . we cannot ever count on the fact that our love of a husband will not require the spiritual death of a best friend and mentor, that fidelity to a wife will not require cruelty to a former lover."[64] The main problem with Nussbaum's injunction is that it ignores the financial contingencies that guarantee the success of Maggie's plan: the Prince and Charlotte are unable to marry because they have no money; Maggie's father has essentially "bought" both spouses. Nussbaum presents the novel as a "coming-of-age" story, in which a young woman breaks away from her father and finally reaches full sexual maturity in the arms of her husband. This reading, strangely for one focused on "awareness" and noticing, ignores the fact that Maggie and the Prince already have a young child; the idea of her attainment to womanhood seems therefore of symbolic significance. In this, it perhaps ignores a harsher reality: the fact that sexual closeness, once surpassed or lost, cannot necessarily be recovered by decision. Not only is such a decision here forced on the dependent characters by economic considerations, it is the product of the role *The Golden Bowl* plays in crowning the fantasy-configuration of the typical Jamesian narrative scenario.

Nussbaum's psychological reading disregards the peculiar effect of Charlotte's dual status as friend and stepmother; its blurring of adultery with the motif of the "primal scene," the discovery of parental sexuality. From their earliest beginnings, James's novelistic narratives create an ambiguous fusion of this motif with a scenario of adult sexual betrayal. He uses this conflation to evoke a ward-mentor relation coalesced around a third object of desire (which both figures either long for or wish to "be"), a dynamic that usually precipitates betrayal of the child by the mentor. The later novels show a tendency toward a reversal of this trajectory, with Milly Theale turning the tables on her false mentors with a gift at her early tragic death, and Strether, himself both mentor and ward, deceived by his would-be stepson. Maggie represents a unique case of the child- or ward-figure achieving an apparently nonsymbolic, living and actual, triumph: replacing the patron-figure, and attaining the coveted love-object for herself. The fact that the one functioning nuclear-familial unit found in James's work is affirmed only with the very last sentence of his last novel[65] offers reason to suspect that this gesture is a valedictory, in some ways purely punctuational, resolution of a conflict that played out endlessly over his oeuvre. Maggie is, when considered in this wider perspective, less a daughter than the young protégé whose position is consonant with James's ambition of making an artistic life possible, and who becomes preoccupied with being outwitted sexually by those not subject to the sublimation such a life demands.

Nussbaum's assimilation of James's work to a female coming-of-age narrative mirrors her criteria for assessing the moral usefulness of other canonical literature. Samuel Beckett, whose topographical representation of the formative corporeal and psychical development of his fragmented protagonists she takes literally rather than parodically, would better not have written at all.[66] Even Proust, to whom she unfavorably compares the "parochial" Irish modernist, must be considered suspect for his exploration of the possibility that love is a solipsism in the individual himself, or concomitantly, a triangular phenomenon, only apparent on the appearance of a rival.[67] The argument and its terms are brought full circle by opposing Proust's notion of love to a short story by Anne Beattie.[68] This raises a legitimate contrast between love as fleeting epiphany and love as enduring care, since the story features a child with special needs (though some would quarrel with Nussbaum's view of the mother-figure's ideality). However, its purpose is again to introduce the priority of the awakening-of-female-sexuality narrative, and the contentiousness of the juxtaposition with Proust undermines the fundamental association governing Nussbaum's book, between literary quality and ethical nuance.

The fact that the criteria supporting Nussbaum's central premise, the parallel between literary complexity and refined moral sensibility, are abandoned, shows that the more important component of her argument is the relation between the person poised to make a difficult decision and the victim of their choice, with whom they sorrowfully sympathize. The dyad has an affinity with Rorty's conception of cruelty as a failure to "notice" the suffering of those different from or weaker than ourselves. But rather than consider this "sympathetic identification" an agent of reform, Nussbaum regards it as the mitigating corollary of a necessary "cruelty," one that fails to perceive the privileges and history that have forged its devastating power. Repeated here are the themes surrounding the interpretation of "cruel and unusual." Rorty, like *Furman*'s judgment, extends the gesture of inclusion, replacing "cruelty" with an attempt to correct the creation of "exceptions," while Nussbaum overlooks the preexisting frameworks within which an assessment of what is "cruel" must take place.

In the work of Judith Butler, we see the fundamental relation that dominates their arguments elevated to heightened prominence and intensity. Involving "grief" and not mere "sympathy," it sheds Rorty's public/private division as well as the *realpolitik* that for Nussbaum severs compassionate feeling from final decision. Seeing Butler's primary trope in this comparative light challenges the radicalism of her critique of the conduct of the "war on terror." Juxtaposing it with her evocations of "cruelty" reveals that hers is the latest effort to effect an imaginary erasure of that quality from the American horizon, by enveloping politics in an overwhelming affective drive toward phantasmal recognition and commiseration with suffering.

PICTURES OF US

In her essays following 9/11, Butler does not address the real interests—economic, political, and historical—that precipitate the coercive initiatives she questions, figuring the infliction of "precarious" conditions of life on other populations primarily as a psychical problem for the perpetrating nation, a "narcissistic" denial of bodily and affective vulnerability and a refusal of "mourning" that gives rise to "melancholia."[69] Her arguments focus directly on technologies of representation, "the camera" as "an instrument of war-waging" and "the obituary" as "the instrument by which grievability is publicly distributed," both mechanisms that "recruit" a viewing and reading public to a position of support for aggression or unthinking disregard for the "casualties the United States inflicts."[70] As this terminology indicates, Butler's emphasis ignores the possibility that—as in the case of Britain, mentioned only as an accomplice to the violation of the Geneva accords[71]—media persuasion and popular consent are not decisive for securing the political option of war, and the United States's own war dead (the actual "recruited") are themselves largely effaced from view, showing that the opportunity for military experiment depends on an already constituted inequality, whereby the economic benefits of participation appeal mainly to those Butler would call, speaking of more comprehensively ravaged territories, "the dispossessed."[72]

Indeed both the designations "war" and "the state" are naturalized in Butler's argument—with such phrases as "contemporary war"; "the current wars"; "state violence"[73]—as if their manifestation in the nature of the US interventions in Iraq and Afghanistan, and their meaning in the amorphous slogan "war on terror," were the predictable next step on a Clausewitzian continuum. In fact, the prosecution of both conflicts seems the result of a hijacking of state power by private interests, which while they may underpin the long-standing economic priorities of the American state, were never so directly in a position both to benefit from the outsourcing of belligerent activities nor from the appropriation of the resources of invaded countries. A parallel with the structure of the American state itself was suggested by the allocation of occupier attention following the seizure of control in Baghdad, where US government protection was accorded to the oil ministry but looting of cultural treasures went unchecked. Butler's refusal to consider whether the United States, which pursued these military engagements, is a state like any other, or like those to which it might most nearly be compared, is demonstrated by the logic of an essay "Sexual Politics, Torture, and Secular Time," elucidating American relegation of Islam to a backward or uncivilized temporal stage with reference to official policies and cultural discourses on immigration and gay rights in Europe.[74]

The tactic of sexual humiliation in torture inflicted by American soldiers is connected to the "presumptively modern"[75] deployment of images of homosexual affection in the testing of low-income immigrants to the Netherlands, and to the double oppression, in France, of a cultural (secularized Catholic-universal) reliance on the foundational symbolic importance of the patriarchal heterosexual family, used both to criticize the unruliness of protesting immigrant groups and to prevent the legalization of gay adoption. By aligning these as instances of "state coercion,"[76] Butler not only achieves her declared aim of challenging an antithesis between religion and progressive modernity, she also makes it seem as though the United States is, domestically, an interventionist welfare state of the sort that, alongside the provision of care to citizens, tends to generate adherence to particular norms as concomitant instruments of policy. Aside from avoiding the question of what immigration and domestic rights policies the United States has been pursuing contemporaneously with its prosecution of "the recent and current wars,"[77] the argument restores as fundamental sites of struggle the categories of embattled identity on which it focuses—Moslem, immigrant, homosexual—rather than exploring the more comprehensive question of how the "state," now turned into the most important object of critique and provocation to political resistance, performs the function of securing the well-being of its citizens as well as regulating social life.

Butler's view affects her ability to read the images she foregrounds as the crucial means of access to the reality of unvalued lives. In a discussion of the Abu Ghraib photographs, conducted through a dialogue with Susan Sontag's *Regarding the Pain of Others*,[78] Butler criticizes Sontag's claim that a photograph cannot move us to political reaction without the addition of a caption or discursive interpretation. Sontag's

position is not, as Butler contends, contradicted by the visual products
of "embedded reporting," since the meaning of such images depends
on the discursive "frame"—to use Butler's pivotal term—which generates the significance of these images .[79] Rather, Sontag's main concern is the declining impact of reportage independent enough in its
recording of horror to incite popular outrage. Butler appears ambivalent on the question of whether the Abu Ghraib pictures can fall into
such a genre: "There seems to be no sense that the photographs, at
the time they were taken, are intervening as an instrument of moral
inquiry, political exposure, or legal investigation." The reason for the
absence of this sense is, as Butler mentions, the role of the security
personnel themselves, who appear in the scenes recorded, "clearly at
ease with the camera, indeed playing to it."[80] She tentatively asks, but
does not answer, the question of whether the photographs shocked
because they were "articulating . . . the widely shared social norms
of the war?"[81] This is essentially the more fundamental question of
"whether it is possible to photograph the frame itself," a possibility
that the images are not cited to exemplify. The analysis goes on to
criticize Johanna Bourke's argument that the aesthetics of pornography legitimized the callousness of these perpetrators and chroni-
clers, dismissing Bourke's perspective as a belief that "the abuse is
performed *by* the camera," or that "the camera, digitalization, or the
pornographic gaze is finally to blame for these actions."[82] Finally Butler's discussion returns to Sontag, criticizing her "outrage and exas-
peration" in response to the torture images as a similar attempt to
render the medium culpable, a "frustration" with "the photograph"
as such, its "failure how to show her how to transform that affect into
political action."[83] Sontag's controversial statement that the pictures
are "photographs of us" is acknowledged only with a parenthetical
"she may be right."[84]

The reason for Butler's reluctance to treat the photographs unequiv-
ocally as pictures of the "frame" or of the "norms" of the war is connected with her obfuscation of the character of the belligerent state.
The photographs signal a war effort partly delegated to "private" initiative and built on the dissemination of amorphous prejudice, popular ignorance—which explains the role of "pornography," colliding
with the army-manual stereotype of "the Arab mind," in de-realiz-
ing the pain of the victims and the culpability of their warders. To
acknowledge that the structure of the war (its frame and its brutality) is evident in the content, source, and internal construction of the

pictures, would be to limit the possibility of the type of apprehension of the precariousness of other lives and experiences of suffering that Butler seeks in the visual image. This kind of exposure to the other she finds rather in the multitude of lesser-known images of torture often mislabeled and mischronicled by army records, which news organizations have released with faces obscured, in order to protect the privacy of victims. Such images allow us to apprehend "the very mark of humanity"; "a mark, in other words, not registered through a norm, but by the very fragments that follow in the wake of an abrogation of the normatively human"; "a double or trace of what is human that confounds the norms of the human or, alternatively, seeks to escape its violence"; a condition that "do[es] not readily conform to a visual, corporeal or socially recognizable identity."[85]

We can see in this affirmation of the ghostly "trace" of the human not only Butler's fetishization of other famous tracelike manifestations of the violence of the "war on terror"—the sign of the forcible reduction of humanity to animality in the first official photographs of prisoners released from Guantanamo Bay; the claim to a disallowed humanity articulated in the fragments of poetry she analyzes by prisoners at the same site[86]—but the figure that inaugurated Butler's theorizing about identity: that of the drag queen, whose "performance" of gender amounts not to an "alternative" standard but the deconstruction of the norm as such.[87] Repeated focus on a figure or trace that offers the prospect of an encounter with the formal dismantling of the elements that would have gone into the making of a culturally consumable or conformist archetype of identity centers theoretical critique on an aesthetic demand, rather like the search for an art that refuses to "resolve[] objective contradictions in a spurious harmony" and instead "expresses the idea of harmony negatively by embodying the contradictions, pure and uncompromised, in its innermost structure."[88] This pursuit of an essentially aesthetic experience in the visual trace of political violence, one whose epistemological criteria are the same as those sought from the cultural phenomenon of staged performance, is also always juxtaposed with the attempt to identify "cruelty" in the images.

Whereas international outcry saw "revenge, cruelty" and "self-satisfied" flouting of legal convention in the first pictures from Guantanamo, Butler sees the human/animal opposition.[89] Where Bourke's reflections on Abu Ghraib suggest that "perhaps the camera promises a festive cruelty" or "there is some mix of cruelty and pleasure here that

we need to think about,"[90] Butler rejects these coordinates as nonpo-
litical inquiries, and along with them an investigation of the particular
barbarity that could produce not only the torture depicted but also its
trivialization and preservation as private trophy. To concede the full
integration of the image into the apparatus of warfare in this case, and
to prioritize the acquisition of real knowledge, as well as the reshap-
ing of political interests and their preconditions, over the importance
of any subjection to visual media, would be to break the importance
of the central scene that Butler valorizes, one similar to Rorty's insistence on "noticing" suffering and to Nussbaum's on the fine-tuning of
sensibility even in the act of annihilatory decision. Although she ends
with the view that the "critical role for visual culture" during times
of war is to "thematize the forcible frame, the one that conducts the
dehumanizing norm"[91] the very focus on visual signs, and the refusal
to accept that it has been uncritical "thematizations" that have provided the greatest spur to opposition, marks this agenda as the wish
to uphold the primacy of an encounter with an other who must be
included, recognized, who has been previously outcast and must be
absorbed within the political community. That this dyadic structure is
fundamental to all Butler's explorations of cultural conflict—whether
involving the claims of sexuality or religion—already suggests its link
to the will to overcome an arbitrary and primary racial hierarchy in
Furman v. Georgia's restitution of the Eighth Amendment. Additionally, its resonances with the preoccupation with "cruelty" as a problem
of recognizing and "noticing" suffering in American philosophy prove
that, while the legal defenses of torture are marked by the imprint of
slavery, progressive critique, in thrall to the same legacy, is just as likely
(though following an alternate agenda) to obscure the predeterminants
of the suffering it confronts.

ACKNOWLEDGMENTS

An earlier version of Chapter 2 appeared as "'Some Things Which Could Never Have Happened': Fiction, Identification, and Benito Cereno," *Nineteenth-Century Literature* 61.1 (2006): 32–66; and an earlier version of Chapter 3 appeared as "Murder and 'Point of View,'" *Comparative Literature* (winter 2013): 62–84. I am grateful to both of these journals for permission to reprint. I would like to express my gratitude for the advice and support of Aileen Douglas, Ruth Franklin, John Guillory, Neil Hegarty, Barbara Johnson, Rebecca Krug, Christie McDonald, and Scott Newstok. This book is dedicated to them, to my parents, and to my sisters, Helen and Phoebe.

INTRODUCTION: "THE STRANGE AND FAMILIAR WORD"

1. Antonin Artaud, "Le Théâtre et son double," in *Oeuvres complètes, vol. IV* (Paris: Gallimard, 1967), 173. Translations are mine unless otherwise indicated.

2. Clément Rosset, *Le Principe de cruauté* (Paris: Minuit, 1988), 18.

3. Andrew Lintott, "Cruelty in the Political Life of the Ancient World," in *Crudelitas: The Politics of Cruelty in the Ancient and Medieval World,* ed. Toivo Viljamaa, Asko Timonen, and Christian Krötzl (Krems: Medium Aevum Quotidianum, 1992), 10.

4. Daniel Baraz, *Medieval Cruelty: Changing Perceptions, Late Antiquity to the Early Modern Period* (Ithaca, NY: Cornell University Press, 2003), 14. See also Daniel Baraz, "Seneca, Ethics, and the Body: Cruelty in Medieval Thought," *Journal of the History of Ideas* 59.2 (1998): 195–215.

5. Baraz modifies the translation given in J. W. Basore's Loeb Classics edition (which reads "harshness"). See Baraz, *Medieval Cruelty,* 14; and "On Mercy," in Seneca, *Moral Essays,* trans. J. W. Basore, ed. Jeffrey Henderson (Cambridge, MA: Harvard University Press, 1928), 437. Susanna Braund renders the word as "barbarousness." Seneca, *De Clementia,* ed. and trans. Susanna Braund (Oxford: Oxford University Press, 2009), 145.

6. Cicero, *Pro Marco Caelio,* ed. Andrew R. Dyck (Cambridge: Cambridge University Press, 2013), 59.

7. Seneca, "De Ira," in *Moral Essays, vol. I,* ed. Jeffrey Henderson, trans. John W. Basore (Cambridge, MA: Harvard University Press, 1928), 176–77.

8. Seneca, "De Ira," 258–59. In the *Nicomachean Ethics,* Aristotle in fact uses the example of anger to make clear the distinction between passions and virtues. Anger in itself is neither praise- nor blameworthy; it depends on degree and on the mode in which it is deployed. Aristotle, *Nicomachean Ethics, The Complete Works of Aristotle, vol. II,* trans. J. L. Ackrill, ed. Jonathan Barnes (Princeton, NJ: Princeton University Press), 1746.

9. Seneca, *De Clementia,* trans. Braund, 144–45.

10. Aristotle, *Nicomachean Ethics,* 1815.

11. Socrates argues that the first irrevocably determinate act of the tyrant is the legally rigged killing of relatives: "as he rubs out a man's life his unholy

mouth and lips taste the blood of a butchered kinsman." Plato, *The Republic,* ed. G. R. F. Ferrari, trans. Tom Griffith (Cambridge: Cambridge University Press, 2000), 280.

12. Lintott, "Cruelty in the Political Life," 16.

13. Ibid., 9.

14. Ibid., 26–27.

15. Seneca, *De Clementia,* 144–51.

16. "There is no one, whatever else he may lack, who does not win my favor by the fact of his being human," intones Seneca, putting words into the mouth of Nero. *De Clementia,* 94–95.

17. *Augustine, Confessions, vol. 1,* ed. James J. O'Donnell (Oxford: Oxford University Press, 1992), 65. The English translation cited here is by Henry Chadwick (Oxford: Oxford University Press, 1991), 100–101.

18. Peter Brown, "Late Antiquity," in *A History of Private Life I: From Pagan Rome to Byzantium,* ed. Paul Veyne (Cambridge, MA: The Belknap Press of Harvard University Press, 1987), 306–8.

19. Daniel Dombrowski, "St. Augustine, Abortion, and libido crudelis," *Journal of the History of Ideas* 49:1 (1988): 153.

20. Typical of the terms in which the Roman desire for mastery is discussed is book 4, chapter 3 of *De Civitate Dei contra paganos II,* lib. iv, capp. iii–iv (ca. 410), trans. William M. Green (Cambridge, MA: Harvard University Press, 1963), 12.

21. Sigmund Freud, "Die sexuellen Abirrungen," in *Drei Abhandlungen zur Sexualtheorie* (Frankfurt: Fischer, 2004), 61; Erich Fromm, *The Anatomy of Human Destructiveness* (New York: Penguin, 1977), 322–24.

22. Hans Blumenberg, *Die Legitimität der Neuzeit* (Frankfurt: Suhrkamp, 1966), 79.

23. Thomas Aquinas, *Summa Theologiæ 44 (2a2æ. 155–170): Well-Tempered Passion,* Latin text and English trans., ed. Thomas Gilby O.P. (Cambridge: Cambridge University Press, 2006), 159, I: 76–77.

24. Aquinas, *Summa Theologiæ,* 78–81.

25. Paulo D. Barrozo, "Punishing Cruelly: Punishment, Cruelty, and Mercy," *Criminal Law and Philosophy* (2007); Harvard Public Law Working Paper No. 08–04: 7, 18.

26. See the chapter entitled, "The Early Middle Ages—An Age of Silence?", in Baraz, *Medieval Cruelty,* 47–74.

27. Steven Pinker, in his recent book on the decline in homicidal violence, states, "Medieval Christendom was a culture of cruelty" (*The Better Angels of Our Nature: Why Violence has Declined* [New York: Penguin, 2011], 132). His view is corroborated by historians of medieval society focusing on specific contexts, for instance, Barbara Hanawalt's work on murder rates in medieval England, which notes the savagery of the kinds of killings that took place and the fact that they seemed not to attract extensive legal or cultural attention; see Barbara Hanawalt, "Violent Death in Fourteenth- and Fifteenth-Century England," *Comparative Studies in Society and History* 18.3 (1976): 313–15. Jody Enders, who demonstrates the close relationship between theatrical performance and the epistemological rationale of torture, suggests that medieval exhibitions of violence challenge any notion of cruelty as an excess

or asymmetry; see Jody Enders, *The Medieval Theater of Cruelty: Rhetoric, Memory, Violence* (Ithaca, NY: Cornell University Press, 1999), 11. Norbert Elias's classic study of the gradual repression of natural "drives" in European society notes the uninhibited enjoyment of suffering that attended medieval popular rituals, as well as the casual acceptance of violence (especially torture and execution) in the portrayal of everyday life; see Norbert Elias, *Über den Prozess der Zivilisation, Soziogenetische und psychogenetische Untersuchungen I: Wandlungen des Verhaltens in den weltlichen Oberschichten des Abendlandes* (Frankfurt: Suhrkamp, 1976), 281–90.

28. Elias cites the strengthening of the state apparatus and its borrowing of the behavioral and cultural standards of the aristocratic court as the main cause of the diminution of physical violence in everyday life. Robert Muchembled adduces instead an older pedagogical program, directed in particular at the taming of European male youth. See Robert Muchembled *Une histoire de la violence: De la fin du Moyen-Âge à nos jours* (Paris: Éditions du Seuil, 2008). The central challenge to the idea that such a development constitutes progress comes chiefly from Nietzsche and Foucault, discussed later in this chapter. A more immediate (in all senses) contradiction of it is articulated by Étienne Balibar's description of the current global zoning of citizenship and access to political participation in terms of cruelty; see Étienne Balibar, "Outlines of a Topography of Cruelty: Citizenship in an Era of Global Violence," *Constellations* 8.1 (2001): 15–29.

29. Jacques Derrida, *États d'âme de la psychanalyse* (Paris: Galilée, 2000), 11.

30. Machiavelli, *The Prince*, ed. Quentin Skinner, trans. Russell Price (Cambridge: Cambridge University Press, 1988), 33.

31. Ibid., 31.

32. For the primary importance of this value in Machiavelli and its implications, see Leo Strauss, *Thoughts on Machiavelli* (Chicago: University of Chicago Press, 1978), 175–79.

33. See, for example, Quentin Skinner's discussion of Machiavelli's misappropriation of the claims of Cicero's *De officiis,* Introduction to *The Prince,* xix–xx.

34. Judith Shklar, *Ordinary Vices* (Cambridge, MA: The Belknap Press of Harvard University Press, 1984), 9.

35. These pleas are found, respectively, in "De la cruauté" *Essais I* (Paris: Garnier, 1962), 474; in the phrase repeated in both of Montaigne's essays on the topic, which aver that anything that goes beyond plain death constitutes cruelty: "De la cruauté," 473, and "Couardise, mère de la cruauté," *Essais II* (Paris: Garnier, 1962), 105.

36. Shklar, *Ordinary Vices*, 42–43.

37. Thomas Hobbes, *Leviathan*, ed. Richard Tuck (Cambridge: Cambridge University Press, 1996), 44.

38. "For I cannot see what drunkenness or cruelty (which is vengeance without regard to future good) contribute to any man's peace or preservation" (Thomas Hobbes, *On the Citizen*, ed. Richard Tuck and Michael Silverthorne [Cambridge: Cambridge University Press, 1998], III: 27n, 54).

39. James A. Steintrager, *Cruel Delight: Enlightenment Culture and the Inhuman* (Bloomington: Indiana University Press, 2004), 6–8.

40. Shaftesbury, *An Inquiry Concerning Virtue or Merit* in *Characteristics of Men, Manners, Opinions, Times,* ed. Lawrence E. Klein (Cambridge: Cambridge University Press, 1999), 227.

41. Adam Smith, *The Theory of Moral Sentiments,* ed. Knud Haakonssen (Cambridge: Cambridge University Press 2002), 164–65.

42. See, for example, Voltaire's use of the words "cruelty" and "barbarity" at the beginning of Chapter 4, where the former word evokes a cycle of violence, the latter a degenerate state of propensity to its infliction. Voltaire, *Traité sur la tolérance* (Paris: Gallimard, 1975), 29.

43. John Langbein, *Torture and the Law of Proof: Europe and England in the Ancien Régime* (1976; reprint, Chicago: University of Chicago Press, 2006), 10, 64–69.

44. Gustave de Beaumont and Alexis de Tocqueville, *On the Penitentiary System in the United States and its Application in France,* trans. Francis Lieber (Philadelphia, PA: Carey, Lea and Blanchard, 1833), 16–17.

45. Beaumont and Tocqueville, *On the Penitentiary System in the United States,* 296–97. Charles Dickens, *American Notes for General Circulation* (London: Chapman and Hall, 1842; reprint, London: Penguin, 2000), 74.

46. Michel Foucault, *Surveiller et Punir: Naissance de la Prison* (Paris: Gallimard, 1975), 50, 239.

47. Ernst Jünger, "Über den Schmerz," in *Sämtliche Werke Zweite Abteilung Bd. 7 Essays I Betrachtungen zur Zeit* (Stuttgart: Klet-Cotta, 1980), 188.

48. Marquis de Sade, *La Philosophie dans le boudoir* (Paris: Domaine Français 1999), 130.

49. Marquis de Sade, *Histoire de Juliette II* (Paris: Domaine Français, 1999), 455.

50. Thomas Jefferson, "Declaration of the Causes and Necessity of Taking up Arms," in *Political Writings,* ed. Joyce Appleby and Terence Ball (Cambridge: Cambridge University Press, 1999), 81, 86. "A Declaration by the Representatives of the United States of America, in General Congress Assembled" (Jefferson, 99).

51. Alexis de Tocqueville, *De la démocratie en Amérique II* (Paris: Gallimard, 1986), 234–35.

52. Lautréamont, *Maldoror, Œuvres complètes,* ed. Jean-Luc Steinmetz (Paris: Gallimard, 2009), 41.

53. Henry James, "Charles de Bernard and Gustave Flaubert," in *Literary Criticism II* (New York: Library of America, 1984), 182.

54. This is James's description of the story in answer to the queries of Frederic Myers. Henry James, *Letters IV 1895–1916,* ed. Leon Edel (Cambridge, MA: Harvard University Press, 1984), 88.

55. Maurice Blanchot, "La Raison de Sade," in *Lautréamont et Sade* (Paris: Éditions de Minuit, 1963), 45. This definition is quoted by Georges Bataille *L'Érotisme* (Paris: Éditions de Minuit, 1957), 193–94; and implicitly

adopted by Simone de Beauvoir's analysis of Sade, *Faut-il Brûler Sade?* (Paris: Gallimard, 1955).

56. Chapter 4 discusses Lacan's references to the logic of anti-Semitism as diagnosed by Ernest Renan's *Vie de Jésus,* in "Kant avec Sade," *Écrits II* (Paris: Seuil, 1966), 266–67, and to the status of Jews in Kant's Prussia and (implicitly) Nazi Germany and occupied France ("Kant avec Sade," 262).

57. See Chapter 4 for the rewriting of Nietzsche in combination with Sade in Theodor Adorno and Max Horkheimer, *Dialektik der Aufklärung* (Frankfurt: Fischer, 2000), 119–20.

58. For a discussion of texts in American philosophy that associate cruelty with a failure to notice suffering, see Chapter 5. Defining cruelty as an avoidance of love occurs in Stanley Cavell's essay on King Lear in *Disowning Knowledge in Seven Plays of Shakespeare* (Cambridge: Cambridge University Press, 2003), 39–123.

I. THE FORMS OF THE PERVERSE

1. *Poe and His Times: The Artist and his Milieu,* ed. Benjamin Franklin Fisher IV (Baltimore, MD: The Edgar Allan Poe Society, 1990); this work gives an overview of Poe's reception and its determinants.

2. Whitman's remark in *Specimen Days* is quoted in Eric W. Carlson, *The Recognition of Edgar Allan Poe: Selected Criticism Since 1829* (Ann Arbor: University of Michigan Press, 1970), 66. Eliot's comments are in the chapter "From Poe to Valéry," in *To Criticize the Critic and Other Writings* (Lincoln: University of Nebraska Press, 1991), 27. Henry James's comment appears in the essay "Charles Baudelaire," in *Literary Criticism: French Writers; Other European Writers; The Prefaces* (New York: Library of America, 1984), 154.

3. Eliot's essay makes the importance of Poe's formal poetic influence on the symbolists clear, as does Louis Seylaz, *Edgar Poe et les premiers symbolistes français* (Geneva: Slatkine Reprints, 1979).

4. Mallarmé's translations of the poetry were explicitly presented as "prose" works; see *Les Poèmes d'Edgar Poe* (Paris: Léon Vanier, 1889). For Valéry's (prose) paean to Eureka, see "Au sujet d'*Eurêka*," *Œuvres I* (1957): 854–67.

5. Patrick Quinn relies on this psychological explanation for Poe's impact on Baudelaire; see *The French Face of Edgar Poe* (Edwardsville: Southern Illinois University Press, 1957), 81. Haskell M. Block asserts that "a feeling of personal affinity was a primary force in Baudelaire's dedication to his task [of translating Poe's work]" ("The Writer as Translator: Nerval, Baudelaire, Gide," in *Translation Spectrum: Essays in Theory and Practice*, ed. Marilyn Gaddis Rose [Albany: State University of New York Press, 1981], 120).

6. Régis Messac, *Le 'Detective novel' et l'influence de la pensée scientifique* (Geneva: Slatkine reprints, 1975).

7. Walter Benjamin, *Das Passagen-Werk, Gesammelte Schriften, vol. V:1,* ed. Rolf Tiedemann (Frankfurt: Suhrkamp, 1982), 553–54. The citations from Messac on this page (in the section titled "Der Flaneur") show

the importance of Messac for Benjamin's thinking about the spatial arrangements and reciprocal influences of literary modernity.

8. Students of W. T. Bandy uncovered the American sources for Baudelaire's two essays on Poe; see W. T. Bandy, "New Light on Baudelaire and Poe," *Yale French Studies* 10 (1953): 65–69. The plagiarism is also alluded to by Lois Davis Vines, "Poe in France," in *Poe Abroad: Influence, Reputation, Affinities* (Iowa City: University of Iowa Press, 1999), 10.

9. The phrase is Meunier's translation of the line from "The Black Cat"; see Baudelaire, *Œuvres complètes, vol. II*, ed. Claude Pichois (Paris: Gallimard, 1976), 278.

10. Baudelaire, *Œuvres complètes, vol. II*, 317.

11. Ibid., 322, 323.

12. Edgar Allan Poe, "The Imp of the Perverse," in *Poetry and Tales*, ed. Patrick E. Quinn (New York: Library of America, 1984), 827.

13. Baudelaire, *Œuvres complètes, vol. II*, 323.

14. Poe, *Poetry and Tales*, 829.

15. Baudelaire, *Œuvres complètes, vol. I*, 629–34.

16. Poe, *Poetry and Tales*, 603.

17. An instance of the former view, relevant to the texts and authors discussed here, is Jared Gardner's *Race and the Founding of American Literature 1787–1845* (Baltimore, MD: Johns Hopkins University Press, 2000). A later study that emphasizes the conflictual, fragmentary, and multiracial basis of US literary nationalism is Robert Levine's *Dislocating Race and Nation: Episodes in Nineteenth-Century American Literary Nationalism* (Chapel Hill: University of North Carolina Press, 2008).

18. Recent studies emphasize the precise sources and consequences of colonial impact on indigenous collectivities. Treating of the early colonial period, Bernard Bailyn attributes the viciousness of wars waged against the first Americans to the intensity of the puritans' own struggle against their original political oppressors in Europe; see Bernard Bailyn, "Abrasions, Utopians and Holy War," in *The Barbarous Years: The Peopling of British North America: The Conflict of Civilizations 1600–1675* (New York: Alfred A. Knopf, 2013), 417–48. Alan Taylor highlights the implications of the Revolutionary War itself for hastening indigenous decline, as well as the effects on food supply of colonial advance; see Alan Taylor, *The Divided Ground: Indians, Settlers and the Northern Borderland of the American Revolution* (New York: Random House, 2006). Joyce E. Chaplin delineates the impact of disease, and asserts its role in consolidating white-racialist hierarchical thinking; see Joyce E. Chaplin, *Subject Matter: Technology, the Body and Science on the Anglo-American Frontier 1500–1676* (Cambridge MA: Harvard University Press, 2001).

19. The classic reading in this instance is Richard Slotkin's argument that American literature constitutes a transformation of the practical confrontations of colonization into symbolization, a process that becomes progressively self-reflexive and self-critical, see Richard Slotkin, *Regeneration Through Violence: The Mythology of the American Frontier 1600–1860* (Norman: University of Oklahoma Press, 1973). Perry Miller posits a comparable

progressive structural transformation of empirical physical experience and its accompanying politics into literary forms, styles and gestures. See the chapters "From Edwards to Emerson" and "Nature and the National Ego," in Perry Miller, *Errand into the Wilderness* (Cambridge, MA: Harvard University Press, 1956), 184–216.

20. Walter Benjamin, *Gesammelte Briefe: 1938–1940, vol. VI*, ed. Christoph Gödde and Henri Lonitz (Frankfurt: Suhrkamp, 2000), 412.

21. Poe, *Poetry and Tales*, 401, 407–10.

22. Ibid., 418. Baudelaire *Œuvres complètes, vol. II*, ed. Yves Florenne (Paris: Club français du livre, 1966), 179. All references to Baudelaire's translations are from this edition of his complete works. Other references are to *Œuvres complètes*, edited by Claude Pichois (1976).

23. Jean-Jacques Rousseau, *La nouvelle Héloïse, Œuvres complètes de J-J Rousseau, vol. IV* (Paris: Poincot, 1788), 379.

24. Poe, *Poetry and Tales*, 431.

25. Baudelaire, *Œuvres complètes, vol. II*, 324.

26. Poe, *Poetry and Tales*, 406.

27. Ibid., 427.

28. Baudelaire, "Note Postliminaire à *l'Aventure sans pareille d'un certain Hans Pfaall*," in *Œuvres complètes, vol. II*, 292–95.

29. Poe, *Poetry and Tales*, 996, 993.

30. Ibid., 1179.

31. Ibid., 1180.

32. Malini Johar Schueller notes that Pym describes the Native American Peters as a white man. The gesture symbolically encapsulates the erasure of American Indians, their absorption into a white colonial expansionism (in the imaginary Poe constructs, based on slavery), accelerated by measures such as the Indian Removal Act of 1830, which secured expansion into the Southwest through a forced migration that precipitated tens of thousands of deaths from nonviolent causes; see Malini Johar Schueller, *U.S. Orientalisms: Race, Nation, and Gender in Literature 1790–1890* (Ann Arbor: University of Michigan Press, 1998), 111.

33. Poe, *Poetry and Tales*, 1095.

34. Ibid., 1097. Baudelaire, *Œuvres complètes, vol. II*, ed. Yves Florenne (1966), 801.

35. Poe, *Poetry and Tales*, 1097. Baudelaire, *Œuvres complètes, vol. II*, ed. Yves Florenne (1966), 801.

36. T. W. Adorno "Extrablatt," in *Minima Moralia: Reflexionen aus dem beschädigten Leben* (Frankfurt: Suhrkamp, 2003), 268–72.

37. In his *Memoirs*, Carwin's discovery of the potential of "biloquiusm" is quickened by his "perverse and pernicious curiosity." Charles Brockden Brown, *Wieland Or The Transformation and Memoirs of Carwin the Biloquist* (Oxford: Oxford University Press, 1994), 231.

38. Stephen Shapiro offers the most sustained attempt to clarify the relation between the three main phases of *Wieland*'s plot, arguing that they represent three distinct modern forms of power, with the last (the emergence of a medico-legal order, and the return of a European-located, feudal kind of

marriage) representing the failure of the second (the democratic American community) to take root and find standards of arbitration. The difficulty with this claim, and with its conclusion that such an inwardly contradictory form signals the collapse of the radical romance into the novel of entertainment, is that it underplays the connections (and lack of connection) between the three phases, or the economics of perpetration, innocence, guilt, enjoyment, and forgetting that their articulation constructs; see Stephen Shapiro, *The Culture and Commerce of the Early American Novel: Reading the Atlantic World-System* (Philadelphia: Pennsylvania State University Press, 2008), 209–58. Nina Baym argues that Brown's novel has no inner logic, following only the provocations of sensation: see Nina Baym, "A Minority Reading of *Wieland*," in *Critical Essays on Charles Brockden Brown*, ed. Bernard Rosenthal (Boston: G. K. Hall & Co, 1981), 87–103.

39. John Carlos Rowe, *Literary Culture and U.S. Imperialism from the Revolution to World War, vol. II* (Oxford: Oxford University Press, 2000), 36–38.

40. Leslie Fiedler, *Love and Death in the American Novel* (Champaign, IL: Dalkey Archive Press, 1960); Ann Douglas, *The Feminization of American Culture* (New York: Alfred A. Knopf, 1977), 236–40.

41. Recognizing the structural affinities between "Rip van Winkle," "Sleepy Hollow," and "The Specter Bridegroom" with their simultaneous emphasis on death and virtual living-on would help to resolve disagreements over tone and implication, such as that been Caleb Crain and David Greven: where Crain sees "Sleepy Hollow"'s allusion to John André as a mark of homosocial "sympathy," Greven reads the encounter on Ichabod's journey home as the perpetration of homosocial violence; see Caleb Crain, "Introduction: The Ghost of André," in *American Sympathy* (New Haven, CT: Yale University Press, 2001), 1–15; and David Greven "Troubling Our Heads about Ichabod: 'The Legend of Sleepy Hollow,' Classic American Literature, and the Sexual Politics of Homosocial Brotherhood," *American Quarterly* 56.1 (2004): 83–109.

42. Washington Irving, "Rip van Winkle," in *History, Tales and Sketches* (New York: Library of America, 1983), 785.

43. Michael Warner's recent argument against dismissing Irving's generative importance for American literature affirms his bachelorhood and the purely literary significance of the sketches as sources of cultural power— without noticing the emphasis on raw physical life in Irving's generic and historiographical excurses; see Michael Warner, "Irving's Posterity," *ELH* 67.3 (2000): 773–99.

44. Douglas, *Feminization*, 238.

45. Irving, *History, Tales and Sketches*, 766.

46. Ibid., 802–7.

47. Irving, "Traits of Indian Character" and "Philip of Pokanoket," both in *History, Tales and Sketches*, 1002–28.

48. Wai Chee Dimock, "Hemispheric Islam: Continents and Centuries for American Literature," *American Literary History* 21.1 (2009): 40.

49. Irving, "A History of New York," in *History, Tales and Sketches*, 596, 389.

50. Terrance Whalen argues that Poe formulated an "average racism" that promotes sentimental bonds between black "servants" and white masters, without mentioning or evoking the legal apparatus of slavery, in order to create a fundamentally "depoliticized" aesthetic that would appeal to a mass audience; see Terrance Whalen, *Edgar Allan Poe and the Masses: The Political Economy of Literature in Nineteenth-Century America* (Princeton, NJ: Princeton University Press, 1999), 142–46.

51. Edgar Allan Poe, "James Fenimore Cooper," in *Essays and Reviews* (New York: Library of America, 1984), 474.

52. Philip Fisher, *Hard Facts: Setting and Form in the American Novel* (Oxford: Oxford University Press, 1987), 39.

53. Wai Chee Dimock, *Residues of Justice: Literature, Law, Philosophy* (Berkeley: University of California Press, 1997), 36–56.

54. Fisher, *Hard Facts*, 54.

55. Ibid., 60.

56. James Fenimore Cooper, *The Deerslayer: or The First War-Path* in *The Leatherstocking Tales, vol. II* (New York: Library of America 1985), 956.

57. Ibid., 837.

58. Ibid., 528.

59. Walter Benjamin, *Das Passagen-Werk, Gesammelte Schriften, vol. V:1*, ed. Rolf Tiedemann (Frankfurt: Suhrkamp, 1982), 551–55.

60. Jonathan Culler, "Baudelaire and Poe," *Zeitschrift für französische Sprache und Literatur* 100 (1990): 61–73.

61. Poe, *Poetry and Tales*, 830.

62. Charles Baudelaire, *Œuvres complètes, vol. I,* ed. Claude Pichois (Paris: Gallimard, 1976), 720.

63. Sonya Stephens, *Baudelaire's Prose Poems: The Practice and Politics of Irony* (Oxford: Oxford University Press, 1999), 67.

64. Marquis de Sade, *Les 120 Journées de Sodome* (Paris: Domaine Français, 1998), 426–28.

65. Walter Benjamin, *Charles Baudelaire: ein Lyriker im Zeitalter des Hochkapitalismus,* ed. Rolf Tiedemann (Frankfurt: Surhkamp, 1974), 41.

66. Jacques Derrida, *Donner le Temps I: la fausse monnaie* (Paris: Galilée, 1991), 210.

67. Baudelaire, "Liste de titres et canevas de romans et nouvelles," in *Œuvres complètes, vol. I,* 595.

68. Baudelaire, *Œuvres complètes, vol. I,* 68.

69. Choderlos de Laclos, *Les Liaisons dangereuses* (Paris: Gallimard, 2011), 243.

70. Poe, *Poetry and Tales,* 900, 903–4.

71. Baudelaire, *Œuvres complètes, vol. I,* 778.

72. Stephens makes this argument, 155, 157. Fancioulle's "failure" is also posited by Ross Chambers, "'L'Art sublime du comédien' ou le regardant et le regardé," *Saggi e ricerche di letteratura francese II* (1971): 250–51; and Charles Mauron, *Le Dernier Baudelaire* (Paris: José Corti, 1966), 19.

73. Ducasse lists "un cabinet de travail en compagnie d'un corbeau" (a study together with a raven) among the maudlin poetic clichés of the age

and negates the sense of Baudelaire's "Le Crépusule du matin," as well as his claims concerning the nature of the autonomy of poetry in "Notes nouvelles sur Edgar Poe," *Poésies I*, Lautréamont, *Œuvres complètes*, ed. Jean-Luc Steinmetz (Paris: Gallimard, 2009), 278, 281, 287.

74. Lautréamont, *Œuvres complètes*, 174.

75. Ibid., 243.

76. Maurice Blanchot, *Lautréamont et Sade* (Paris: Éditions de Minuit, 1963), 76.

77. Marquis de Sade, *La Philosophie dans le boudoir* (Paris: Paris: Domaine Français, 1999), 130; Marquis de Sade, *Histoire de Juiliette, vol. II* (Paris: Domaine Français, 1999), 455.

78. Lautréamont, *Œuvres complètes*, 41.

79. Ibid., 86–89.

80. Ibid., 220, 184; 135–39.

81. Julia Kristeva focuses on this aspect in *La Révolution du langage poétique* (Paris: Seuil, 1985), 310–16.

82. Lautréamont, *Œuvres complètes*, 39–40.

83. The exemplary discussion of Baudelaire's use of the adverb comme and the anomalous manner of its deployment in "Correspondances" is Paul de Man's "Anthropomorphism and Trope in the Lyric," in *The Rhetoric of Romanticism* (New York: Columbia University Press, 1984), 239–62.

84. Lautréamont, *Œuvres complètes*, 51.

85. Ibid., 66, 50.

86. Ibid., 161.

87. Ibid., 164.

88. Ibid., 212.

89. Walter Benjamin, "Der Surrealismus: Die letzte Momentaufnahme der europäischen Intelligenz," in *Gesammelte Schriften, vol. II:1*, ed. Rolf Tiedemann and Hermann Schweppenhäuser, 7 vols. (Frankfurt am Main: Suhrkamp, 1997), 305–6.

90. Poe, "The Philosophy of Composition," in *Essays and Reviews* (New York: Library of America, 1984), 13–25.

91. Benjamin, *Gesammelte Briefe, vol. VI*, 412.

2. "SOME THINGS WHICH COULD NEVER HAVE HAPPENED"

1. See Hershel Parker, *Herman Melville: A Biography, vol. 2, 1851–1891* (Baltimore, MD: Johns Hopkins University Press, 2002), 130.

2. Herman Melville, letter to Nathaniel Hawthorne, 13 August 1852, in his *Correspondence*, ed. Lynn Horth, vol. 14 of *The Writings of Herman Melville: The Northwestern-Newberry Edition* (Evanston and Chicago, IL: Northwestern University Press and The Newberry Library, 1993), 237. Hereafter referred to as *Correspondence*.

3. See James C. Wilson, introduction to *The Hawthorne and Melville Friendship: An Annotated Bibliography, Biographical and Critical Essays, and Correspondence Between the Two*, ed. Wilson (Jefferson, NC: McFarland and Co., 1991), 10–13.

4. See Herman Melville, "Benito Cereno," in *The Piazza Tales and Other Prose Pieces, 1839–1860*, ed. Harrison Hayford, Alma A. MacDougall, G. Thomas Tanselle, and others, vol. 9 of *The Writings of Herman Melville* (Evanston and Chicago, IL: Northwestern University Press and The Newberry Library, 1987), 46–117. Further citations are from this edition and appear in the text. For the real-life Delano's narratives referred to in this essay, see Amasa Delano, *Delano's Voyages of Commerce and Discovery: Amasa Delano in China, the Pacific Islands, Australia, and South America, 1789–1807*, ed. Eleanor Roosevelt Seagraves (Stockbridge, MA: Berkshire House Publishers, 1994), 245–68.

5. See Sidney Kaplan, "Herman Melville and the American National Sin: The Meaning of Benito Cereno," *Journal of Negro History* 42 (1957): 12; and Joyce Adler, "Melville's *Benito Cereno*: Slavery and Violence in the Americas," *Science and Society* 38 (1974): 19, 36.

6. F. O. Matthiessen objects that the tale, "though pictorially and theatrically effective," is "comparatively superficial" because of "Melville's failure to reckon with" the injustice of slavery (see F. O. Matthiessen, *American Renaissance: Art and Expression in the Age of Emerson and Whitman* [New York: Oxford University Press, 1941], 508).

7. See Crain, "Lovers of Human Flesh: Homosexuality and Cannibalism in Melville's Novels," *American Literature* 66 (1994): 46–48.

8. See Herman Melville, letter to Nathaniel Hawthorne, [1 June?] 1852, in *Correspondence*, 192–93. Charlene Avallone points out that, more than any other magazine, *Holden's* was for Melville "a gauge of popular taste and provided him with models of writing geared to that taste," extensively influencing aspects of *Pierre* (Charlene Avallone, "Calculations for Popularity: Melville's *Pierre* and *Holden's Dollar Magazine*," *Nineteenth-Century Literature* 43 [1988]: 84).

9. Herman Melville, letter to Nathaniel Hawthorne, [16 April?] 1851, in *Correspondence*, 187, 185. In his argument, Crain does not mention this letter.

10. Herman Melville, letter to Nathaniel Hawthorne, 29 June 1851, in *Correspondence*, 196.

11. As Diana Fuss has suggested, the psychoanalytic distinction between identification and desire remains an unstable one, disrupted, as she shows, within both metaphor and narrative (see Diana Fuss, *Identification Papers* [London and New York: Routledge, 1995], 11–12). Rey Chow's view of identification as a form of usurpation is also discernible in Melville's metaphorical, epistolary aggression (see Rey Chow, *Writing Diaspora: Tactics of Intervention in Contemporary Cultural Studies* [Bloomington and Indianapolis: Indiana University Press, 1993], 53).

12. Herman Melville, letter to Nathaniel Hawthorne, November 1851, in *Correspondence*, 212–13.

13. Herman Melville, letter to Nathaniel Hawthorne, 17 July 1852, in *Correspondence*, 230. Hershel Parker speculates that this letter may betray Melville's sense of something that "would become a recurrent phenomenon for the rest of his life, that he was being eclipsed by Hawthorne; but

the publication of *Pierre* was two weeks away, and Melville could still pretend that nothing was wrong. A young man who had achieved instant fame and an older man who had inched his way out of anonymity, Melville and Hawthorne had met as equals, only months after the simultaneous laudatory reviewing of *The Scarlet Letter* and *White-Jacket*" (*Herman Melville: A Biography, vol.* 2, 119). As I have suggested, however, Melville's previous letters are equally preoccupied with Hawthorne's success, also registering it in terms of public visibility, through reference to his name, initials, book titles, etc. Further, although Hawthorne and Melville may have met on a footing of "equality," Melville's expression of his literary ambition through an identification with Hawthorne's work and its assimilation to his own dates from that period, since, as Marvin Fisher argues, "Hawthorne and His Mosses" (1850) "reviewed [Melville's] own progress and prospects, revealed his own ambitions" (Fisher, "Portrait of the Artist in America: 'Hawthorne and His Mosses,'" in *The Hawthorne and Melville Friendship*, 119). The uncharacteristic absence of cannibalistic metaphors in the note of 17 July 1852 perhaps indicates the exhaustion of Melville's zealous, competitive incorporation of his friend's literary significance and labor. Instead it posits a contrast between Hawthorne's acceptability in the respectable domestic sphere (since his book is seen in the hands of a clergyman, and two of the instances of his name being uttered involve women—one of them Elizabeth Shaw Melville—drawing *The Blithedale Romance* [1852] to the attention to their husbands), and Melville's condition as "an utter idler and a savage" who must now resume work instead of taking up his addressee's invitation to visit (see Melville, *Correspondence*, 231). As I am proposing, the "Agatha" letter and its "skeleton" may be read as the displacement of this will to productivity, demoralized by the reception of *Pierre*, onto a reconception of the identification with Hawthorne.

14. Parker proposes that Melville wrote the "Agatha" story as *The Isle of the Cross*, whose manuscript, remaining unpublished, is now lost (see Hershel Parker, "Herman Melville's *The Isle of the Cross*: A Survey and a Chronology," *American Literature* 62 [1990]: 1–16). Echoing previous exploration of the links between "Agatha" and Sketch Eight of "The Encantadas" (1854, 1856), Basem L. Ra'ad challenges this claim with the convincing argument that the "Isle of the Cross" is nothing other than "Norfolk Isle and the Chola Widow" (see Ra'ad, "'The Encantadas' and 'The Isle of the Cross': Melvillean Dubieties, 1853–54," *American Literature* 63 [1991]: 316–23).

15. *Correspondence*, 234. See Robert Sattelmeyer and James Barbour, "The Sources and Genesis of Melville's 'Norfolk Isle and the Chola Widow,'" *American Literature* 50 (1978): 408–9.

16. Harrison Hayford, in "The Significance of Melville's 'Agatha' Letters," *ELH* 13 (1946): 305–6, drew on the letters to refute a then-prevailing critical assumption that Melville considered *Pierre* to be the last work of his career.

17. *Herman Melville: A Biography, vol.* 2, 131.

18. See Herman Melville, letters to Nathaniel Hawthorne, 13 August 1852 and 25 October 1852, in *Correspondence*, 234, 240, 237. In the 25

October letter Melville suggests that the story include an exploration of Robinson's "latitudinarian notions" (*Correspondence*, 240). Parker points out that "the theme of the disappearing and reappearing father could not help stirring up intense feelings in Melville" (*Herman Melville: A Biography, vol. 2*, 115), but the motif of the father's disappearance also resonates with Hawthorne's biography.

19. See Herman Melville, letter to Nathaniel Hawthorne, between 3 and 13 December 1852, in *Correspondence*, 242.

20. See William B. Dillingham, *Melville's Short Fiction, 1853–1856* (Athens: University of Georgia Press, 1977), 98.

21. See Melville, *Correspondence*, 234. Hawthorne was finishing the *Life of Franklin Pierce* (1852) when the letter arrived, though he was not yet resolved on accepting a political appointment from his subject. Hawthorne's lack of interest in the possibilities of "Agatha" is perhaps indicated by his characterization of the "new romance" that he wrote of to Horatio Bridge on 13 October 1852 as "more genial" than *The Blithedale Romance*, hardly a recognizable description of "Agatha"'s story (see Parker, *Herman Melville: A Biography, vol. 2*, 136–37). Edward G. Lueders argues that Hawthorne's decision not to use the tale should not be added to the evidence of growing estrangement (Lueders, "The Melville-Hawthorne Relationship in *Pierre* and *The Blithedale Romance*," in *The Hawthorne and Melville Friendship*, 139), but, as his remarks on Hawthorne's possible "presence" in *Pierre* and Melville's in *Blithedale* demonstrate, the literary record of their relation exhibits a decisive contrast of perspectives and positions (see "The Melville-Hawthorne Relationship," 140–49).

22. Sattelmeyer and Barbour argue that the concerns of the "Chola Widow" section of *The Encantadas*, which echoes the projected themes of "Agatha"'s story, "fixes with more precision" the point of Melville's turn toward a covertly critical aesthetic ("The Sources and Genesis of Melville's 'Norfolk Isle and the Chola Widow,'" 417).

23. See H. Bruce Franklin, "Slavery and Empire: Melville's 'Benito Cereno,'" in *Melville's Evermoving Dawn: Centennial Essays*, ed. John Bryant and Robert Milder (Kent, OH: Kent State University Press, 1997), 148. John Haegert notes that the story "abounds in precisely the sort of 'overplotting' that we usually associate with [the] popular forms . . . which Melville presumably disdained" ("Voicing Slavery Through Silence: Narrative Mutiny in Melville's *Benito Cereno*," *Mosaic* 26.2 [1993]: 23). Peter Coviello identifies an attitude of undeclared "hatred" for the reader in the story (see "The American in Charity: 'Benito Cereno' and Gothic Anti-Sentimentality," *Studies in American Fiction* 30 [2002]: 166).

24. Though he argues that Melville's "expectations and his disappointments with regard to Hawthorne flicker in and out" of Melville's short fiction, Dillingham deals with their presence in "Benito Cereno" in an oddly displaced, encoded manner, seeing it as a dialogue between two friends of opposing worldviews, "Dominick" and "Bachelor" (see *Melville's Short Fiction*, 17, 267–70). Michael Paul Rogin suggests that "Benito Cereno" implicitly criticizes the view of slavery expressed in the Hawthorne biography of

Pierce; that it would, if left alone, "vanish like a dream": "When the dream on the *San Dominick* vanishes, slavery is still in place" (*Subversive Genealogy: The Politics and Art of Herman Melville* [New York: Alfred A. Knopf, 1983], 219).

25. Recent arguments have revised the view that Melville's later writings show an involuted recoil from direct engagement with, as Maurice S. Lee puts it, "the meaning of America" (see "Melville's Subversive Political Philosophy: 'Benito Cereno' and the Fate of Speech," *American Literature* 72 [2000]: 495). See also Nicola Nixon, "Compromising Politics and Herman Melville's *Pierre*," *American Literature* 69 (1997): 719–41.

26. Melville, "Benito Cereno," 48.

27. See Eric J. Sundquist, *To Wake the Nations: Race in the Making of American Literature* (Cambridge, MA: Belknap Press of Harvard University Press, 1993), 173. See also Lee, "Melville's Subversive Political Philosophy," 504.

28. Later in this chapter I explore the figurehead's implications for the story's allegory, whose structure is seen as or inadvertently shown to be problematic in critical accounts.

29. Alexis de Tocqueville, *Democracy in America* (1835–40, 1848), trans. Arthur Goldhammer (New York: Literary Classics of the United States, 2004), 659.

30. For example, Saidiya V. Hartman's argument, in its interrogation of the reader's responses to images of slavery, seems as anxious to revive the nineteenth-century abolitionist recourse to the "solution" of identificatory empathy, as it is to explore the latter's suffusion with enjoyment (see *Scenes of Subjection: Terror, Slavery, and Self-Making in Nineteenth-Century America* [New York: Oxford University Press, 1997], 42). Lauren Berlant gives a deft theoretical summary of the problems created by American "liberal sentimentality" and the "acts of identification" it promotes (see Lauren Berlant, "Poor Eliza," *American Literature* 70 [1998]: 636). Berlant ultimately suggests that these are dissipated by the resistance of the unruly body to sentimental appropriation and by the way in which unexpected (or failed) identifications disrupt conformist imitation and historical continuity (see "Poor Eliza," 659, 662). Her analysis, however, neglects (regarding it as having been effaced by cultural and historical trends) James Baldwin's view, cited in her epigraph (one that could also serve for "Benito Cereno" itself) that sentimentality can be "the mask of cruelty" (see "Poor Eliza," 635, 656). Other arguments that safeguard the value of sympathy even in the midst of their stringent critique of it include Elizabeth Barnes's rigorous refusal, in *States of Sympathy: Seduction and Democracy in the American Novel* (New York: Columbia University Press, 1997), 92, of any oppositional stance regarding sentiment's tendency to render its objects equivalent. Karen Sánchez-Eppler, in *Touching Liberty: Abolition, Feminism, and the Politics of the Body* (Berkeley and Los Angeles: University of California Press, 1993), 48–49, produces a positively inflected evaluation of the same phenomenon, in her claim that sympathy's very effacement of racial characteristics attests to the body's importance as a marker of identity. Having outlined, like Berlant,

the drawbacks of sentimental narrative strategies, Shirley Samuels, in her introduction to *The Culture of Sentiment: Race, Gender, and Sentimentality in Nineteenth-Century America*, ed. Samuels (New York: Oxford University Press, 1992), 5–6, rejects the criticism that these strategies constitute a retreat into the passivity of the body on the grounds that "the bodies for whom such reform efforts are enacted are only to a limited extent culturally and critically malleable"—a defense that elides the specific effects of establishing sympathetic identification as a primary political and aesthetic value.

31. Stanley T. Williams, "'Follow Your Leader': Melville's 'Benito Cereno,'" *Virginia Quarterly Review* 23 (1947): 67, 70.

32. Rosalie Feltenstein, "Melville's 'Benito Cereno,'" *American Literature* 19 (1947): 248, 251.

33. Kaplan, "Herman Melville and the National Sin," 13, 22, 12.

34. Matthiessen, *American Renaissance*, 508.

35. Maggie Montesinos Sale, *The Slumbering Volcano: American Slave Ship Revolts and the Production of Rebellious Masculinity* (Durham, NC: Duke University Press, 1997), 163.

36. Gloria Horsley-Meacham, "Bull of the Nile: Symbol, History, and Racial Myth in 'Benito Cereno,'" *New England Quarterly* 64 (1991): 229.

37. Arvin, *Herman Melville* (Westport, CT: Greenwood Press, 1950), 239.

38. Susan Weiner argues, "By eliminating vital points within the story line, either by omission of information and detail or by the lack of an authoritative narrative viewpoint, [Melville] creates gaps or points at which new forces can enter" (Susan Weiner, "'Benito Cereno' and the Failure of Law," *Arizona Quarterly* 47.2 [1991]: 10). Joyce Adler argues that "the light from other works [by Melville] may . . . show, in a newly revealed larger context, unconcealed elements which help to clarify what was previously obscured" (Adler, "Melville's *Benito Cereno*: Slavery and Violence in the Americas," 21). Carol Colatrella proposes, "A sympathetic reading of the slave cause as led by Babo must be provided by the authorial audience [awareness of the narrator's position] and by drawing connections with other fictions by Melville" (Carol Colatrella, "The Significant Silence of Race: *La Cousine Bette* and 'Benito Cereno,'" *Comparative Literature* 46 [1994]: 262).

39. See Marianne DeKoven, "History as Suppressed Referent in Modernist Fiction," *ELH* 51 (1984): 140–43.

40. Karcher, *Shadow over the Promised Land: Slavery, Race, and Violence in Melville's America* (Baton Rouge: Louisiana State University Press, 1980), 140, 141.

41. Guy A. Cardwell makes the point that stressing the obviousness of the conspiracy courts the danger of echoing a nineteenth-century concern with the potential treacherousness of Africans (see Guy A. Cardwell, "Melville's Gray Story: Symbols and Meaning in 'Benito Cereno,'" *Bucknell Review* 8 [1959]: 154–67). Nevertheless, the arguments that implicitly or explicitly assume that Delano should be able empirically to "recognize" the occurrence of slave revolt are numerous; see Jean Fagan Yellin, "Black Masks: Melville's 'Benito Cereno,'" *American Quarterly* 22 (1970): 678–89; Howard Welsh, "The Politics of Race in 'Benito Cereno,'" *American Literature*

46 (1975): 558; Adler, "Melville's *Benito Cereno*: Slavery and Violence in the Americas"; Dekoven, "History as Suppressed Referent," 137–52; James H. Kavanagh, "That Hive of Subtlety: 'Benito Cereno' and the Liberal Hero," in *Ideology and Classic American Literature*, ed. Sacvan Bercovitch and Myra Jehlen (Cambridge: Cambridge University Press, 1986), 352–83; Weiner, "'Benito Cereno' and the Failure of Law"; Colatrella, "The Significant Silence of Race"; and Jeannette Idiart and Jennifer Schulz, "American Gothic Landscapes: The New World to Vietnam," in *Spectral Readings: Towards a Gothic Geography*, ed. Glennis Byron and David Punter (New York: St. Martin's Press, 1999), 127–39. The persistence of this emphasis is shown by its background appearance in arguments not directly concerned with slavery and slave rebellion; see, for example, Nicola Nixon, "Men and Coats; or, The Politics of the Dandaical Body in Melville's 'Benito Cereno,'" *PMLA* 114 (1999): 359–72.

42. See Kavanagh, "That Hive of Subtlety," 373. Kavanagh proposes that an image of the Africans fighting with "their red tongues loll[ing], wolf-like, from their black mouths" ("Benito Cereno," 102) represents a "rendering of the personal courage of black men and women . . . remarkable . . . in American literature for any year, let alone 1855."

43. Gesa Mackenthun, "Postcolonial Masquerade: Antebellum Sea Fiction and the Transatlantic Slave Trade," in *Early America Re-Explored: New Readings in Colonial, Early National, and Antebellum Culture*, ed. Klaus H. Schmidt and Fritz Fleischmann (New York: Peter Lang, 2000), 541.

44. Melville, "Benito Cereno," 48–49.

45. See Joshua Leslie and Sterling Stuckey, "The Death of Benito Cereno: A Reading of Herman Melville on Slavery," *Journal of Negro History* 67 (1982): 297.

46. Kavanagh, "That Hive of Sublety," 372.

47. Adler refers obliquely to the figurehead in asking the reader to consider the political meanings created by "the skeleton of the work as a whole" ("Melville's *Benito Cereno*: Slavery and Violence in the Americas," 19).

48. See Coviello, "The American in Charity," 155–80.

49. Nixon, "Men and Coats," 362, 365.

50. See Lee, "Melville's Subversive Political Philosophy," 500, 503. Other arguments that register a sense of the pointlessness of subjecting "Benito Cereno" to allegorical decoding (but decline to theorize the significance of this apparent interpretative redundancy) include Welsh, "The Politics of Race in 'Benito Cereno'"; and Cardwell, "Melville's Gray Story."

51. Eric Sundquist, "Suspense and Tautology in 'Benito Cereno,'" *Glyph* 8 (1981): 117, 115. Other arguments that focus on an interpretative and political deadlock in "Benito Cereno" include Dillingham, *Melville's Short Fiction*, 231; and Philip Fisher, "Democratic Social Space: Whitman, Melville, and the Promise of American Transparency," *Representations*, no. 24 (1988): 91. Sundquist's analysis, however, expresses the strongest sense of the loss of identificatory possibility that this paralysis entails.

52. See Lee, "Melville's Subversive Political Philosophy," 503. See also Melville, "Benito Cereno," 102.

53. Lee, "Melville's Subversive Political Philosophy," 507.

54. Ibid., 511.

55. Sundquist, "Suspense and Tautology in *Benito Cereno*," 112, 115.

56. Melville, "Benito Cereno," 107.

57. See Benjamin D. Reiss, A Madness and Mastery in Melville's 'Benito Cereno,'" *Criticism* 38 (1996): 139. Reiss's Foucauldian focus on a "gaze of power" in the scene obscures the logic of "reflection" that it sets up, in which the "whites," rather than being scrutinized by a new, opposing authority, are confronted with the image of their own former power.

58. See Robert S. Levine, *Conspiracy and Romance: Studies in Brockden Brown, Cooper, Hawthorne, and Melville* (Cambridge: Cambridge University Press, 1989), 219. Levine sees Babo's "remarks" simply as atavistic outpourings; proof of "the sadistic energies unleashed by the black rebellion" (219–20).

59. Sundquist, *To Wake the Nations*, 170.

60. Ibid.

61. Sanborn, *The Sign of the Cannibal: Melville and the Making of a Postcolonial Reader* (Durham, NC: Duke University Press, 1998), 176.

62. Franklin, "Slavery and Empire," 147.

63. Diana J. Schaub, "Master and Man in Melville's 'Benito Cereno,'" in *Poets, Princes, and Private Citizens: Literary Alternatives to Postmodern Politics*, ed. Joseph M. Knippenberg and Peter Augustine Lawler (Lanham, MD: Rowman and Littlefield, 1996), 55.

64. See Morrison, "Unspeakable Things Unspoken: The Afro-American Presence in American Literature," *Michigan Quarterly Review* 28 (1989): 15.

65. Levine, *Conspiracy and Romance*, 218, 200.

66. See Sundquist, *To Wake the Nations*, 180; and Weiner, "*Benito Cereno* and the Failure of Law," 21–22.

67. Sundquist refers to the "ridiculous" nature of the conversation about the knot (see "Suspense and Tautology in *Benito Cereno*," 117).

68. This is one of Newton Arvin's main complaints about the aesthetics of "Benito Cereno" (see *Herman Melville*, 240). As I indicate, Arvin's observation remains valuable, with the qualification that this narrative "wastefulness" can be said to serve a political purpose.

69. Melville, "Benito Cereno," 47.

70. See Herman Melville, *Mardi, and A Voyage Thither*, ed. Harrison Hayford, Hershel Parker, and G. Thomas Tanselle, vol. 3 of *The Writings of Herman Melville* (Evanston and Chicago, IL: Northwestern University Press and The Newberry Library, 1970), 186. The (white) "veiled" appearance of Lima itself plays a key role in the construction of *Moby-Dick*'s allegory, with its overtones of racial significance (see Herman Melville, *Moby-Dick, or The Whale*, ed. Harrison Hayford, Hershel Parker, and G. Thomas Tanselle, vol. 6 of *The Writings of Herman Melville* [Evanston and Chicago, IL: Northwestern University Press and The Newberry Library, 1988], 192–93). While "Benito Cereno" also holds up the "horror" of whiteness, its narrative strategies here create an allegory that enacts both its own attempts to avoid racialized significance and the cultural impossibility of doing so.

71. Melville, "Benito Cereno," 53.

72. See Glenn C. Altschuler, "Whose Foot on Whose Throat? A Re-examination of Melville's *Benito Cereno*," *CLA Journal*, 18 (1975): 386. Altschuler makes similar use of Cereno's statement, "So far may even the best man err, in judging the conduct of one with the recesses of whose condition he is not acquainted" (Melville, "Benito Cereno," 115; see Altschuler, "Whose Foot on Whose Throat," 391). Newton Arvin's response to this line, despite his dismissiveness of the tale as a whole, is perhaps more appropriate to its obvious hollowness: "To be sure!" (*Herman Melville*, 240).

73. Melville, "Benito Cereno," 72.

74. Ibid.

75. In "The American in Charity," Coviello explores the generic dimensions of Delano's racism.

76. Melville, "Benito Cereno," 116.

77. See Feltenstein, "Melville's 'Benito Cereno,'" 253.

78. Matthiessen, *American Renaissance*, 508.

79. Melville, "Benito Cereno," 102.

80. Ibid., 99.

81. See Sanborn, *Sign of the Cannibal*, 195; and Robert Kiely, *Reverse Tradition: Postmodern Fictions and the Nineteenth Century Novel* (Cambridge, MA: Harvard University Press, 1993), 73.

82. See Sanborn, *Sign of the Cannibal*, 200.

83. Melville, "Benito Cereno," 61.

84. See Dillingham, *Melville's Short Fiction*, 241.

85. Sanborn, *Sign of the Cannibal*, 196.

86. Levine, *Conspiracy and Romance*, 210.

87. Melville, "Benito Cereno," 116, 59.

88. Haegert, "Voicing Slavery Through Silence," 35.

89. Sanborn, *Sign of the Cannibal*, 194.

90. Coviello, "The American in Charity," 165.

91. Again, Arvin's disdainful view of the tale—"a greater portentousness of moral meaning is constantly suggested than is ever actually present" (*Herman Melville*, 240)—can be rewritten to describe a strategy, rather than a failing, of Melville's narrative, one that is insufficiently acknowledged in readings that give due weight to its political and historical significance.

92. Melville, "Benito Cereno," 88.

93. Reinhold J. Dooley, "Fixing Meaning: Babo as Sign in 'Benito Cereno,'" *American Transcendental Quarterly* 9 (1995): 41–50.

94. See Sundquist, *To Wake the Nations*, 164.

95. Timothy Marr, "Melville's Ethnic Conscriptions," *Leviathan: A Journal of Melville's Studies* 3.1 (2001): 22.

96. Sanborn, *Sign of the Cannibal*, 173.

97. Michael Paul Rogin argues that "Babo tortures his lord by feigning obedience to him," thereby emptying the positions within slavery of their substantiality (*Subversive Genealogy*, 217).

98. Peter Coviello observes hatred of the reader in "Benito Cereno"'s political project, without theorizing the relation between the two (see "The

American in Charity," 166–76). As I am suggesting, the skeleton's reference to the 1852 letter indicates the formal transformation of such "personal" feeling into political commentary.

3. MURDER AND "POINT OF VIEW"

1. Henry James, *Literary Criticism: French Writers; Other European Writers; The Prefaces to the New York Edition* (New York: Library of America, 1984), 861, 865, 404.

2. Peter Brooks, *Henry James Goes to Paris* (Princeton, NJ: Princeton University Press, 2007), 154, 155, 128.

3. See Pierre Walker, *Reading Henry James in French Cultural Contexts* (DeKalb: Northern Illinois University Press, 1995); and Edwin S. Fussell, *The French Side of Henry James* (New York: Columbia University Press, 1990).

4. David Gervais, *Flaubert and Henry James: A Study in Contrasts* (New York: Barnes and Noble, 1978), 85.

5. Peter Brooks, *The Melodramatic Imagination: Balzac, Henry James, Melodrama and the Mode of Excess* (New Haven, CT: Yale University Press, 1995).

6. Philip Grover, *Henry James and the French Novel: A Study in Inspiration* (London: Elek Press, 1973).

7. Brooks, *Henry James Goes to Paris*, 2.

8. James, *Literary Criticism*, 330.

9. Brooks, *Henry James Goes to Paris*, 65.

10. Gustave Flaubert, *Correspondance, vol. IV* (Paris: Gallimard, 1998), 164.

11. Brooks, *Henry James Goes to Paris*, 121.

12. James, *Literary Criticism*, 133, 131–32.

13. Brooks, *Henry James Goes to Paris*, 61.

14. Dorothy Hale, "Henry James and the Invention of Novel Theory," in *The Cambridge Companion to Henry James,* ed. Jonathan Freedman (Cambridge: Cambridge University Press, 1998), 82.

15. See José Antonio Álvarez Amorós, "Henry James, Percy Lubbock, and Beyond: A Critique of the Anglo-American Conception of Narrative Point of View," *Studia Neophilologica* 66.1 (1994): 47–57; Timothy P. Martin, "Henry James and Percy Lubbock," *Novel: A Forum on Fiction* 14.1 (1980): 20–29; Barbara Hardy, *Henry James, The Later Writing* (Plymouth, UK: Northgate House, 1996), 83.

16. Martin idenifies *The Craft of Fiction* as "a kind of defense of the modern psychological novel" (Martin, "Henry James and Percy Lubbock," 26).

17. Percy Lubbock, *The Craft of Fiction* (London: BibiloBazaar, 2007), 111.

18. James, *Prefaces*, 1095.

19. Ibid., 1322.

20. Max Beerbohm, "Jacobean and Shavian," in *Henry James: A Collection of Critical Essays,* ed. Leon Edel (Englewood Cliffs, NJ: Prentice-Hall, 1963), 19, 24.

21. Brooks, *Henry James Goes to Paris*, 141.

22. James, *Prefaces*, 1323.

23. Ibid., 1054–55.

24. Ibid., 1086.

25. Winfried Fluck, "Power Relations in the Novels of James: The 'Liberal' and the 'Radical' Version," in *Enacting History in Henry James*, ed. Gert Buelens (Cambridge: Cambridge University Press, 1997), 26.

26. James, *Prefaces*, 1096.

27. Ibid., 1331.

28. Ibid., 1169; see also Brooks, *Realist Vision*, 192-93.

29. James, *Prefaces*, 1185.

30. Sarah B. Daugherty, "James and the Ethics of Control: Aspiring Architects and Their Floating Creatures," in *Enacting History in Henry James,* ed. Gert Buelens (Cambridge: Cambridge University Press, 1997), 74.

31. Brooks, *Henry James Goes to Paris*, 162.

32. Henry James, *Letters, Vol. 4: 1895–1916*, ed. Leon Edel (Cambridge, MA: Harvard University Press, 1984), 634.

33. Henry James, *Letters, vol. 3: 1883–1895,* ed. Leon Edel (London: Macmillan, 1981), 28.

34. James, *Literary Criticism*, 861.

35. Ibid., 182.

36. Ibid., 181.

37. Ibid., 182.

38. Edmond and Jules de Goncourt, *Soeur Philomène* (Paris: Charpentier/Fasquelle, 1904), 310.

39. Ibid., 95, 204–6, 285–91.

40. Ibid., 99.

41. Ibid., 243–48.

42. Brooks, *Henry James Goes to Paris*, 4.

43. Colm Toibin, *The Master* (London: Scribner, 2005); David Lodge, *Author, Author* (London: Viking, 2004).

44. Henry James, *Letters to A. C. Benson and Auguste Mond,* I: vii (London: Scribner's, 1930).

45. Leon Edel, *Henry James: The Treacherous Years* (London: Hart-Davis, 1969), 246–47.

46. Fred Kaplan, *Henry James: The Imagination of Genius* (London: The Johns Hopkins University Press, 1992), 33.

47. James, *Prefaces*, 1159.

48. Edmund Wilson famously assimilates the governess of *Turn* to "one of [James's] familiar themes": "the thwarted Anglo-Saxon spinster"; see Edmund Wilson, "The Ambiguity of Henry James," in *A Casebook on Henry James's* The Turn of the Screw, ed. Gerald Willen (New York: Thomas Y. Crowell Co.), 121. Fleda Vetch was assigned to this category by Louis Auchincloss, *Reflections of a Jacobite* (Boston: Houghton Mifflin Reprints, 2008), 215, but also in a recent reading from Deborah Wynne "The New Woman: Portable Property and *The Spoils of Poynton*," *The Henry James Review* 31.2 (2010): 143.

49. James, *Prefaces*, 138–40.

50. Henry James, *Notebooks*, ed. F. O. Matthiessen and Kenneth B. Murdock (Chicago: University of Chicago Press, 1981), 178.

51. James, *Letters*, 3:411.

52. Ibid., 3:516.

53. William James, *Correspondence*, vol. 2, ed. Ignas K. Skrupskelis and Elizabeth M. Berkeley (Charlottesville: University Press of Virginia, 2004), 416.

54. Edel, *Henry James*, 159.

55. Hugh Stevens, *Henry James and Sexuality* (Cambridge: Cambridge University Press, 1998), 34.

56. Henry James, *Novels 1896–1899* (New York: Library of America, 2003), 73.

57. Sigmund Freud, *Schriften zur Krankheitslehre der Psychoanalyse* (Frankfurt: Fischer, 2006), 260.

58. "Both "Inversion" and "konträre Sexualempfindung" were used by Krafft-Ebing in his 1886 text *Psychopathia sexualis* (Munich: Matthes & Seitz, 1984); the second was placed in the foreground by Albert Moll *in Die konträre Sexualempfindung* (Berlin: Fischer, 1891 [1899]). Havelock Ellis observed that in the English context—notably in the 1901 defense of homosexuality by J. A. Symonds, on which James amusedly commented—the first term was used to translate the second; see Havelock Ellis, *Studies in the Psychology of Sex*, vol. 2 (Philadelphia, PA: Davis, 1927), 14–15.

59. Henry James, *A Small Boy and Others* (London: Gibson Square Books, 2001), 217.

60. Michael Moon, *A Small Boy and Others: Imitation and Initiation in American Culture from Henry James to Andy Warhol* (Durham, NC: Duke University Press, 1998), 17–27.

61. G. W. F. Hegel, *Vorlesungen über die Ästhetik I* (Frankfurt: Suhrkamp, 1970), 1:511–16.

62. E. T. A. Hoffmann, *Nachtstücke* (Stuttgart: Reclam, 2007), 21–22.

63. Sigmund Freud, *Der Moses der Michelangelo: Schriften über Kunst und Künstler* (Frankfurt: Fischer, 2008), 151–52.

64. Jacques Lacan *Le Séminaire, Livre VII: L' éthique de la psychanalyse* (Paris: Seuil, 1986), 133.

65. James, *Prefaces*, 1187.

66. Roger Lockhurst, "Knowledge, Belief and the Supernatural at the Imperial Margin," in *The Victorian Supernatural,* ed. Nicola Bown, Carolyn Burdett, and Pamela Thurschwell (Cambridge: Cambridge University Press, 2004), 197–216.

67. James, *Prefaces*, 1185.

68. Ibid., 1096.

69. James, *Letters*, 3:88.

70. Jacques Lacan, *Le Séminaire, Livre XI: Les quatre concepts fondamentaux de la psychanalyse* (Paris: Seuil, 1973), 189.

71. Bruce Robbins, "Shooting Off James's Blanks: Theory, Politics, and *The Turn of the Screw*," *Henry James Review* 5.3 (1984): 195.

72. Shoshana Felman, "Turning the Screw of Interpretation," in *Literature and Psychoanalysis: The Question of Reading: Otherwise* (Baltimore, MD, and London: The Johns Hopkins University Press, 1977), 130, 132.

73. Henry James, *The Turn of the Screw* (London: W. W. Norton, 1999), 2–3.

74. Ibid., 3.

75. Ibid., 6.

76. Felman, "Turning the Screw of Interpretation," 121.

77. James, *Turn of the Screw*, 4.

78. Jacques Lacan, *Le Séminaire, Livre I: Les Écrits techniques de Freud* (Paris: Seuil, 1975), 194.

79. James, *Turn of the Screw*, 5.

80. John Carlos Rowe, *The Theoretical Dimensions of Henry James* (Madison: University of Wisconsin Press, 1984), 136–37.

81. James, *Turn of the Screw*, 5.

82. Lacan, *Les Écrits techniques de Freud*, 219, 225.

83. Sigmund Freud, *Das Ich und das Es: metapsychologischen Schriften* (Frankfurt: Fischer, 2005), 53.

84. James, *Turn of the Screw*, 6–7.

85. Ibid., 10.

86. Ibid., 3.

87. Ibid., 10.

88. Ibid., 11.

89. Pericles Lewis, "'The Reality of the Unseen': Shared Fictions and Religious Experience in the Ghost Stories of Henry James," *The Arizona Quarterly* 61. 2 (2005): 49.

90. James, *Turn of the Screw*, 11.

91. Ibid., 14, 31, 12.

92. Ned Lukacher, *Primal Scenes: Literature, Philosophy, Psychoanalysis* (Ithaca, NY: Cornell University Press, 1986), 120.

93. James, *Turn of the Screw*, 5.

94. Ibid., 79.

95. Ibid., 85.

96. Ibid., 14–15.

97. Ibid., 15.

98. Lacan, *Les Écrits techniques de Freud*, 129.

99. James, *Turn of the Screw*, 7, 72.

100. Ibid., 54–55, 85.

101. Ibid., 26.

102. Ibid., 9.

103. Ibid., 27.

104. Ibid., 49.

105. Ibid., 49.

106. Ibid., 4.

107. Ibid., 38.

108. Freud, *Schriften über Kunst und Künstler*, 39–40.

109. Lacan, *L'Éthique de la psychanalyse,* 133.

110. Erich Fromm, *The Anatomy of Human Destructiveness* (New York: Penguin, 1977), 322–24.

111. James, *Turn of the Screw,* 53.

112. Ibid., 72.

113. Ibid., 82.

114. Lacan, *Les Quatre concepts fondamantaux de la psychanalyse,* 46.

115. James, *Turn of the Screw,* 52.

116. Ibid., 50.

117. Ibid., 2.

4. THE MARQUIS DE SADE IN THE TWENTIETH CENTURY

1. Marcel Proust, *In Search of Lost Time, vol. I: Swann's Way,* trans. C. K. Scott Moncrieff and Terence Kilmartin (New York: Modern Library, 2003), 232. *À la recherche du temps perdu* (Paris: Gallimard, 2002), 137. References to the English translation and the French text are hereafter given in parenthesis following the quotation.

2. See Martin Puchner, *Stage Fright: Modernism, Anti-Theatricality, and Drama* (Baltimore, MD: Johns Hopkins University Press, 2011), 1–30.

3. For two directly opposed views, see François Tonelli, *L'Esthétique de la cruauté: Étude des implications esthétiques du 'Théâtre de la cruauté' d'Antonin Artaud* (Paris: A. J. Nizet, 1972), 10; and Maggie Nelson, *The Art of Cruelty: A Reckoning* (New York: W. W. Norton, 2011), 15–16. Tonelli sees the term as a "key to the spiritual crisis of the twentieth century"; Nelson, criticizing the contradictions and hypocrisies in Artaud's approach, which she considers typical of the avant-garde in general, concludes that the word has no meaning other than that arbitrarily given it by Artaud himself.

4. Jacques Derrida, "Le théâtre de la cruauté et la cloture de la représentation," in *L'Écriture et la différence* (Paris: Seuil, 1967), 343.

5. Friedrich Nietzsche, *Birth of Tragedy,* trans. Douglas Smith (Oxford: Oxford University Press, 2000), 25. Friedrich Nietzsche, *Die Geburt der Tragödie aus dem Geiste der Musik, Werke, vol. III.1,* ed. Giorgio Colli and Mazzino Montinari (Berlin: de Gruyter, 1972), 28.

6. Nietzsche extols the "Kühnheit" (boldness) of noble races "ihre Gleichgultigkeit und Verachtung gegen Sicherheit, Leib, Leben, Behagen, ihre entsetzliche Heiterkeit und Tiefe der Lust in allem Zerstörten, in allen Wollüsten des Siegs und der Grausamkeit" (Friedrich Nietzsche, *Jenseits von Gut und Böse; Zur Genealogie der Moral,* ed. Giorgio Colli and Mazzino Montinari [Berlin: de Gruyter, 1999], 275); English translation: "Their indifference to and contempt for security, body, life, comfort, their hair-raising cheerfulness and profound joy in all destruction, in all the voluptuousness of victory and cruelty" (*On the Genealogy of Morals* and *Ecce Homo,* trans. Walter Kaufmann [New York: Random House, 1967], 42).

7. Comte de Lautréamont, *Maldoror,* ed. Jean-Luc Steinmetz (Paris: Gallimard, 2009), 1.4, 42.

8. André Breton, *Manifestes du surréalisme* (Paris: Gallimard, 1979), 10.

9. Antonin Artaud, "In Total Darkness, or the Surrealist Bluff" (1927), in *Selected Writings*, ed. Susan Sontag (Berkeley: University of California Press, 1976), 141. "À la grande nuit ou le bluff surréaliste," Antonin Artaud *Oeuvres complètes, vol. I.1* (Paris: Gallimard, 1976), 62.

10. Louis Aragon, "Lautréamont et nous," in Lautréamont, *Oeuvres complètes,* ed. Jean-Luc Steinmetz (Paris: Gallimard, 2009), 528–46.

11. André Breton and Philippe Soupault, *Les Champs magnétiques* (Paris: Gallimard, 1967), 52.

12. Artaud, *Selected Writings,* 156. Artaud, "Le théâtre Alfred Jarry," in *Oeuvres complètes, vol. II* (Paris: Gallimard, 1980), 16.

13. Ernst Jünger, "Über den Schmerz," in *Sämtliche Werke Zweite Abteilung Bd. 7 Essays I: Betrachtungen zur Zeit* (Stuttgart: Klet-Cotta, 1980), 188.

14. Artaud, *Selected Writings,* 157. Artaud, "Le théâtre Alfred Jarry," *Oeuvres complètes, vol. II,* 17.

15. Artaud, *Selected Writings,* 258; 255. Antonin Artaud, *Oeuvres complètes, vol. IV* (Paris: Gallimard, 1978), 94, 80.

16. Artaud, *Selected Writings,* 256; Artaud, "En finir avec les chefs-d'oeuvres," *Oeuvres complètes, vol. IV,* 77.

17. Artaud, *Selected Writings,* 77–78; Artaud, "Lettres sur la cruauté," *Oeuvres complètes, vol. IV,* 98.

18. Artaud, *Selected Writings,* 251. Artaud, "Le théâtre de la cruauté" (premier manifeste), *Oeuvres complètes, vol. IV,* 96.

19. Maurice Blanchot, "La Raison de Sade," in *Lautréamont et Sade* (Paris: Éditions de Minuit, 1963), 19.

20. Ibid., 27.

21. Ibid., 32.

22. Ibid., 33.

23. Ibid., 45.

24. Ibid.

25. Marquis de Sade, *La Philosophie dans le boudoir* (Paris: Domaine Français, 1999), 130.

26. This feature of the novel (and the role of the compact between libertines in general) is pointed out by Jane Gallop, *Intersections: A Reading of Sade with Bataille, Blanchot and Klossowski* (Lincoln and London: University of Nebraska Press, 1981), 15. Confusion over this problem of the contract is evident in the striking contrasts between critical assertions concerning it. Gilles Deleuze insists that the idea of a contract is utterly repugnant to Sade: "His hostility towards the contract, toward any appeal to contract, or any idea or theory of contract, is without limits" (Gilles Deleuze *Présentation de Sacher-Masoch* [Paris: Éditions de Minuit, 1967], 67). Without mentioning the question of gender, Roland Barthes sums up Sade's contradictory representation of the issue: "Contracts and pacts are at once eternal ('this is an adventure that will unite us forever') and revocable from one day to the next: Juliette throws Olympe Borghèse into Vesuvius and ends up poisoning Clairwil" (Roland Barthes, *Sade, Fourier, Loyola* [Paris: Éditions du Seuil, 1971], 31).

27. Sade, *Juliette II,* 433.

28. Marquis de Sade, *120 Journées de Sodome* (Paris: 10/18, 1975), 426–28.

29. Ibid., 455.

30. Pierre Klossowski, *Sade mon prochain* (Paris: Éditions du Seuil, 1971), 96–104.

31. Ibid., 117–22.

32. Ibid., 122.

33. Sade, *Philosophie,* 241.

34. Klossowski, *Sade mon prochain,* 86.

35. Sade, *La Philosophie dans le boudoir,* 252. "Gardez vos frontiers et restez chez vous" (Protect your frontiers and stay at home).

36. Simone de Beauvoir, *Faut-il Brûler Sade?* (Paris: Gallimard, 1955).

37. Ibid., 25–26.

38. Ibid., 44.

39. Ibid., 63.

40. Ibid., 70.

41. Ibid., 71–72.

42. Georges Bataille, *L'Érotisme* (Paris: Éditions de Minuit, 1957), 25, 48.

43. Ibid., 194.

44. Ibid., 195.

45. Ibid., 211.

46. Ibid., 89.

47. Ibid., 87, 87–89.

48. Jacques Lacan, "Kant avec Sade," *Écrits II* (Paris: Seuil, 1966), 254.

49. Ibid., 266.

50. Ibid., 269.

51. Ibid., 247.

52. Ibid., 246.

53. Ibid., 262.

54. Ernest Renan, *Vie de Jésus* (Paris: Gallimard, 1974), 393.

55. Ibid., 394.

56. Ibid., 400.

57. Ibid., 268.

58. Max Horkheimer and Theodor W. Adorno, *Dialektik der Aufklärung* (Frankfurt: Fischer, 2000), 119–20.

59. Hannah Arendt, *Eichmann in Jerusalem: A Report on the Banality of Evil* (New York: Penguin, 2006), 136.

60. Ibid., 252.

61. Ibid., 12.

5. AMERICAN CRUELTY

1. David Cole, "Introductory Commentary," in *The Torture Memos: Rationalizing the Unthinkable* (New York: The New Press, 2009), 35.

2. Jonathan Schell, "Cruel America," *The Nation*, October 17, 2011.

3. Interview with Alberto Mora, *Torturing Democracy*, available at: http://www.gwu.edu/~nsarchiv/torturingdemocracy/interviews/alberto_mora.html

4. Colin Dayan, *The Story of Cruel and Unusual* (Cambridge, MA: MIT Press, 2007).

5. Thomas Jefferson, "Declaration of the Causes and Necessity of Taking up Arms," in *Political Writings,* ed. Joyce Appleby and Terence Ball (Cambridge: Cambridge University Press, 1999), 81, 86; "A Declaration by the Representatives of the United States of America, in General Congress Assembled," 99.

6. Alexis de Tocqueville and Gustave de Beaumont, although promoting solitary confinement (at least in nighttime hours) as a way to avoid mutual corruption among prisoners, condemn its absolute use: "This absolute solitude, if nothing interrupt it, is beyond the strength of man; it destroys the criminal without intermission and without pity; it does not reform, it kills" (Alexis de Tocqueville and Gustave de Beaumont, *On the Penitentiary System in the United States and its Application in France; with an Appendix on Penal Colonies and also, Statistical Notes,* translated from the French by Francis Lieber [Philadelphia: Carey, Lea and Blanchard, 1833], 5). A greater partisan of the system, Harriet Martineau, nevertheless noted "an enormous amount of wrong must remain in a society where the elaboration of a vast apparatus for the infliction of human misery, like that required by the system of solitary imprisonment, is yet a work of mercy" (Harriet Martineau, *Society in America, vol. II* [Paris: Baudry's European Library, 1837], 195).

7. Charles Dickens, *American Notes* (London: Penguin, 2000), 111.

8. Alexander Hamilton, James Madison and John Jay, *The Federalist Papers*, ed. Ian Shapiro (New Haven, CT: Yale University Press, 2009), 26, 30.

9. Hamilton in ibid., 385, 376.

10. Mark Twain, "To the Person Sitting in Darkness" (1901), quoted in Amy Kaplan, *The Anarchy of Empire in the Making of U.S. Culture* (Cambridge, MA: Harvard University Press, 2005), 92.

11. Naval Inspector General, Vice Admiral Albert T. Church, III, Report on Department of Defense Interrogation Operations, "Executive Summary," March 10, 2005, 2–3. The Church Report notes seventy-one substantiated cases of detainee abuse. It invokes a comprehensive vagueness of definition to suggest conformity to recognized standards: "While no universally accepted definitions of 'torture' or 'abuse' exist, the theme that runs throughout the Geneva Conventions, international law, and U.S. military doctrine is that detainees must be treated 'humanely.'" The Fay/Jones Report makes clear the "homemade" status of abuse as a category: "defined as treatment of detainees that violated US criminal law or international law or treatment that was inhumane or coercive without lawful justification," Investigation of Intelligence Activities at Abu Ghraib, Investigation of the Abu Ghraib Prison and 205th Military Intelligence Brigade, LTG Anthony R. Jones, Investigation of the Abu Ghraib Detention Facility and 205th Military Intelligence Brigade, MG George R. Fay, August 2004, 4. See also p. 22. Interestingly, both reports confirm the critique suggested by W. J. T. Mitchell in his study of the iconography of the released photographs of "abuse" from Abu Ghraib: that the making public of only these images of the US torture policy consolidates an official effort to damn the practices represented as the work of a few "bad apples" (W. J. T. Mitchell, *Cloning Terror* [Chicago: University of Chicago

Press, 2011], 119). Both reports refer to the recorded Abu Ghraib abuse as if it were "iconic," while also categorizing it as exceptional: "The events at Abu Ghraib have become synonymous with the topic of detainee abuse" (Church Report 2); "Clearly abuses occurred at the prison at Abu Ghraib" (Fay/Jones 2). They also strive to separate abuse and interrogation techniques, a claim that, instead of succeeding in marginalizing it, links it to the wider culture of the war whose reverberations Mitchell analyses.

12. Department of Defense, Army Regulation 15–16: Investigation into FBI Allegations of Detainee Abuse at Guantanamo Bay, Cuba Detention Facility, June 9, 2005, 2.

13. Arthur J. Schlesinger, Final Report of the Independent Panel to Review Department of Defense Operations, August 2004, 5, 29.

14. Schlesinger, Final Report, Appendix G, 1–3.

15. International Committee of the Red Cross, *ICRC Report on the Treatment of Fourteen "High Value Detainees"* in CIA Custody (February 2007) available at http://www.nybooks.com/icrc-report.pdf 5, 24.

16. Convention Against Torture and Other Cruel, Inhuman or Degrading Treatment of Punishment (CAT), art. 16 ¶ 2, 1465 UNTS 85 (June 26, 1987).

17. August 1, 2002, memo for Alberto R. Gonzales, 17; US Department of Justice, Office of Legal Counsel, Memorandum for William J. Haynes II, General Counsel of the Department of Defense, Re: Military Interrogation of Unlawful Alien Combatants Held Outside the United States, March 14, 2003, available at http://www.justice.gov/olc/docs/memo-combatantsoutsideunitedstates.pdf, 51; Department of Defense Legal Task Force, Working Group on Detainee Interrogations in the Global War on Terrorism: Assessment of Legal, Historical, Policy, and Operational Considerations, March 6, 2003, http://www.slate.com/features/whatistorture/legalmemos.html, 2; May 30 memo for John A. Rizzo, 21.

18. March 14, 2003, memo for William J. Haynes II, 1,10.

19. Dayan, *Story of Cruel and Unusual,* 27–49.

20. The "self-defense" argument appears without reference to Eighth Amendment cases in the August 2002 memo for Alberto R. Gonzales, 45–46, and recurs in connection with such cases in Haynes, 61, and in the Working Group memo, 39.

21. May 30, 2005, memo for John A. Rizzo, 26.

22. Cole, "Introductory Commentary," 173.

23. John H. Langbein, *Torture and the Law of Proof: Europe and England in the Ancien Régime* (Chicago, IL: University of Chicago Press, 2006), 15, quoted in May 10 memo for John A. Rizzo, 19. The contrast between the investigative use of torture (to confirm circumstantial evidence) in the pre-nineteenth-century European judicial system described by Langbein, and the political antagonism and potentially indefinite duration framing its deployment in the "war on terror" challenges the (apparently transhistorical) distinction he wishes to maintain between torture and punishment.

24. May 30, 2005, memo for John A. Rizzo, 39.

25. Antonin Scalia, the main figure associated with originalism, confirms its use of historical reference to decide what legal prohibitions mean: "It is

entirely clear that capital punishment, which was widely in use in 1791, does not violate the abstract moral principle of the Eighth Amendment" (Antonin Scalia, *A Matter of Interpretation: Federal Courts and the Law* [Princeton, NJ: Princeton University Press, 1997], 145).

26. 1 Annals of Congress 754 (1789).

27. Stephen Breyer, *Making Our Democracy Work: A Judge's View* (New York: Alfred A. Knopf, 2010), 76.

28. Ronald Dworkin, *Justice in Robes* (Cambridge, MA: Harvard University Press, 2006), 120.

29. *Trop v. Dulles*, 356 U.S. 86 (1958) at 100–101, cited in *Furman v. Georgia* 4080 U.S. 238 (1972): 269–70.

30. *O'Neil v. Vermont*, 144. U.S.339 (1892) (Field, J., dissenting). Cited in Furman v. Georgia at 272.

31. *Furman v. Georgia* at 273.

32. Ibid., 255.

33. Ibid., 318

34. Ibid., 331.

35. Ibid., 375 n16.

36. Ibid., 366.

37. Richard Rorty, *Contingency, Irony, and Solidarity* (Cambridge: Cambridge University Press, 1989), xv.

38. Judith N. Shklar, *Ordinary Vices* (Cambridge, MA: Belknap Press of Harvard University Press, 1984), 7, 43.

39. Ibid., 10–12.

40. Hobbes, whose establishment of the basic preconditions for the state can be regarded as antecedent rather than antithetical to liberalism, deems cruelty merely senseless, not morally objectionable; it is inexplicable both within the state of a general war for self-preservation and the framework of a sovereign monopoly of violence. See *De Cive*: "for I cannot see what drunkenness or cruelty (which is vengeance without regard to future good) contribute to any man's peace or preservation" (Thomas Hobbes, *On the Citizen*, ed. Richard Tuck and Michael Silverthorne [Cambridge: Cambridge University Press, 1998], III 27n, 54). See also *Leviathan*: "for, that any man should take pleasure in other mens great harmes, without other end of his own, I do not conceive it possible" (Thomas Hobbes, *Leviathan,* ed. Richard Tuck [Cambridge: Cambridge University Press 1991], VI, 44). The attitude of a liberal reformer like Kaunitz in the eighteenth century shows, along with a moral repugnance for the terrible modes of execution envisaged by the *Nemesis Theresiana*, a concern with the (presumably economic and social) "value of men," as well as a distaste for the "laughable" futility of elaborate physical punishment. See Franz A. J. Szabo, *Kaunitz and Enlightened Absolutism, 1753–1780* (Cambridge: Cambridge University Press, 1994), 183–84.

41. See the introduction for a discussion of the meaning of Machiavelli's use of the word "cruelty." Shklar compares Machiavelli to Nietzsche, and to Hannah Arendt's characterization of post-WWI demagoguery: all elevate "cruelty" into a "virtue" in revolt against the "hypocrisy" of "religion, philanthropy and compassion" (Shklar, *Ordinary Vices,* 42).

42. Shklar's historical overview creates the impression of a seamless continuity between eighteenth-century reformism and abolition: "The age of reform that began in the eighteenth century was fueled by an increasing revulsion against cruelty. It may not have been put first, but enough people hated cruelty so intensely that the mores and institutions of the Anglo-American world were significantly altered. As A. V. Dicey, the eulogist of that age, reminds us, it was not the inalienable rights of the Declaration of Independence but a new sense of the suffering of slaves that brought about the abolition of slavery in the South. The effect attributed to *Uncle Tom's Cabin* speaks of the same power of pity" (Shklar, *Ordinary Vices,* 35).

43. See Pierre Rosanvallon, *La Société des Egaux* (Paris: Seuil, 2011), 124.

44. Rorty, *Contingency,* 141.

45. Vladimir Nabokov, *Lolita* (1955; reprint, New York: Vintage International, 1997), 316, 213.

46. Rorty, *Contingency,* 163.

47. Nabokov's aesthete protagonists are characterized as "cruelly incurious" (163) in their "failure to notice suffering" (159); content to "turn the lives of other human beings into images on a screen, while simply not noticing that these other people are suffering" (157). "Cruelty" is thus made identical with human incuriosity in the service of aestheticism, and rendered a problem of observation rather than direct action, despite the careers of the cold heroes Nabokov traces.

48. Rorty, *Contingency,* 144, 146.

49. Ibid., 177, 183–87.

50. Ibid., 68.

51. Ibid., 93.

52. Ibid., 99–100, 103–4, 106–8.

53. Ibid., 109–20.

54. Ibid., 32.

55. "Despite the efforts of such writers as Fromm and Marcuse, Freudian moral psychology cannot be used to define social goals, goals for humanity as opposed to goals for individuals" (ibid., 34). However, the theory Fromm offers regarding the origins of cruelty—that it is the inverted, negative expression of a necessary connection to the human environment—shows no incompatibility with Rorty's own goal for humanity, the cultivation of sympathetic identification. See Erich Fromm, *The Anatomy of Human Destructiveness* (1973; reprint, New York: Holt, 1992), 300–61.

56. Rorty, *Contingency,* 63.

57. Michel Foucault, *Histoire de la folie à l'âge classique* (Paris: Gallimard, 1974), 239.

58. Rorty, *Contingency,* 126–33.

59. The danger of such humiliation is central to Rorty's ethics of the disjunction between public and private: Rorty, *Contingency,* 89, 91. It seems more obviously a feature of the language games with the proper name of Derrida's interlocutor in *Limited Inc.* (Evanston, IL: Northwestern University Press, 1977), 29–110.

60. Rorty, *Contingency*, 102–3.

61. Nussbaum critiques this aspect of Proust; it is given anthropological universality by René Girard, *Deceit, Desire and the Novel* (1961; reprint, Baltimore, MD: Johns Hopkins University Press, 1965), 93–228.

62. Martha Nussbaum, *Love's Knowledge: Essays on Philosophy and Literature* (Oxford: Oxford University Press, 1990), 65.

63. Ibid., 135.

64. Ibid., 133.

65. This is pointed out by Jonathan Freedman, "Introduction: The Moment of Henry James," in *The Cambridge Companion to Henry James* (Cambridge: Cambridge University Press, 1998), 5.

66. Nussbaum, *Love's Knowledge, 308.*

67. Ibid., 45, 308, 272–74.

68. Ibid., 274–85.

69. Judith Butler, *Precarious Life: The Power of Mourning and Violence* (London: Verso, 2004), 7, 29; "I am as much constituted by those I do grieve for as by those whose deaths I disavow"(46).

70. Judith Butler, *Frames of War: When Is Life Grievable* (London: Verso, 2010), xi; Butler, *Precarious Life,* 34; Butler, *Frames of War,* xii.

71. Butler's belief that it is representational politics that has prevented current "war-waging" from sparking a domestic "popular revolt" (xvi) ignores not only the political disregard for British popular rejection of the war, but the kinds of circumstances that have provoked full-scale revolts in the past. Her reference to Britain in connection with the Geneva Conventions appears on 79.

72. Butler, *Frames of War,* x.

73. Ibid., 3, 28, 32.

74. Ibid., 101–35.

75. Ibid., 105.

76. Ibid., 132.

77. Ibid., 32, 125.

78. Susan Sontag, *Regarding the Pain of Others* (London: Penguin, 2003).

79. Butler, *Frames of War,* 66.

80. Ibid., 88.

81. Ibid., 83.

82. Ibid., 88, 91.

83. Ibid., 99.

84. Ibid., 100.

85. Ibid., 94, 95.

86. Butler, *Precarious Life,* 78; Butler, *Frames of War,* 56–62.

87. Judith Butler, *Gender Trouble* (1990; reprint, New York: Routledge, 2007), 186–89.

88. Theodor Adorno, "Cultural Criticism and Society," *Prisms* (Cambridge, MA: MIT Press, 1967 1983), 32.

89. Butler, *Precarious Life,* 78.

90. Butler, *Frames of War,* 83, 87.

91. Ibid., 100.

INDEX